641

TESTED

RECIPES

FROM THE

Sealtest

TRADE MARK

KITCHENS

To Our Homemaker Friends,

Homemaking is much more than a routine job. It's the challenge of keeping a home running smoothly . . . of keeping a family happy and healthy. And one of the best ways we know of doing this is to serve attractive, nourishing, well-cooked food.

We of the Sealtest Consumer Service staff have the pleasant job of developing recipes for you . . . new exciting dishes featuring our fine dairy products. We strive to make our recipes simple and easy to prepare, economical, nutritious and attractive as we think of the millions of homes to which our products go.

Every recipe in this book has been carefully worked out in our ultra modern kitchens. To assure perfect results, each recipe has been tested over and over again using varied equipment and ingredients. The recipes are arranged in chapters which follow each other like the courses in a meal, with a few exceptions. For example, you will find a chapter devoted to cottage cheese in main dishes because we want you to know what an excellent cooking ingredient cottage cheese is. And you will find a chapter on ice cream with many ideas for using this popular food in a variety of ways.

We hope you'll enjoy using this book. May our recipes contribute to the health and happiness of your family.

The Sealtest Kitchen Staff

"The people who have achieved, who have become large, strong vigorous people, who have reduced their infant mortality, who have the best trades in the world, who have an appreciation of art, literature and music, who are progressive in science and in every activity of the human intellect, are the people who have used liberal amounts of milk and its products."

DR. E. V. McCOLLUM
Emeritus Professor of Biochemistry
THE JOHNS HOPKINS UNIVERSITY

CONTENTS

APPETIZERS—hors d'oeuvres, canapes, salads . . . 7

SOUPS 15

MEATS, POULTRY, FISH 23

COTTAGE CHEESE IN MAIN DISHES 41

AMERICAN CHEESE, EGGS, MACARONI 48

VEGETABLES IN MAIN DISHES 52

SALADS—kinds, helpful pointers, nineteen intriguing, fruit and cottage cheese, meat and cottage cheese, vegetable and cottage cheese, molded with cottage cheese, salad plates, miscellaneous 59

SALAD DRESSINGS 87

BREADS 91

SANDWICHES—kinds, breads, cutting, pantry shelf fillings, deliciously different, open face, triple decker, hot main course, party 101

DESSERTS—custards, puddings, molded, shortcakes, cakes and cookies, cheese cakes, pastries, confections . . 113

ICE CREAM—Alaskas, small fry favorites, parfaits, sherbet cups, sundae glamour, toppings, frosty tricks and treats 155

BEVERAGES—ice cream, chocolate, sherbet, egg nog, milk, cream, buttermilk 186

SOUR CREAM AND YOGURT 201

HELPFUL INFORMATION—what makes a good cook, how to measure 206

PLANNING FAMILY MEALS—a daily food guide, nutrients, what to have with what, holiday reminders . . . 210

MENUS—children's parties, wedding fare, anniversary parties, outdoor picnics, card party fare, teen-age-get-togethers, out-of-the-ordinary breakfasts, TV tray lunches, special dinners, party refreshments, year of holiday menus 217

MILK AND OTHER DAIRY FOODS—important nutrition facts . . . milk, homogenized milk, buttermilk, skim milk, chocolate drink, cottage cheese, ice cream, sherbet, sour cream, yogurt 229

INDEX 236

DAIRY MEASURES, ABBREVIATIONS, OVEN TEMPERATURES 255

DAIRY FOODS ARE LOW IN CALORIES 256

Appetizers

There's something festive about appetizers. Whether you serve them at the table or pass them around on trays in living room, garden or terrace, you'll want them to *look* as interesting as they'll *taste!*

Actually, there are three distinct categories of appetizers:

HORS D'OEUVRES—page 8, small tidbits, often served on toothpicks stuck in a polished eggplant or grapefruit.

CANAPES—page 11, tiny morsels on bite-sized bits of toast, crackers or miniature cream puffs.

SALADS—page 14, small, seasoned salads served on individual plates at the table.

Cottage cheese—so easy to handle, so delicate in flavor—makes a wonderful base for all three types.

HORS D'OEUVRES

APPETIZER CHEESE CAKE

Prepare this the day before—then whisk it out of the refrigerator ready to serve.

2 cups finely crushed cheese crackers, 1 six-oz. pkg.
1 green pepper, finely chopped
½ cup finely chopped, stuffed green olives
½ cup finely chopped celery
2 tbsp. lemon juice
1 small onion, minced
1 tsp. salt
¼ tsp. paprika
1 tsp. Worcestershire sauce
Dash of Tabasco
2 cups Sealtest sour cream

Line deep, 8" round or square pan with waxed paper, leaving good margin at sides to fold over finished cake. Brush bottom and sides with melted butter, and line pan with part of the crushed crackers, making a layer about ¼" thick.

Mix remaining ingredients, except crackers, and add to sour cream; stir just enough to mix. Spread sour cream mixture about ½" thick over crushed cracker lining, and fill pan with alternate layers of sour cream and crushed crackers, ending with cracker layer.

Fold sides of waxed paper over cake. Place in refrigerator for at least 24 hrs. Turn out on serving plate; peel off waxed paper. Cut in small wedges or "fingers" to serve. One 8" cake. This will keep several days in your refrigerator.

CHEESE SHORTBITS

¼ cup butter, softened
¼ lb. Old English cheese, grated
¾ cup sifted flour

Mix butter and cheese together until smooth and well-blended (using a spoon or rotary beater). Mix in flour until thoroughly blended.

Shape dough in balls about 1" in diameter (or pat out and cut in bars about 1" x 2" x ¼"). Place on ungreased cookie sheet. Chill until dough is firm. Bake in hot oven, 400°F., 10 min. Serve hot or cold. About 2½ doz.

COTTAGE CHEESE PASTRY HORS D'OEUVRES

Divide Cottage Cheese Pastry dough, recipe below, in quarters; make some of each of the following:

CHEESE PASTRY STRAWS: Roll out pastry ⅛" thick. Cut in 8" x ½" strips. Roll each strip, with edges overlapping, around paper straws ¼" in diameter. Bake. Cool. Slip out paper straws. Fill Pastry Straws with seasoned cream cheese. ¼ recipe makes 30.

OLIVE PINWHEELS: Roll out pastry ⅛" thick. Cut in strips 8" x 1". Wrap each strip around a large green stuffed olive. (Pickled onions may be used, too.) Secure the end with a toothpick. Bake. ¼ recipe makes 16.

LILY NIBBLES: Roll out pastry ⅛" thick. Cut in 2½" rounds. Place two small strips of bologna in center of each round. Fold over edges to center to form a cornucopia or lily shape; seal. Bake. ¼ recipe makes 20.

RUFFLED CHEESE ROUNDS: Roll out pastry ⅛" thick. Cut in 1¾" rounds. Bake. When cool, top each round with a rolled anchovy, a slice of olive, or sprig of parsley and add a ruffle of cream cheese, using a decorator's tube. ¼ recipe makes 20.

COTTAGE CHEESE PASTRY

An easy, elegant, never-fail, puff-type pastry
for hors d'oeuvres and a variety of uses

1 cup butter or margarine — **2 cups flour**
1 cup Sealtest cottage cheese

Cut butter into flour with pastry blender, or two knives, until mixture resembles coarse meal. Add cottage cheese and mix until well-blended. (This dough may be stored, well-wrapped in wax paper, in refrigerator 1 to 2 weeks and used as you need it.)

Roll out dough on well-floured board to required thickness and cut into shapes. (See recipes above.) Bake all pastries on ungreased, brown paper lined cookie sheet in a very hot oven, 500°F., 5 min. or until golden brown.

If a glaze is desired on pastries, brush pastry before baking with mixture of 1 beaten egg yolk and 2 tbsp. milk.

COTTAGE CHEESE CRISPS

1 cup sifted flour
¼ tsp. salt
½ tsp. baking powder
1 tsp. celery seed
6 tbsp. butter
½ cup Sealtest cottage cheese
1 tbsp. milk
Paprika

Mix and sift flour, salt and baking powder. Stir in celery seed. Cut in butter with 2 knives or pastry blender.

Combine cottage cheese and milk. Add to first mixture, stirring in quickly.

Turn dough onto a floured board; roll to ⅛" thickness. Cut into strips, rounds or other shapes, using floured knife or cutters.

Place on a buttered baking sheet. Brush with milk or cream. Sprinkle with paprika. Bake in hot oven, 425°F., 10 to 12 min. or until a delicate brown. 35 to 40 crisps.

DEVILED EGGS A LA INDIA

4 hard-cooked eggs, halved
2 tbsp. mayonnaise
2 tsp. vinegar
¼ tsp. dry mustard
½ tsp. curry powder
½ cup Sealtest cottage cheese
Salt and pepper to taste

Remove egg yolks from whites. Mash yolks; mix with remaining ingredients until well blended and fluffy. Fill egg whites with yolk mixture. Garnish with paprika. 8 halves.

DEVILED EGG BASKETS

When preparing deviled eggs, add about a tbsp. Sealtest cottage cheese for each yolk. Top each egg with the scored rind of a cucumber slice to make basket handle.

SIMPLE 'N SPEEDY HORS D'OEUVRES

BACON BALLS: Wrap stuffed olives in bacon. Broil, to cook the bacon; serve on toothpicks.

COTTAGE CHEESE POPS: Mix equal amounts of Sealtest cottage cheese and blue cheese; season with a little grated onion. Form in little balls with small measuring spoon; roll in finely chopped parsley; serve on toothpicks. (Tricky to make but worth it.)

NUT SHELLS: Arrange pecan halves, in pairs, with cream cheese between.

PERKY CUCUMBER SLICES: Soften ¼ lb. cream cheese with spoon; add 1 tsp. prepared mustard and ⅛ tsp. salt; mix well. Cut 1 medium cucumber in thin slices, about ⅛" thick. Place small dab of cheese mixture on each slice. Top with a caper or tiny piece of parsley. About 3 doz. slices.

SALMON POPS: Cut ¼ lb. cream cheese into about 32 tiny cubes. Shape each cube in a ball with fingers. Cut ¼ lb. smoked salmon in 32 little strips, about 3" x ½". Wrap each strip around a cheese ball; secure with toothpick. Dip in chopped parsley to add color if desired. 32 pops.

CANAPES

TOASTED BREAD CUT-OUTS

Remove crust from day old bread; cut slices in interesting shapes with knife, round biscuit cutters, or cookie cutters. Toast on one side in small amount butter in frying pan, or spread with butter, and toast under broiler. Butter untoasted side and spread with any of the Tasty Dips and Spreads, page 12.

PETITE PARTY CREAM PUFFS

Delicious with your favorite filling

½ cup water	½ cup sifted flour
¼ cup butter	2 eggs

Heat water and butter to boiling point in saucepan. Mix in flour all at once. Stir constantly until mixture leaves sides of pan and forms into a ball, about 1 min. Remove from heat. Cool about 5 min.

Beat in eggs one at a time, beating until smooth after each addition. Whip mixture until velvety. Drop by leveled teaspoonfuls in small mounds on lightly greased baking sheets. Bake in hot oven, 400°F., about 20 min.

Cool puffs and cut off tops. Fill with chicken salad, tuna salad, your favorite Sealtest cottage cheese mixture or any favorite sandwich filling. 40 small puffs.

TASTY DIPS AND SPREADS

Marvelous for TV snacks

Want to make life easy for yourself and keep your guests pleasantly occupied? Place any of the tasty mixtures described below in a bowl flanked by heaps of crackers or potato chips—and let everyone dip in. If your guests are not of the dipper-in class—spread the same mixtures on Toasted Bread Cut-outs or Party Cream Puffs, page 11, or on any plain cracker.

CHICKEN OLIVE: Mix 1 cup chopped cooked chicken, 1/4 cup chopped celery, 1/4 cup chopped ripe olives, 1/4 cup mayonnaise, few drops Worcestershire, salt and pepper to taste. 1 2/3 cups.

CHILI CHEESE: Mix together lightly 1 cup sieved Sealtest cottage cheese and 2 tbsp. chili sauce. 1 generous cup.

CLAM CHEESE: Mix together well 1 cup Sealtest cottage cheese, 2 tbsp. drained canned minced sea clams, 1 tsp. finely cut chives and a few drops Tabasco and Worcestershire. 1 generous cup.

COTTAGE CHEESE DATE COCONUT: Mix 1 cup finely chopped dates, 1/2 cup shredded coconut and 1 cup Sealtest cottage cheese. Let stand awhile to blend flavors. Decorate with whole dates and shredded coconut. 2 1/3 cups.

COTTAGE CHEESE RELISH: Mix 1/2 cup drained sweet pickle relish with 1 cup Sealtest cottage cheese. About 1 1/4 cups.

DEVILED HAM CHEESE: Mix together lightly 1 cup sieved Sealtest cottage cheese and 1/4 cup deviled ham. 1 generous cup.

FLUFFY COTTAGE CHEESE: Mix 1 cup sieved Sealtest cottage cheese and 1/4 cup sour cream lightly together, just enough to blend. Season with salt and pepper to taste. 1 generous cup.

HORSERADISH CHEESE: Mix together well 1 cup Sealtest cottage cheese, dash of celery salt, 3 tsp. drained bottled horseradish and a pinch of salt. 1 cup.

PIMIENTO CHEESE: Mix together lightly 1 cup Sealtest cottage cheese and 1/4 cup chopped drained pimiento. 1 generous cup.

PINEAPPLE CHEESE: Mix together lightly 1 cup Sealtest cottage cheese and ½ cup drained crushed pineapple. Decorate with bits of pineapple. 1½ cups.

SPICY BEET CHEESE: Mix together well 1 cup Sealtest cottage cheese, 2 tbsp. drained bottled horseradish, 1 tsp. garlic salt, ½ cup finely chopped canned beets. 1½ cups.

TANGY ROQUEFORT: Mix ¾ cup Sealtest cottage cheese, ¼ lb. crumbled Roquefort cheese and 1 tbsp. sour cream just enough to blend. Add few drops of Worcestershire sauce. Pile in serving dish, and decorate with small fingers of Roquefort cheese. 1¼ cups.

BACON SPRINKLES

Spread cream cheese on toasted bread rounds; top with diced crisp bacon.

CHEESE BELLS

Soften American cheese; spread on bell-shaped toasted bread cut-outs. Edge with cream cheese.

PARSLEY FLOWERS

Spread Sealtest cottage cheese on fancy toasted bread cut-outs; garnish with chopped parsley.

SNAPPY TRIPLE DECKERS

Spread 4 thin slices buttered or unbuttered pumpernickel with Beet Cream Cheese Filling, recipe below. Spread another 4 slices with Herring Cream Cheese Filling, recipe below.

Now make up 4 triple-decker sandwiches as follows: Place a Beet Cheese layer on a Herring Cheese layer and top with a plain slice buttered or unbuttered bread. Cut each triple decker into 4 strips. 16 small sandwiches.

BEET CREAM CHEESE FILLING: Blend together ¼ lb. cream cheese, ½ cup grated cooked beets, 1½ tsp. grated onion and ½ tsp. garlic salt.

HERRING CREAM CHEESE FILLING: Blend together ¼ lb. cream cheese and ⅓ cup chopped pickled herring.

SALADS

Salads make an intriguing first course.

EGG ASPIC APPETIZER

3 hard-cooked eggs, halved
2 tbsp. sour cream
¼ cup sieved Sealtest cottage cheese
¼ tsp. prepared mustard
Salt and pepper
Paprika
Lettuce
Tomato aspic, canned or home-made
Watercress

Mash egg yolks with fork. Add sour cream and mix until smooth. Fold in cheese and mustard lightly until blended. Season with salt and pepper. Fill egg whites with yolk mixture. Sprinkle with paprika. Chill.

Place one egg half on small lettuce leaf. Garnish with cubes of aspic, or small wedges of tomato, and watercress. 6 servings.

SPRINGTIME DINNER
Egg Aspic Appetizer
Ham Steak
Glazed Pineapple Rings Buttered Lima Beans
Rolls and Currant Jelly
Rhubarb Pie with Ice Cream
Milk Coffee with Cream

LIME APPETIZER SALAD

1½ cups boiling water
1 pkg. lime-flavored gelatin
3 tbsp. cider vinegar
½ tsp. salt
1 cup Sealtest cottage cheese
10 radishes, thinly sliced
1 medium cucumber, diced
1 medium onion, diced

Add boiling water to gelatin, stirring until dissolved. Stir in vinegar and salt. Cool.

When gelatin mixture is cool, add remaining ingredients, mixing until well-blended. Pour into 6 to 8 individual molds or an 8" square pan.

Chill until firm; unmold on lettuce or other salad greens. Serve with sour cream or any desired dressing. 6 to 8 servings.

Soups

Ah, for the infinite variety of soup! There is consomme—clear and light enough to tickle the most fastidious appetite. There are thick, rich soups full of nourishing ingredients. There's hot soup and cold soup, spicy or bland—each with its own wonderful aroma, its own distinctive color, taste and texture.

Soup can be a very economical course especially when you have bits of meat or vegetables left over, which you want to use to new advantage. And you'll find that different garnishes and accompaniments can add distinction to the family's favorite soup.

BASIC CREAM SOUP

Hot and hearty to "hit the spot", this basic soup can be made into endless varieties.

2 tbsp. minced onion
4 tbsp. butter
4 tbsp. flour
3½ cups Sealtest milk
About 1½ cups chopped or sieved cooked vegetable and vegetable liquid (such as carrot, celery, spinach)
Salt and pepper

Cook onion in butter in heavy saucepan over low heat until tender but not brown, stirring occasionally. Add flour; mix until smooth. Pour in milk all at once and immediately stir vigorously over moderate heat until thickened.

Shortly before serving, add vegetable and enough vegetable liquid to give desired consistency. Reheat. Season to taste with salt and pepper. 6 servings.

NEW ENGLAND-STYLE CLAM CHOWDER

1 qt. fresh clams or 2 cans minced clams, 10½ oz.
Water
4 slices bacon, finely diced
2 medium onions, sliced
4 medium potatoes, peeled and diced
2 cups Sealtest milk
Salt and pepper

Drain clams, reserving liquid. If fresh clams are used, grind in food chopper, using fine or medium blade. Add enough water to clam liquid to make 2 cups.

Cook bacon in large heavy kettle until crisp. Drain off all but 2 tbsp. of the fat. Add onions and cook, stirring occasionally, until tender and yellow. Add clam liquid and potatoes. Cover and cook until potatoes are tender, about 15 min. Add clams and milk. Continue cooking only until clams and milk are hot. Season with salt and pepper. 4 to 6 servings.

SOUP SUPPER

New England-Style Clam Chowder
Toasted Tomato and Lettuce Sandwiches
Fruit Cup
Cookies
Milk

SAVORY CHEESE SOUP

4 tbsp. butter
4 tbsp. flour
1 qt. Sealtest milk
2 beef bouillon cubes
2 tsp. grated onion
½ tsp. Worcestershire sauce
1 lb. Old English cheese, grated

Melt butter in large heavy saucepan. Add flour and stir until blended. Add milk all at once, and bouillon cubes. Cook, stirring constantly, until sauce is thickened and bouillon cubes are dissolved.

Add remaining ingredients. Cook over low heat, stirring constantly, until cheese is melted. Season with pepper, if desired. 6 generous servings.

VARIATIONS:

1. Cut luncheon meat (one 12-ounce can) in very small cubes. Cook until crisp and browned in frying pan. Drain and add to cheese soup.

2. Cook 2 to 3 cups of chopped celery in a small amount of water until tender. Add celery and ½ cup of the cooking liquid to cheese soup.

BLUSTERY WEATHER LUNCH

Savory Cheese Soup
Melba Toast   Hard Rolls
Fruit Salad Dessert
Coffee with Cream   Hot Chocolate

ONION SOUP DELUXE

2 tbsp. butter
3 cups thinly sliced onions
1 small clove of garlic, minced
2½ cups leftover turkey or chicken stock
1 cup Sealtest whipping cream
Salt and pepper

Melt butter in heavy saucepan. Add onions and garlic. Cook over low heat until onions are tender and yellow. Add turkey stock. Cover and simmer over low heat about 2 hours. Add cream just before serving and reheat. Season with salt and pepper. If desired, serve garnished with small toast triangles and grated cheese. 4 to 6 servings.

ONION MILK SOUP

1½ cups thinly sliced onion	Salt and pepper
2 tbsp. butter	¼ tsp. onion salt
1 qt. Sealtest milk	Grated American cheese
4 tbsp. flour	6 small toast rounds

Cook onion in the butter in heavy pan until soft and golden brown, stirring frequently.

Add a little cold milk to flour; blend to smooth paste; stir in remaining milk. Pour over onions all at once. Cook, stirring constantly, until thickened. Season with salt, pepper and onion salt.

Sprinkle cheese on toast rounds; brown under broiler. Serve on soup. 4 to 6 servings.

PARTY OYSTER STEW

1 qt. oysters with liquor	1 pint Sealtest whipping cream
8 tbsp. butter	Celery salt
2 tbsp. flour	Salt
3 cups Sealtest milk	Freshly ground pepper

Pick over oysters, removing bits of shell. Drain, saving the liquor.

Melt butter in top of large double boiler. Stir in flour, mixing until smooth. Gradually add oyster liquor, milk, and cream, stirring until smoothly blended. Cook over boiling water, until slightly thickened and thoroughly heated. Stir occasionally. Season with celery salt, salt and pepper.

About 5 min. before serving time, add oysters. Continue cooking only until oysters are plump and their edges begin to curl. Serve immediately. 8 servings.

COMPANY SUPPER

Party Oyster Stew
Crisp Crackers
Mixed Green Salad with Roquefort
Cheese Dressing
Hot Crusty French Bread
Garlic Butter
Lemon Meringue Pie   Coffee

PIMIENTO BISQUE

Pink and pretty and as good as it looks

2½ tbsp. butter
2½ tbsp. flour
5 cups Sealtest milk
½ tsp. grated onion
¾ cup pimiento
Salt and pepper

Melt butter in heavy saucepan. Add flour; mix well. Add milk all at once. Cook, stirring constantly, until thickened.

Add onion and coarsely sieved pimiento. Season with salt and pepper. Reheat, stirring most of the time. *Do not boil.* If desired, top with a few slivers of avocado. 6 servings.

SAVORY POTATO CHOWDER

3 medium potatoes, peeled and sliced
2 tbsp. butter
¼ cup chopped onion
½ cup finely cut sliced dried beef
2 tbsp. flour
3 cups Sealtest milk
⅛ tsp. pepper

Cook potatoes in 1½ cups boiling salted water (½ tsp. salt) until just tender. Do not drain. Break up potatoes slightly with fork.

Melt butter in saucepan. Add onion; cook until golden brown, stirring occasionally. Add beef; cook, stirring frequently, until edges curl. Add flour; mix well. Add milk all at once. Cook, stirring constantly, until thickened. Add pepper, potatoes and potato water. Reheat. 6 servings.

SOUR CREAM POTATO SOUP

3 cups diced raw potatoes
½ cup chopped celery
½ cup chopped onion
3 cups water
2 cups scalded Sealtest milk
2 chicken bouillon cubes
3 tbsp. butter
1 cup Sealtest sour cream
1 tbsp. flour
Salt and pepper

Cook potatoes, celery and onion in the water in covered pan until very tender. (Do not drain.) Press through sieve. Add milk, bouillon cubes and butter.

Mix sour cream with flour until smooth. Add to soup, and cook, stirring constantly, until thickened and bouillon cubes are dissolved. Season with salt and pepper. 6 servings.

CHAMPION'S CHOWDER

Smackin' good cottage cheese and salmon soup

1 eight-oz. can salmon
1 cup Sealtest milk
2 tbsp. butter
2 tbsp. chopped onion
2 tbsp. flour
Dash of Tabasco
2 cups Sealtest cottage cheese

Drain salmon; add liquid to milk. Melt butter in heavy saucepan; add onion and cook slowly until tender, stirring occasionally. Add flour; mix well. Add milk mixture all at once. Cook over moderate heat, stirring constantly, until thickened.

Add Tabasco, cheese and flaked salmon; reheat, stirring constantly. As mixture heats it thins to desirable consistency. Serve piping hot. This soup has a rather tart, deliciously unusual flavor. 4 servings.

SURPRISE TOMATO SOUP

1 can condensed tomato soup
1 1/3 cups Sealtest milk
Dash of salt
1/2 tsp. celery salt
1 1/2 cups Sealtest cottage cheese, warmed to room temperature

Pour tomato soup into heavy saucepan. Stir in milk, salt and celery salt until blended. Heat thoroughly, but do not boil; stir constantly.

Just before serving add cottage cheese, and beat with rotary beater just enough to break up curds. Heat a minute longer (*no more*) stirring constantly. The soft tender cheese curds give an interesting new addition to soups, in a class with egg balls, custard cubes, etc. Overcooking toughens them.

Remove soup from heat; serve *immediately* in hot dishes. If desired, garnish with slice of hard-cooked egg and chopped parsley. 4 servings.

SPRING "PICK-UP" LUNCHEON

Surprise Tomato Soup
Hot Biscuits or Popovers
Tossed Green Salad with Ham Strips
Strawberry or Hot Fudge Sundae
Coffee with Cream Milk

FROSTY TOMATO BUTTERMILK SOUP

Wonderfully refreshing on wilting days

- 1 can condensed tomato soup
- Sealtest buttermilk
- Tabasco sauce
- Worcestershire sauce

Combine soup with an equal amount of buttermilk. Mix well. Season to taste with Tabasco and Worcestershire. Chill. Serve cold, garnished with chopped chives or parsley. 4 to 6 servings.

SUMMER SNACK LUNCH

Frosty Tomato Buttermilk Soup
Sliced Boiled Ham and Watercress Sandwich
Fresh Fruit Cup with Sherbet
Milk Iced Tea

VICHYSSOISE

- 4 medium potatoes, diced
- 3 medium onions, sliced
- 1 can condensed cream of chicken soup
- 1 tbsp. butter
- 3½ cups Sealtest milk
- ¼ cup Sealtest cream
- Salt and pepper
- Sealtest sour cream
- Chopped chives

Cook potatoes and onions in small amount of boiling salted water until soft. Press through sieve into double boiler. Add chicken soup, butter, milk, cream; mix well. Heat over boiling water, stirring until blended. Season with salt and pepper. Serve hot or icy cold. If served cold, beat until smooth before serving. Garnish with a dab of sour cream and chopped chives. 6 to 8 generous servings.
NOTE: For curry lovers season the sour cream with a smidgeon of curry powder.

TUREEN TRICKS

With milk and canned soup

MUSHROOM SOUP with a new twist: Combine 1 can condensed cream of mushroom soup and 1¼ cups Sealtest milk, stirring until smooth. Add 1 cup cooked or canned mixed vegetables. Heat, stirring occasionally. Season to taste with salt and pepper. 4 servings.

Delicious and unusual **CHICKEN CURRY SOUP:** Mix well 1 can condensed cream of chicken soup, one can condensed cream of mushroom soup, ½ tsp. curry powder and 1½ cups Sealtest milk. Heat, stirring occasionally. Serve garnished with salted whipped cream and grated coconut. 6 servings.

Deliciously different **TOMATO SOUP:** Combine 1 can condensed tomato soup and an equal amount of Sealtest milk. Stir in ½ to 1 cup of sauteed onion rings; heat and serve. 4 servings.

Quick **MONGOLE SOUP:** Try mixing a can of condensed pea soup and a can of condensed tomato soup with an equal amount of Sealtest milk. Heat and garnish with hot croutons rolled in finely chopped parsley. 6 servings.

SOUP GARNISHES AND GO-ALONGS

CLEAR SOUPS: Garnish with . . . grated cheese, thin slices of lemon, whipped cream, minced parsley, celery rings, radish slices, avocado slices or cubes, shredded almonds, sliced cooked mushrooms, asparagus tips.

Pass . . . butter wafers, cheese straws, fancy croutons, carrot strips, Melba toast.

CREAM SOUPS: Garnish with . . . salted whipped cream, shredded toasted almonds, minced chives, pimiento strips, buttered or cheese popcorn, grated cheese, chow mein noodles, buttered ready-to-eat cereals.

Pass . . . crackers, toast croutons, pretzels, wafers, pickles, celery.

JELLIED SOUPS: Garnish with . . . chopped olives, sieved hard cooked egg, watercress, onion slices, chopped chives.

Pass . . . popovers, French bread.

MEAT SOUPS: Garnish with . . . frankfurter slices, sliced lemon.

Pass . . . Melba toast, crisp crackers, relish, bread sticks.

SAVORY CRISPS

SAVORY CRACKERS: Spread a little soft butter on crisp crackers; sprinkle with a little celery salt; heat in moderate oven, 350°F., about 5 min.

CURRY CRISPS: Blend 2 tbsp. soft butter and ¼ tsp. curry powder. Spread on 4 slices French bread. Heat in hot oven, 400°F., 10 min. Cut in strips.

Meats, Poultry, Fish

Human beings cannot live without protein. Probably this vital need in our system makes the foods that supply protein so marvelously satisfying to us.

Meat, fish, eggs, milk and other dairy foods, especially cottage cheese, are all excellent sources of protein. The main course of any meal should contain at least one of these strength-giving foods. When you add a cream sauce or cheese to meat, vegetables, spaghetti and casserole dishes, you not only increase the nutrient value of your meal—you also get a tastier dish!

MEATS

BEEF STROGANOFF

1½ tsp. salt
Pepper
1 tsp. garlic salt
Flour
1½ lbs. round steak, cut in ¾" cubes
3 tbsp. butter
1 cup canned tomatoes
1 cup Sealtest sour cream

Combine salt, pepper, garlic salt and ⅓ cup flour in clean heavy paper bag. Add meat and shake until well coated.

Brown meat slowly in butter in heavy skillet, turning frequently. Use large enough pan, and keep pieces apart for best browning effect. Add tomatoes; stir well. Cover tightly and simmer 1½ to 2½ hrs. or until meat is tender. Stir frequently during cooking; add hot water as mixture becomes dry.

Add 2 tbsp. flour to sour cream; stir until smooth. Add to meat. Cook, stirring constantly, until thickened. If desired, serve on hot noodles. 4 to 6 servings.

SAVORY MEAT LOAF

2½ cups soft bread crumbs
1 cup Sealtest milk
½ green pepper, diced
1 medium onion, diced
⅛ tsp. pepper
½ cup drained canned tomatoes
1 egg
1 lb. ground beef
1½ tsp. salt

Soak crumbs in milk about 10 min. Add remaining ingredients; mix together thoroughly. Pack in 9" x 5" x 3" loaf pan. Bake in moderately hot oven, 375°F., 45 to 60 min. 6 servings.

BUTTERMILK BEEF PUFFS

1 lb. ground beef
1 cup Sealtest buttermilk
¼ tsp. Worcestershire sauce
1¼ to 1½ tsp. salt
Few grains pepper
1 tsp. grated onion

Combine all ingredients; beat well until light and fluffy. Drop by heaping teaspoonfuls into deep hot fat, 300°F., and cook for 2 to 2½ min. Drain on unglazed paper. 24 small balls. 4 to 6 servings.

BUTTERMILK BEEF PINWHEELS

1/3 to 1/2 cup Sealtest buttermilk
1 1/2 cups packaged biscuit mix
1 one-lb. can corned beef hash
1 tbsp. prepared mustard
1/3 cup mayonnaise
Few drops Worcestershire sauce
Salt and pepper

Add buttermilk to biscuit mix. Mix well. (Dough should be soft but not sticky. If too dry, add more buttermilk.) Pat or roll dough into 12" x 14" rectangle on lightly floured surface.

Mix hash, mustard, mayonnaise and Worcestershire. Season with salt and pepper; spread on dough. Roll up firmly, beginning at wide side; cut in 6 slices. Place, cut side up, on greased baking sheet. Bake in hot oven, 425°F., 15 min. or until browned. Serve hot with Tangy Tomato Sauce, recipe below. 6 generous servings.

TANGY TOMATO SAUCE

4 tbsp. butter
4 tbsp. flour
1 1/2 cups Sealtest buttermilk
1/4 cup chili sauce or catsup

Melt butter in heavy saucepan. Add flour; mix well. Pour in buttermilk all at once and immediately stir vigorously over moderate heat until thickened. Add chili sauce, mix well. Season with salt and pepper. Serve hot. 1 1/2 cups sauce. 6 servings.

PANTRY SHELF PARTY

Buttermilk Beef Pinwheels
Buttered Green Beans
Sliced Pineapple
Coffee with Cream Milk

CREAMED DRIED BEEF

2 tbsp. butter
2 tbsp. flour
1 1/4 cups Sealtest milk
1/4 lb. sliced dried beef, cut in pieces
Pepper
3 cornmeal muffins, home-made or baker's

Melt butter in heavy saucepan. Add flour; mix well. Pour in milk all at once and immediately stir vigorously over moderate heat until thickened. Add dried beef. Season with pepper. Serve on hot muffins, split in half. 3 servings.

DRIED BEEF GOLDENROD

For two

2 tbsp. butter
2 tbsp. flour
1 cup Sealtest milk
1 hard-cooked egg
2 oz. sliced dried beef, cut in pieces
Salt and pepper
4 Toast Cases, recipe below

Melt butter in heavy saucepan. Add flour; mix well. Pour in milk all at once and immediately stir vigorously over moderate heat until thickened. Fold in dried beef and sliced egg white. Season with salt and pepper. Reheat. Spoon into Toast Cases. Sprinkle with yolk put through coarse sieve. 2 servings.

TOAST CASES: Trim crusts from 4 slices fresh bread. Press each slice into section of buttered muffin pan. Brush with melted butter. Shortly before serving bake in moderately hot oven, 375°F., about 10 min. or until lightly browned. 4 toast cases.

CURRIED DRIED BEEF

On rice griddle cakes

4 tbsp. butter
4 tbsp. flour
½ tsp. curry powder
2 cups Sealtest milk
¼ lb. sliced dried beef, finely chopped
Rice Griddle Cakes, recipe below

Melt butter in heavy saucepan. Add flour and curry powder; mix well. Pour in milk all at once and immediately stir vigorously over moderate heat until thickened. Add dried beef; mix thoroughly. Reheat. Serve on Rice Griddle Cakes. 4 servings.

RICE GRIDDLE CAKES

3 cups cooked rice
2 eggs, slightly beaten
¼ to ½ tsp. salt
Dash of pepper

Add rice to eggs; mix thoroughly. Add salt and pepper. Drop by spoonfuls on very hot, well greased griddle; cook until golden brown on both sides. Eight 4" griddle cakes.

FRANKFURTER-MACARONI CASSEROLE

- 2 tbsp. butter
- 2 onions, coarsely chopped
- 1 green pepper, coarsely chopped
- 1 can condensed tomato soup, 10½ or 11 oz.
- 2 tbsp. flour
- 2 cups Sealtest milk
- ¼ cup chopped parsley
- Salt and pepper
- 1 lb. frankfurters, sliced
- 4 cups cooked elbow macaroni

Melt butter in large, heavy skillet or saucepan. Add onions and green pepper. Cook over low heat, stirring occasionally, until tender. Add soup, stirring until blended.

Mix flour with a little of the milk to a smooth paste; add remaining milk, mixing thoroughly. Add to soup mixture; cook, stirring constantly, until thickened. Add parsley. Season with salt and pepper. Remove from heat.

Add frankfurters and macaroni, stirring until just blended. Turn into 2-qt. casserole. Bake in moderate oven, 350°F., 30 min. 6 servings.

HEARTY FRANKFURTER STEW

- 1 lb. frankfurters
- 2 qts. boiling water
- 3 or 4 large potatoes, peeled and cut in large cubes
- 12 to 16 small white onions, peeled
- 6 carrots, scraped and cut in 1" diagonals
- 6 stalks celery, cut in 1" pieces
- ⅓ cup chopped parsley
- 3 cups Sealtest milk
- ½ cup flour

Drop frankfurters in large kettle of boiling water. Cover and simmer 5 to 8 min. Remove from water; cut in 1" chunks. Save water.

Add potatoes, onions, carrots, and celery to water in which frankfurters were cooked. Cover; bring to a boil; cook until vegetables are tender, about 20 to 30 min. Drain off all but 1 cup of cooking water.

Gradually add milk to flour, mixing until smoothly blended. Add frankfurters, parsley, and milk mixture to vegetables. Return to heat and cook, stirring constantly but gently, until thickened. 6 servings.

SAVORY SQUARES

Creamy gravy and frankfurters on savory bread dressing

- 1 qt. bread cubes, from left-over bread
- 1 cup Sealtest milk
- 1 small onion, chopped
- 2 tbsp. butter
- 1 tsp. salt
- 1/8 tsp. pepper
- 1 tsp. sage
- 1 egg, slightly beaten

Soak bread in milk few min. Brown onion lightly in butter; add to bread. Add remaining ingredients; mix well. Spread in buttered shallow 8" square pan. Bake in hot oven, 400°F., 20 to 25 min. Cut in squares.

TOPPING: Cut 3 frankfurters in half crosswise; then split halves lengthwise. Fry slowly in 2½ tbsp. butter; place on bread squares. Add 2½ tbsp. flour to drippings; mix well. Pour in 1½ cups milk all at once and immediately stir vigorously over moderate heat until thickened. Season with salt and pepper. Serve on the bread squares. 4 to 6 servings.

SOUTHERN-STYLE CASSEROLE

With corn bread topping

- 2 large green peppers, diced
- 2 medium onions, diced
- 3 tbsp. butter
- 1 twelve-oz. can luncheon meat, cubed
- 2 cups whole kernel corn, drained
- 1/3 cup flour
- 3 cups Sealtest milk
- Salt and pepper
- 1 pkg. corn muffin mix, 11¾ oz.

Cook green peppers and onions in butter, in large skillet or kettle, until tender but not browned. Add luncheon meat and corn; cook over moderate heat, stirring occasionally, until lightly browned. Sprinkle flour over meat mixture; stir until blended. Add milk and cook, stirring constantly, until thickened. Pour into large casserole or 13" x 9" baking dish.

Prepare corn muffin mix according to pkg. directions. Drop by large spoonfuls over top of meat mixture in casserole. Bake in moderately hot oven, 375°F., 20 to 30 min. 6 servings.

HEARTY DINNER PIE

Tasty company casserole . . . with a wonderful cheese pastry crust

- Cheese Pastry, recipe below
- 3 tbsp. butter
- 3 tbsp. flour
- 1½ cups Sealtest milk
- ¼ tsp. salt
- ⅛ tsp. pepper
- ½ tbsp. prepared mustard
- 1 twelve-oz. can luncheon meat, cubed
- 1 cup drained cooked peas
- 2 hard-cooked eggs, cubed

Prepare Cheese Pastry, recipe below.

Melt butter in heavy saucepan. Add flour; mix well. Pour in milk all at once and immediately stir vigorously over moderate heat until thickened. Season with salt, pepper, mustard. Remove from heat. Add meat, peas, eggs; mix well. Pour into greased baking dish, 10" x 6½" x 2". Let stand while rolling pastry.

Roll pastry to fit top; prick well with fork. Place on meat mixture. Bake in hot oven, 400°F., 20 min. or until crust is golden brown. 6 servings.

CHEESE PASTRY: Stir ¼ cup butter until softened; add ¼ lb. grated Old English process cheese; blend well. Add ¾ cup sifted flour; mix well. Press into ball with fingers. Chill in waxed paper 1 hour.

HAM TETRAZZINI

- 3 tbsp. butter
- 2 medium onions, finely chopped
- 1 medium green pepper, sliced
- ¼ lb. fresh mushrooms, sliced
- 1½ cups Sealtest light cream
- 1½ tbsp. flour
- 1 cup diced left-over cooked ham
- 1 pimiento, sliced
- 1 egg yolk, slightly beaten
- Salt and pepper
- ½ lb. spaghetti, cooked

Melt butter in large, heavy saucepan. Add onions, green pepper and mushrooms; cook, stirring occasionally, until tender and lightly browned. Stir in cream, and flour that has been mixed to a smooth paste with a little water. Cook, stirring constantly, until thickened.

Add ham and pimiento. Reheat, stirring gently. Add a little of this hot mixture to yolk; stir vigorously. Return to mixture in pan; cook, stirring gently and constantly, until reheated. Season with salt and pepper. Serve over hot spaghetti. 6 servings.

CURRIED LAMB AND RICE

1½ lbs. lean lamb shoulder, cut in pieces
Salt, pepper
Flour, butter
1½ cups hot water
1 small onion, sliced
2 tsp. curry powder
1½ cups Sealtest milk
Hot fluffy rice

Sprinkle lamb with salt and pepper; roll in flour. Fry slowly in a little butter until well browned on all sides. Add hot water and onion. Cover. Cook over low heat 1 to 2 hrs. or until tender. Stir occasionally and add more water if necessary.

Mix curry powder and ¼ cup sifted flour; add a little milk to make a smooth paste. Add remaining milk gradually and stir into lamb mixture. Cook, stirring constantly, until thickened. Season with salt and pepper. Serve on hot rice mixed with a little melted butter. 6 servings.

MAIN DISH PASTRY TURNOVERS

½ recipe Cottage Cheese Pastry, page 9
2 cups chopped, cooked meat or 2 cups cooked vegetables

Roll out pastry about ⅛" thick on floured board. Cut in six 6" squares; place ¼ to ⅓ cup filling in center of each. Fold diagonally, moisten edges and seal. Prick tops with fork. Brush lightly with mixture of 1 beaten egg yolk and 2 tbsp. milk.

Bake on brown-paper-lined baking sheet in very hot oven, 500°F., about 5 to 10 min. or until golden brown. Serve with Mushroom Sauce, recipe below. 6 servings.

MUSHROOM SAUCE

Mix 1 can condensed cream of mushroom soup with half as much Sealtest milk. Heat, stirring occasionally, and serve over Turnovers.

PORK CHOPS IN CREAM GRAVY

4 medium pork chops
Salt and pepper
2 tbsp. flour
1½ cups Sealtest milk

Cut some fat from chops and fry it slowly in heavy frying pan. Sprinkle chops with salt and pepper. Fry in the fat slowly until brown on both sides. Cover tightly and cook slowly, turning occasionally, for 45 to 50 min. or until tender. Remove from pan.

Add flour to drippings. Mix to smooth paste. Add milk all at once and immediately stir vigorously over moderate heat until thickened. Add more salt if desired. Serve on pork chops. 4 servings.

SAVORY VEAL

Delicious with buttermilk gravy

2 lbs. cubed lean veal shoulder
Salt, pepper, flour
3 tbsp. butter
1 cup hot water
1 small onion, sliced
2 cups Sealtest buttermilk

Sprinkle veal with salt and pepper. Roll in flour. Fry in butter until well browned on all sides. Add water and onion. Cover. Cook over low heat 1 to 2 hrs. or until tender, adding more water if necessary.

Mix 3½ tbsp. flour with a little buttermilk to make smooth paste. Add remaining buttermilk, mix well and stir into veal.

Cook over low heat, stirring constantly, until thickened. Add salt and pepper if desired. 6 servings.

ELEGANT VEAL BIRDS

1¼ lbs. veal steak, very thin
1¼ cups soft bread crumbs
½ cup chopped celery
2 tsp. chopped onion
⅛ tsp. sage
¼ tsp. salt
Few grains pepper
Butter, flour
1 cup boiling water
1 cup Sealtest sour cream

Trim veal; cut in 6 portions. Combine crumbs, celery, onion, sage, salt, pepper, 3 tbsp. melted butter; mix well; put a spoonful on each piece of meat. Roll up, fasten with toothpicks, sprinkle with salt and pepper, roll in flour. Fry in 2 tbsp. butter until brown, turning frequently. Add the water, cover tightly, simmer 1 to 2 hours or until tender. Turn occasionally, add water if necessary. Remove meat from pan, take out toothpicks.

Mix sour cream and 2⅓ tbsp. flour until smooth; add to meat gravy. Cook, stirring constantly, until thickened. Season with salt and pepper. Thin with water if desired. Add veal birds; reheat. 6 servings.

JULIENNE VEAL STEW

Cream . . . sweet or sour . . . garbs any dish in party dress

- 3 tbsp. butter
- 1½ lbs. lean shoulder of veal, in one piece
- 7 tbsp. flour
- 1½ cups hot water
- 3 medium onions, sliced crosswise
- 3 medium carrots, cut in thin strips
- 3 medium potatoes, cut in thin strips
- 1 small green pepper, cut in thin strips
- 2 cups Sealtest sour cream

Melt butter in large, heavy saucepan. Cut veal in thin strips; roll in 3 tbsp. of the flour; cook in butter until browned. Add water and onion slices. Simmer until meat is almost tender (about 30 min.). Add carrot and potato; cook until almost tender. Add green pepper. Cook until meat and vegetables are tender.

Mix sour cream and remaining 4 tbsp. flour until smooth. Add to stew. Stir until blended. Cook over moderate heat, stirring until thickened. Season with salt and pepper. 6 servings.

VEAL AND NOODLE CASSEROLE

- 1 lb. lean shoulder veal, cubed
- 1 small onion, diced
- 2 tbsp. melted butter
- ½ cup water
- 1 eight-oz. pkg. wide noodles
- ¼ lb. mushrooms, sliced
- ⅔ cup Sealtest sour cream
- 1 tbsp. flour
- Salt and pepper
- Buttered fresh bread crumbs

Brown veal and onion in the butter. Add water. Cover and simmer until veal is tender, adding more water if necessary.

Cook noodles in boiling, salted water until tender. Drain. Add to veal. Cook mushrooms in a little butter over low heat about 5 min.

Mix sour cream and flour together until smooth. Add mushrooms and sour cream to veal and noodles. Mix well. Season with salt and pepper.

Pour into 2-qt. casserole. Sprinkle with bread crumbs. Bake in moderate oven, 350°F., about 30 min. 6 servings.

POULTRY

CHICKEN A LA REGENT

5 tbsp. butter
5 tbsp. flour
2 cups Sealtest milk
2 tsp. grated onion
¼ tsp. basil
¼ tsp. salt
⅛ tsp. pepper
1 one-half lb. pkg. process American cheese, grated
2 cups big pieces cooked chicken
2 pimientos, cut in strips
6 slices toast, cut diagonally

Melt butter in double boiler. Add flour; mix well. Pour in milk all at once and immediately stir vigorously over moderate heat until thickened. Add onion, basil, salt, pepper; mix in well.

Sprinkle cheese over top a little at a time and stir in. Continue to stir until all is melted. Add chicken; heat through, stirring occasionally. Fold in pimiento; reheat. Serve on toast. 6 servings.

CHICKEN AND BROCCOLI MORNAY

2 cups medium white sauce, recipe page 58
½ cup grated process American cheese
Slices or pieces of cooked chicken, heated
6 stalks broccoli, cooked
Salt and pepper

Season white sauce with salt and pepper. Add cheese; stir until melted. Arrange chicken on heated plates, top with broccoli and pour sauce over all. Serve immediately. 6 servings.

CHICKEN BAKED IN CREAM

1 frying chicken cut in pieces, 3 to 3½ lbs.
Flour
Salt
4 tbsp. butter
½ cup Sealtest milk
1 cup Sealtest cream

Roll chicken in flour seasoned with salt. Fry in butter slowly until brown on all sides. Cover. Cook over low heat until very tender.

Combine milk and cream; add a little of it to 2 tbsp. flour to make smooth paste. Add remaining milk and cream gradually, stirring constantly. Pour over chicken.

Bake, covered, in moderate oven, 350°F., ½ to ¾ hr. 4 servings.

CURRY INDIENNE

Chicken, turkey, lamb, veal or shrimp

For wonderful and easy entertaining have a curry party and spend your time with your guests. Prepare curry the day before—then reheat to serve. Keep rice hot in a ring mold set in hot water, ready to turn out. Put accompaniments in small dishes—and let guests serve themselves buffet-style.

- 8 tbsp. butter
- 6 medium onions, thinly sliced
- 1 clove garlic, minced
- 1½ apples, peeled and diced
- 3 tbsp. curry powder
- 1 tsp. turmeric
- ½ cup fresh coconut milk
- 2 cups chicken stock or broth (or 2 chicken bouillon cubes and 2 cups hot water)
- 2 cups Sealtest whipping cream
- 4 cups diced cooked chicken, turkey, lamb, veal or shrimp
- Hot cooked rice
- Assorted accompaniments, below

Melt butter in large, heavy kettle or skillet. Add onions, garlic and apple. Cover and cook over low heat, stirring occasionally, until onions are tender and yellow. Mix in curry powder (use less if desired) and turmeric. Continue cooking over low heat 15 min. Add chicken stock and coconut milk; mix thoroughly. Bring to a boil, then lower heat; cover and simmer about 3 or 4 hrs. Stir occasionally.

Stir in cream. Continue cooking over low heat ½ hr. or more, stirring occasionally. Season to taste with salt. Add chicken, turkey, lamb, veal or shrimp; cook until heated through. Serve over hot cooked rice (about 2 cups raw rice) with assorted accompaniments. 8 generous servings.

CURRY ACCOMPANIMENTS

Serve chutney plus any of these:

- Grated fresh coconut
- Salted peanuts, almonds, cashews
- Chopped hard-cooked egg
- Diced green pepper
- Sweet or sour pickles
- Currant or cranberry jelly
- Sliced or fried banana
- Chopped crisp cooked bacon
- Fried onion rings
- Tomato wedges or slices
- Sliced avocado
- Finely chopped orange rind

CURRY PARTY SUPPER

Tomato Juice Cocktail
Curry Indienne   Hot Fluffy Rice
Curry Accompaniments
Tossed Green Salad   French Dressing
Pineapple and Sherbet Cup
Tea with Lemon or Cream

LITTLE CHICKEN PIES

6 tbsp. butter or margarine
6 tbsp. flour
1½ cups Sealtest milk
1¼ cups cold chicken stock
Salt and pepper
Pastry
2 cups diced cooked chicken

Melt butter in heavy saucepan. Add flour; mix well. Pour in milk and stock all at once and immediately stir vigorously over moderate heat until thickened. Season with salt and pepper.

Line 6 individual pie pans with pastry. Fill with chicken. Pour 3 tbsp. sauce over each. Cover with pastry. Seal edges. Cut slits in top. Bake in hot oven, 425°F., 25 to 30 min. Lift gently from tins. Serve with remaining hot sauce. 6 servings.

CREAMY CHICKEN FRICASSEE

1 stewing chicken, cut up (about 3 to 4 lbs.)
⅓ cup finely chopped celery
⅓ cup finely chopped onion
Few celery leaves
2 bay leaves
4 to 5 cups boiling water
2 cups Sealtest milk
10 tbsp. flour
Salt and pepper

Put chicken, celery, onion, celery leaves and bay leaves in a large heavy kettle. Add water. Cover and simmer over low heat 2 hrs. or until chicken is tender. Remove chicken from stock to hot platter. Also remove and discard celery leaves and bay leaves. Skim off excess fat from top of stock. Boil down stock to about 2 cups.

Add milk gradually to flour, stirring until smooth. Add milk-flour mixture to hot stock; mix well. Cook, stirring constantly, until thickened. Season with salt and pepper. Pour gravy over chicken or serve separately. If desired, chicken may be put back in gravy to reheat. Serve with hot fluffy rice, dumplings or biscuits. 4 to 6 servings.

TURKEY-HAM ORIENTAL

3 tbsp. butter
3 tbsp. flour
1 cup Sealtest milk
½ cup Sealtest cream
1 cup diced cooked turkey
1 cup diced cooked ham
Salt and pepper
Chow mein noodles, shoestring potatoes or buttered toast triangles

Melt butter in heavy saucepan. Add flour; mix well. Pour in milk and cream all at once and immediately stir vigorously over moderate heat until thickened.

Fold in turkey and ham. Season with salt and pepper. Reheat, stirring lightly. Serve on warmed noodles, potatoes or toast. 4 to 6 servings.

TURKEY CROUSTADES

4 tbsp. butter or margarine
4 tbsp. flour
¾ cup Sealtest milk
½ cup Sealtest light cream
1 cup cold turkey stock
Salt and pepper
1 cup cooked diced celery
2½ to 3 cups large chunks cooked turkey
6 to 7 croustades

Melt butter in heavy saucepan. Add flour; mix well. Pour in combined milk, cream and stock all at once and immediately stir vigorously over moderate heat until thickened. Season with salt and pepper. Add celery and turkey. Reheat, stirring gently. Serve in croustades. If desired, garnish with pimiento. 6 to 7 servings.

CROUSTADES: Cut bread in 2" thick slices, then in 2½" rounds or squares; hollow out centers. Brush inside and out lightly with melted butter. Bake in moderately hot oven, 375°F., 10 to 12 min.

BUFFET SUPPER

Fruit Bowl with Frosted Grapes
Turkey Croustades
Sparkling Cranberries
Cottage Cheese with Relishes
Mint Parfaits Coffee with Cream

FISH

HOT SALMON MOUSSE

1 one-lb. can salmon
5 tbsp. butter
5 tbsp. flour
½ tsp. salt
¼ tsp. nutmeg
Few grains pepper
1½ cups Sealtest milk
2 eggs, separated

Drain salmon; flake finely with fork. Melt butter in heavy saucepan. Add flour, salt, nutmeg and pepper; mix well. Pour in milk all at once and immediately stir vigorously over moderate heat until thickened.

Add sauce gradually to salmon beating constantly with rotary beater. When thoroughly blended and smooth, add egg yolks. Beat well.

Beat egg whites until stiff but not dry. Fold into fish mixture. Pour into buttered 1½-qt. casserole. Bake in moderate oven, 325°F., 45 min. or until a knife inserted in center comes out clean. 4 to 6 servings.

LITTLE SALMON LOAVES

For hearty nourishing noon-day lunch

1 one-lb. can salmon
About ⅔ cup Sealtest milk
1 tbsp. lemon juice
2 tbsp. butter
2 tbsp. flour
Salt, pepper, onion salt
½ cup packaged dry bread crumbs
⅔ cup finely chopped celery
1 egg, slightly beaten with fork

Drain salmon; add enough milk to salmon liquid to make 1 cup. Flake salmon with fork; sprinkle with lemon juice.

Melt butter in heavy saucepan. Add flour; mix well. Pour in milk mixture all at once and immediately stir vigorously over moderate heat until thickened. Season with salt, pepper, onion salt. Pour over salmon. Stir in crumbs, celery, then egg; mix lightly but well. Spoon into well-greased custard cups. Bake in moderate oven, 350°F., about 30 min.

Turn out of cups; garnish with lemon wedges. 5 servings.

SALMON A LA KING

1 one-lb. can salmon
½ cup Sealtest milk
4 tbsp. butter or margarine
2 tbsp. finely chopped onion
4 tbsp. flour
Dash of Tabasco
1½ cups Sealtest cottage cheese
Hot fluffy rice, waffles, or French fried potato sticks

Drain salmon; add salmon liquid to milk. Gently break salmon in large pieces. Melt butter in heavy saucepan. Add onion and cook slowly until tender but not browned, stirring occasionally. Blend in flour. Pour in milk and salmon liquid all at once and immediately stir vigorously over moderate heat until it begins to thicken. Add Tabasco.

Immediately fold in cottage cheese; reheat, stirring gently. Add salmon; reheat, stirring gently. Serve immediately on rice, waffles or potato sticks. 6 servings.

HOMEY SUPPER
Hot Tomato Bouillon
Salmon A La King
Pickle Relish in Lettuce Cup
Lemon Tarts
Coffee with Cream Milk

FISH ROLL-UPS

4 white fish fillets, ¼" to ½" thick, about 1½ lbs.
8 slices process American cheese, 3½" x 3½" x ⅛"
1 tsp. oregano or thyme
¼ cup finely chopped parsley
2 tbsp. butter
2 medium onions, chopped
2 tbsp. flour
1 tsp. salt
⅛ tsp. pepper
1½ cups Sealtest milk

Cover each fish fillet with 2 slices cheese. Top cheese with generous sprinkling of oregano and parsley. Roll up fillets and fasten with toothpicks or skewers.

Melt butter in heavy saucepan. Add onions and cook until tender and yellow. Add flour, salt and pepper; mix well. Pour in milk all at once and immediately stir vigorously over moderate heat until thickened. Pour into shallow baking dish or 9" pie pan. Arrange fish rolls in sauce. Bake in hot oven, 400°F., 20 to 25 min. 4 servings.

SCALLOPED OYSTERS

1 cup fine saltine crumbs
¾ cup Sealtest milk
2 doz. fresh oysters, drained
Salt and pepper
2 tbsp. butter

Sprinkle ⅓ of crumbs in buttered 8″ oven-glass pie plate. Moisten carefully with part of milk. Cover with half of oysters, sprinkle with salt and pepper, then cover with more crumbs. Repeat, ending with crumbs. Moisten carefully with milk. Dot with butter.

Bake in moderately hot oven, 375°F., 40 to 45 min. or until brown. Serve immediately. 3 to 4 servings.

CREAMED SHRIMP AND EGGS

2¼ tbsp. butter or margarine
2¼ tbsp. flour
1¾ cups Sealtest milk
Salt and pepper
1 to 1½ cups cooked or canned shrimp
4 hard-cooked eggs
6 Toast Cases, recipe page 26

Melt butter or margarine in heavy saucepan. Add flour; mix well. Pour in milk all at once and immediately stir vigorously over moderate heat until thickened. Season with salt and pepper; add shrimp and sliced eggs. Reheat. Serve in Toast Cases. 6 servings.

TUNA SCALLOP

4 tbsp. butter
4 tbsp. flour
2 cups Sealtest milk
½ cup Miracle Whip salad dressing
2 seven-oz. cans tuna, drained
½ cup canned sliced mushrooms
1 tbsp. lemon juice
Hot toast or French fried potato sticks
Salt and pepper

Melt butter in heavy saucepan. Add flour; mix well. Pour in milk all at once and immediately stir vigorously over moderate heat until thickened. Blend in salad dressing. Add tuna and mushrooms. Cook over moderate heat until tuna is heated through; stir constantly. (Break up tuna into large chunks.) Add lemon juice, and salt and pepper to taste. Serve over toast, or potato sticks. 4 to 6 servings.

TUNA DINNER TREAT

Scrumptious easy-do double cheese casserole

- 1 pkg. Kraft Dinner
- 2 cups Sealtest cottage cheese
- 1 tsp. grated onion
- 1 seven-oz. can tuna, drained
- 1/3 cup finely rolled cheese crackers

Prepare Kraft Dinner exactly as directed on pkg. Add cottage cheese, onion and flaked tuna; mix well. Pour into well-buttered 1½ qt. casserole. Sprinkle with cracker crumbs. Bake in moderately hot oven, 375°F., 30 min. or until piping hot. 6 servings.

BUFFET SUGGESTION

Tuna Dinner Treat
Buttered Green Beans Tossed Salad
Celery, Olives Assorted Relishes
Buttered Hot Ready-to-Serve Rolls
Lemon Sherbet
Milk Coffee with Cream

MARINER'S CASSEROLE

Tart spicy pickled beets and onions go well with this

- 3 tbsp. butter
- ½ to 2/3 cup coarsely chopped onions
- ½ cup flour
- 1 cup cooked or canned tomatoes
- 1 cup cooked rice
- 2 cups Sealtest milk
- 1 thirteen-oz. or 2 seven-oz. cans tuna, drained and flaked in large pieces
- 1/8 tsp. ground thyme
- 1 tsp. salt
- Dash of cayenne

Melt butter in large heavy saucepan. Add onions; cover and cook over low heat until onions are soft but not brown. Add flour, mix well.

Add tomatoes, stirring until blended. Add milk. Cook over moderate heat, stirring constantly, until thickened.

Add rice, tuna, thyme, salt and cayenne. Mix well. Continue cooking over moderate heat until tuna and rice are thoroughly heated. Stir occasionally. Serve in individual casseroles; garnish with toasted buttered bread croutons and parsley. 6 servings.

Cottage Cheese in Main Dishes

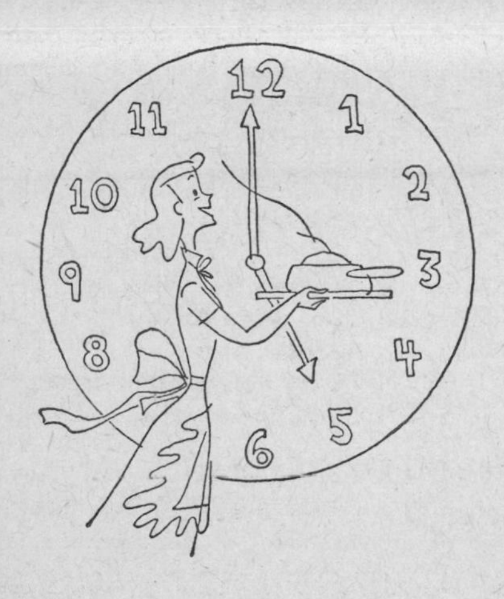

Women are discovering that they can *cook* with cottage cheese! It's always ready to use any hour of the day . . . no advance preparation . . . no waste. It handles easily, adds its own delicious flavor to an amazing variety of dishes. And, of course, it gives you a good share of those all-important proteins at low cost. Do find out for yourself what a wonderful time-and-money-saver cottage cheese can be!

The recipes on the following pages all use cottage cheese as their chief ingredient. Most of them are main courses; there are also several that make attractive and nourishing additions to a light meat course.

BLINTZES

1¼ to 1½ cups Sealtest milk
1 cup packaged pancake mix
1 medium onion, finely chopped
½ green pepper, finely chopped
Sealtest sour cream or chili sauce
2 cups Sealtest cottage cheese

Add milk gradually to pancake mix, stirring until blended. Do not overbeat. Stir in onion and pepper. Drop by spoonfuls on hot, lightly greased griddle. Bake until golden brown on both sides.

Spoon cheese on center of each pancake. Roll up; fasten with toothpick. Serve immediately with spoonful of sour cream or heated chili sauce. 12 to 14 pancakes.

CHEESE AND NOODLE CASSEROLE

3 cups (5 oz.) egg noodles
1 cup Sealtest cottage cheese
1 cup Sealtest sour cream
2 tbsp. grated onion
½ tsp. salt
¼ to ½ clove garlic, minced
2 tsp. Worcestershire
¼ tsp. Tabasco
¼ cup fine dry bread crumbs
¼ cup grated Parmesan cheese

Cook noodles in boiling salted water for 10 min. or until tender; drain. Combine with remaining ingredients except grated cheese; mix well. Place in 1½ or 2 qt. casserole; sprinkle with cheese. Bake in moderate oven, 350°F., 20 to 25 min. or until heated through. 4 to 6 servings.

CHEESE SANDWICH BARBECUE

2 eggs
⅓ cup Sealtest milk
½ tsp. salt
Few grains pepper
⅛ tsp. nutmeg
2 cups Sealtest cottage cheese
12 slices buttered bread
Butter or other fat for frying
Barbecue sauce, bought or homemade

Beat eggs slightly with fork in shallow dish. Add milk, salt, pepper, nutmeg; mix thoroughly.

Spread cheese on 6 slices bread; top with remaining slices. Dip both sides of sandwiches in egg mixture quickly. Fry in butter until golden brown on both sides. Serve immediately with hot barbecue sauce. 6 sandwiches.

COTTAGE CHEDDAR SOUFFLE

Magnificent blending of two popular cheeses

4 eggs, separated
2 tbsp. butter, melted
1½ cups Sealtest cottage cheese
2 tbsp. Sealtest milk
3 tbsp. flour
¾ tsp. salt
⅛ tsp. white pepper
1 cup shredded sharp Cheddar cheese

Beat egg whites until stiff. Beat together yolks and butter with egg beater until well blended. Add cottage cheese, milk, flour, salt, pepper; continue to beat with egg beater until well blended. Fold into whites along with Cheddar cheese.

Pour into unbuttered deep round glass 8″ layer cake pan, 1½ qt. capacity. Bake in slow oven, 300°F., about 1 hr. Serve immediately. 4 to 5 servings.

COTTAGE CHEESE SOUFFLE

4 eggs, separated
¼ cup Sealtest milk
⅓ cup flour
1½ tsp. salt
3 tbsp. finely chopped chives or onions
⅛ tsp. pepper
2 cups Sealtest cottage cheese

Beat egg yolks until light and foamy. Add milk gradually to flour, stirring until smooth. Add to egg yolks. Beat well with electric mixer or hand rotary beater. Add chives, salt, pepper and cottage cheese. (If cheese curds are large, press through a sieve before adding.) Beat until smooth and blended.

Beat egg whites until stiff but not dry. Fold into cheese mixture gently but thoroughly. Bake in 1½ qt. casserole in a slow oven, 300° F., 1 hr. or until set. 4 to 6 servings.

TOP-OF-STOVE SOUFFLE

4 eggs, slightly beaten
1 cup Sealtest cottage cheese
¼ cup Sealtest milk
Few grains pepper
1 tsp. salt

Combine all ingredients in top of double boiler. Cook over boiling water, beating constantly with rotary beater 3 min. Cover and continue cooking over boiling water 15 to 18 min., without uncovering. Serve immediately. 4 to 6 servings.

COTTAGE CHEESE HERBED ONIONS

Flavorful new mainstay dish

2 lbs. baby onions
4 tbsp. butter or margarine
4 tbsp. flour
½ cup Sealtest milk
½ tsp. salt
Dash pepper
¾ tsp. marjoram
1½ cups Sealtest cottage cheese
Buttered fresh bread crumbs

Cook peeled whole onions in boiling salted water 20 min. or until tender. Drain. Turn into buttered shallow baking dish, about 10"x 6" x 2".

Melt butter in heavy saucepan. Add flour; mix well. Add milk all at once. Cook, stirring constantly, for about ½ min. or until just beginning to thicken. Remove from heat; quickly blend in salt, pepper, marjoram, cheese. Spread evenly over onions. Sprinkle with crumbs. Bake in moderately hot oven, 375°F., about 25 min. Serve with a crisp green salad. 6 servings.

BUTTERED FRESH BREAD CRUMBS: Remove crusts from 3 slices fresh bread. Pull bread apart into small bits with fingers or fork. Pour 2 to 3 tbsp. melted butter over top; toss with fork until blended.

HEARTY CHEESE CUSTARD PIE

A main dish that's a welcome change

5 eggs, separated
1 cup Sealtest cottage cheese
1 cup Sealtest light cream
1 tsp. celery flakes, crumbled
1 tsp. salt
⅛ tsp. pepper
2 tbsp. melted butter
1 baked 9" pastry shell

Add egg yolks to cottage cheese. Beat with rotary beater until well-blended and cheese curds are very fine.

Add cream, celery flakes, salt, pepper and melted butter. Beat well with rotary beater until thoroughly blended.

Beat egg whites until stiff but not dry. Lightly fold into cheese mixture.

Pour into pastry shell. Bake in hot oven, 450°F., 10 min. Reduce heat to moderate, 350°F., and continue baking for 20 to 25 min. or until a knife comes out clean when inserted. Serve hot garnished with hard-cooked egg. 4 to 6 servings.

MAINSTAY BAKED STUFFED POTATOES

2 large potatoes
1 cup Sealtest cottage cheese
1 tbsp. chopped chives
1½ tbsp. melted butter
¾ to 1 tsp. salt
⅛ tsp. pepper

Bake potatoes in moderately hot oven, 375°F., about 1 to 1½ hrs. or until done. Cut in half lengthwise.

Scoop out insides (reserving shells); mash. Add remaining ingredients. Beat until light and fluffy.

Fill potato shells with mixture. Dot with extra butter, and sprinkle with paprika. Bake in moderately hot oven, 375°F., about 15 to 20 min. until lightly browned on top and thoroughly heated. 4 servings.

PINT-SIZE PIZZAS

Wonderfully savory individual tomato pies

1¼ cups canned tomatoes
1 six-oz. can tomato paste
½ tsp. garlic salt
½ tsp. salt
Dash pepper
1½ tsp. oregano
½ cup Sealtest milk
2 tbsp. melted butter
2 cups packaged biscuit mix
2 cups Sealtest cottage cheese
¼ lb. Mozzarella or Muenster cheese, grated

Mix together tomatoes, tomato paste, garlic salt, salt, pepper and oregano.

Add milk and butter to biscuit mix; stir quickly and vigorously with fork until dry ingredients are just moistened. Knead gently a few seconds; divide in 6 pieces. Pat out on cookie sheets into 6" circles. Pinch up edges to make slight rims.

Spread cottage cheese on circles; cover with tomato mixture. Sprinkle Mozzarella or Muenster cheese over top. Bake in hot oven, 425°F., 15 min. Reduce heat to moderate, 350°F. Bake 10 to 15 min. longer. 6 individual pies or pizzas.

HEARTY SUPPER

Chicken Bouillon
Pint-Size Pizzas
Tossed Green Salad
Fruited Jello with Whipped Cream
Milk Coffee with Cream

LASAGNA

Low cost hearty substantial meal

1⅔ cups Tomato Sauce, recipe below
½ lb. lasagna noodles (broad noodles)
½ lb. (8 slices) process American cheese
1 cup Sealtest cottage cheese
⅓ cup grated Parmesan cheese

Prepare sauce. While sauce is simmering, cook noodles in 3 qts. rapidly boiling water, with 1 tbsp. olive oil, for about ½ hr. or until tender; drain well.

Pour ⅓ cup sauce into bottom of deep 9" square baking dish; over this place layer of noodles, a layer of cheese slices, 4 or 5 tbsp. cottage cheese and sprinkling of Parmesan. Repeat this process in layers until all ingredients are used. Top layer should be sauce and grated Parmesan. Bake in moderate oven, 350°F., 30 min. or until firm. (Let stand about 15 min. before serving.) 4 to 6 servings.

TOMATO SAUCE: Cook 1 chopped onion and 1 minced clove garlic in 3 tbsp. hot olive oil 3 min. until lightly browned. Add one No. 2 can tomatoes, 1 tbsp. chopped parsley, 3 basil leaves, one 6 oz. can tomato paste and pinch of sugar. Simmer over low heat 1 hr., stirring occasionally. Season with salt and pepper.

PEPPY COTTAGE CHEESE PEPPERS

A man's main dish

3 green peppers, halved
2 tbsp. chopped onion
2 tbsp. butter
2¼ cups cooked rice
½ tsp. thyme
1 tsp. Worcestershire sauce
¼ tsp. salt
1 cup Sealtest cottage cheese
⅔ cup canned tomato sauce
2 strips bacon

Partially cook hollowed-out peppers in boiling salted water 5 to 10 min. Drain.

Cook onion slowly in butter until yellow, stirring occasionally; pour over rice. Add thyme, Worcestershire, salt; mix well. Stir in cheese and tomato sauce. Spoon into peppers. Top with bacon cut in small pieces. Bake in moderately hot oven, 375°F., about 25 min. 6 servings.

PUFFY OMELET WEDGES

Airy triangles of nutritious cottage cheese and egg

4 eggs separated
¼ to ½ tsp. salt
⅛ tsp. pepper
1 cup Sealtest cottage cheese
1½ tbsp. butter

Beat egg whites with egg beater until stiff but not dry.

Beat yolks with the same beater until thick and lemon colored. Add salt, pepper and cheese. Continue beating with beater until smooth and blended. Add egg whites; fold in gently.

Heat butter slowly in 9″ skillet until just moderately hot, not brown. Add egg mixture; cook over low heat about 3 min. or until puffed up and delicately browned on bottom.

Bake in moderate oven, 350°F., 15 min. or until surface is just firm. Cut in wedges. Serve at once, plain or with crisp bacon, or mushroom sauce. 4 to 5 servings.

SCRAMBLED EGGS WITH COTTAGE CHEESE

1 tbsp. butter
1 tsp. salt
Few grains pepper
½ cup Sealtest milk
6 eggs
½ cup Sealtest cottage cheese

Melt butter in medium frying pan over low heat. Add salt, pepper and milk to eggs and beat lightly. Pour into frying pan. Cook over low heat, stirring until the eggs are creamy and firm, but not hard and dry.

Gently fold in cottage cheese. Continue cooking over very low heat only until cheese is warm but not hot. Serve immediately. 4 servings.

For 3 additional cottage cheese main dish combinations see:

MAIN DISH PASTRY TURNOVERS, page 30
SALMON A LA KING, page 38
TUNA DINNER TREAT, page 40

American Cheese, Eggs, Macaroni

If you are budget-conscious (and who isn't nowadays?) you'll find the recipes on the next few pages a great help. Cheese, eggs, macaroni and milk are featured in a variety of interesting combinations which make excellent lenten meals, too.

Our particular favorite is Cheese Souffle, page 49, a real treat for family and friends. Try it the next time company comes—and watch your reputation as a kitchen wizard soar!

CHEESE FONDUE

1½ cups Sealtest milk
1 tbsp. butter
1½ cups small fresh bread crumbs
2 cups grated process American cheese
3 eggs, separated
¾ to 1 tsp. salt
Few grains pepper

Scald milk in double boiler. Stir in butter. Remove from heat; add crumbs and cheese. Mix well.

Beat egg yolks slightly; add first mixture gradually, stirring constantly. Add salt and pepper. Fold in stiffly beaten egg whites. Pour into buttered shallow round 1½ qt. baking dish, 8¼" x 1¾".

Bake in pan of hot water in moderate oven, 350°F., 40 min. or until a knife inserted in center comes out clean. 6 servings.

CHEESE SOUFFLE

A special "cook's pride" dish—but follow directions carefully

3 tbsp. butter
3 tbsp. flour
1 cup Sealtest milk
½ tsp. salt
Dash of cayenne
½ tsp. Worcestershire sauce
½ lb. process American cheese, grated
5 eggs, separated

Melt butter in heavy saucepan. Add flour; mix well. Pour in milk all at once and immediately stir vigorously over moderate heat until thickened. Add salt, cayenne, Worcestershire and cheese; cook over low heat, stirring constantly, until cheese melts. *Remove from heat;* cool slightly. Beat egg yolks well; add to cheese mixture, stirring quickly to blend thoroughly.

Beat egg whites until stiff but not dry. Add cheese mixture gradually, folding it gently but thoroughly into egg whites. Pour into ungreased 2 qt. baking dish or casserole.

If desired, run the tip of a spoon around the mixture 1" from edge of baking dish, making a slight depression. This forms a "box top" lid on souffle as it bakes and puffs up.

Bake in slow oven, 300°F., about 1 hr. 5 min. 6 servings.

CHEESE TOAST SANDWICHES

2 eggs, slightly beaten
½ cup Sealtest milk
4 slices bread
Butter
¼ lb. sliced process American cheese
Few grains salt and pepper

Combine eggs, milk, salt and pepper. Pour into shallow dish.

Dip each slice of bread into egg mixture, turning so that both sides take up liquid.

Fry slices in butter on one side. Turn and top 2 slices with cheese. When the cheese begins to melt and all slices are brown on the bottom, combine sandwich fashion. Serve immediately. 2 servings.

For 7 additional main dish American cheese recipes see:

CHICKEN A LA REGENT, page 33
CHICKEN AND BROCCOLI MORNAY, page 33
COTTAGE CHEDDAR SOUFFLE, page 43
FISH ROLL-UPS, page 38
HEARTY DINNER PIE, page 29
LASAGNA, page 46
TOASTED CHEESE SANDWICH, page 108

CREAMED EGGS IN BOLOGNA CUPS

4 tbsp. butter or margarine
4 tbsp. flour
2 cups Sealtest milk
Salt and pepper
8 hard-cooked eggs
6 slices bologna, skin left on

Melt butter in heavy saucepan. Add flour; mix well. Pour in milk all at once and immediately stir vigorously over moderate heat until thickened. Season with salt and pepper. Add quartered or sliced eggs; reheat, stirring very lightly.

Heat bologna slices slowly in frying pan in small amount butter or other fat until they form cup shapes. Fill with creamed eggs. Sprinkle with paprika, if desired. 6 servings.

For 6 additional main dish egg recipes see:

CREAMED SHRIMP AND EGGS, page 39
CREAMY CORN CUSTARDS, page 53
FRENCH TOAST, page 94
PUFFY OMELET WEDGES, page 47
SCRAMBLED EGGS WITH COTTAGE CHEESE, page 47
TOP-OF-STOVE SOUFFLE, page 43

MACARONI AND CHEESE

- 1 cup elbow macaroni
- 2 tbsp. butter
- 2 tbsp. flour
- 1 cup Sealtest milk
- ½ tsp. Worcestershire
- ¼ tsp. dry mustard
- 2 cups grated Cheddar cheese
- Salt and pepper
- Buttered bread crumbs

Cook macaroni in boiling salted water according to package directions. Drain.

Melt butter in heavy saucepan. Add flour; mix well. Pour in milk all at once and immediately stir over moderate heat until thickened. Add Worcestershire, mustard, macaroni and 1½ cups cheese. Mix until well-blended. Season to taste with salt and pepper.

Pour into 1½ qt. casserole. Sprinkle remaining ½ cup cheese, and crumbs over top. Bake in moderately hot oven, 375°F., 25 min. 4 generous servings.

For 2 additional main dish macaroni recipes see:

FRANKFURTER-MACARONI CASSEROLE, page 27
TUNA DINNER TREAT, page 40

Vegetables in Main Dishes

Vegetables are important because they give us essential vitamins and minerals. They also supply the roughage and bulk we need. But aside from their contribution to our good health, vegetables, if well prepared, make delightful delicious eating!

To retain their flavor and vitamin content, we must treat vegetables with special care and consideration. A generous dab of butter brings out the natural flavor of cooked vegetables; a cream or cheese sauce adds a fine epicurean touch.

BEETS IN SOUR SAUCE

2 tbsp. flour
1 cup Sealtest sour cream
1 tbsp. prepared horseradish
1 tsp. vinegar
3 cups sliced cooked beets, drained
Salt and pepper

Add flour to sour cream. Mix until smooth. Cook in double boiler until thickened, stirring constantly.

Add horseradish and vinegar. Season with salt and pepper. If desired, add more horseradish. Add beets. Reheat, stirring occasionally. 4 to 6 servings.

CABBAGE IN CREAM

2 qts. shredded cabbage
¾ to 1 cup Sealtest light cream
¼ cup butter
Salt and pepper

Cook cabbage in boiling salted water until just tender, about 8 to 15 min. Drain.

Add cream and butter to cabbage. Cook over low heat, stirring lightly but well, until mixture is heated through. Do not boil. Season with salt and pepper. 6 servings.

CREAMY CORN CUSTARDS

3 eggs
1¼ cups Sealtest milk, scalded
1 one-lb. can cream style corn
Salt and pepper

Beat eggs slightly; gradually add milk, beating vigorously. Add corn; season with salt and pepper. Spoon into buttered individual baking dishes. Bake in pan of hot water in moderate oven, 350°F., about 50 min. or until set. Garnish with parsley. 6 servings.

PEAS IN CREAM

2 lbs. fresh peas, shelled
½ to ¾ cup Sealtest cream
2 tbsp. butter
Salt and pepper

Cook peas in boiling salted water until just tender. Drain. Add cream and butter. Heat slowly, stirring lightly. Do not boil. Season with salt and pepper. 4 servings.

ESCALLOPED EGGPLANT AND TOMATO

4 tbsp. butter
2 tbsp. finely chopped onion
1 small eggplant, peeled and cubed
1½ cups cooked tomatoes
1 tbsp. sugar
2 tbsp. flour
½ cup Sealtest sour cream
Salt and pepper

Melt butter in large frying pan. Fry onion and eggplant in butter until lightly browned.

Add tomatoes and sugar. Cook until about half the liquid has evaporated. Cover and cook slowly until eggplant is tender or about 20 min.

Blend flour and sour cream. Add to eggplant mixture. Cook, stirring gently until just thickened. Season with salt and pepper. 4 generous servings.

PEERLESS POTATOES

Deliciously unusual base for anything creamed such as codfish, dried beef or chicken

Scrub 3 medium potatoes; cut in halves lengthwise. With sharp knife cut deep crisscross lines, making a waffle pattern. Brush generously with butter; sprinkle with salt, pepper, paprika. Bake in very hot oven, 450°F., 35 to 45 min. 6 servings.

POTATO PUFFS ON TOMATOES

3 tomatoes
5 medium potatoes
½ to ⅔ cup Sealtest cream, scalded
Salt and pepper

Cut out stem end of tomatoes; cut tomatoes in half crosswise. Place in shallow pan; sprinkle with salt and pepper.

Cook potatoes; mash; season with salt and pepper. Add cream, and beat until smooth and fluffy. (Amount of cream will depend upon dryness of potatoes.) Pile on tomato halves. Bake in hot oven, 400°F., about 15 min. 6 servings.

POTATO PUFF SOUFFLE

¼ cup butter
¼ cup sifted flour
1 cup Sealtest sour cream, sweet milk or cream
2 tsp. grated onion
1½ cups hot, riced potatoes, firmly packed
1½ tsp. salt
Dash of pepper
4 eggs, separated

Melt butter in heavy saucepan. Add flour and mix until smooth. Add sour cream all at once. Cook, stirring constantly, until just thickened. Remove from heat. Add potatoes, onion, salt and pepper. Beat until smooth and thoroughly blended.

Add a small amount of hot mixture to well beaten egg yolks, stirring constantly. Add to remaining hot mixture. Mix well.

Beat egg whites until stiff but not dry. Fold lightly into potato mixture. Pour into buttered 1¼ qt. shallow casserole. Bake in pan of hot water in moderate oven, 325°F., about 50 min. or until a knife, when inserted in the center, comes out clean. 6 servings.

SCALLOPED POTATOES

1¼ qts. raw potatoes, sliced very thin (about 6 medium potatoes)
2½ tbsp. flour
1¼ tsp. salt
Few grains pepper
2½ tbsp. butter or margarine
2½ cups Sealtest milk

Spread about one-third of the potatoes in loose overlapping fashion in greased baking dish about 2¼ qt. capacity.

Sprinkle with one-half of the flour, salt and pepper. Dot with one tbsp. butter or margarine cut in small bits.

Repeat with another layer of potatoes, flour, salt, pepper and butter or margarine. Cover with remaining potatoes and dot with remaining butter or margarine. Pour milk over top.

Cover and bake in moderately hot oven, 375°F., about 30 min.

Uncover and bake for 20 to 40 min. longer or until potatoes are tender. 6 servings.

BAKED BANANAS AND SWEET POTATOES

1½ lbs. sweet potatoes
1 tsp. salt
⅓ to ½ cup warm Sealtest milk
4 tbsp. butter
3 bananas
12 marshmallows, cut in pieces
⅓ cup brown sugar

Cook, peel and mash sweet potatoes. Add salt, 2 tbsp. of butter and enough milk to make light and fluffy. Spread on bottom of individual baking dishes.

Slice bananas. Place on top of sweet potatoes. Dot with marshmallows. Sprinkle with brown sugar and with the remaining 2 tbsp. of butter, melted.

Bake in moderately hot oven, 375°F., about 30 min. 6 servings.

SWEET POTATOES CHANTILLY

6 medium sweet potatoes
1 to 2 tbsp. butter
¼ to ¾ cup Sealtest milk, scalded
Salt and pepper
1½ cups whipped Sealtest cream
¼ cup brown sugar

Cook potatoes in boiling salted water until tender. Peel and mash. Add butter. Season with salt and pepper. Add milk gradually and beat until potatoes are smooth and fluffy. (Amount of milk depends upon dryness of potatoes.) Pile in baking dish.

Season whipped cream with a little salt. Spread over sweet potatoes. Sprinkle with brown sugar.

Bake in a moderately hot oven, 375°F., 20 to 25 min. 6 servings.

BAKED SQUASH

2 acorn squash, cut in half
1 tbsp. melted butter
Salt
1 tbsp. brown sugar
2 tbsp. Sealtest heavy cream

Remove squash seeds and stringy portions. Score inside surface by making several gashes with sharp knife. Brush with butter and sprinkle with salt and brown sugar.

Place in shallow baking dish, cut side up. Bake in moderate oven, 350°F., about one hr. or until tender. Pour a little cream into each half and bake 10 min. longer. 4 servings.

GARDEN GREEN SOUFFLE

Delectable . . . dependable . . . glamorous

½ lb. fresh spinach
Salt
4 tbsp. butter
4 tbsp. flour
1 cup Sealtest milk
3 eggs, separated
Pepper

Wash and dry spinach. Chop fine. Sprinkle with 1 tsp. salt. Melt butter in heavy saucepan. Add flour; mix well. Add milk all at once. Cook, stirring constantly, until it begins to thicken. Remove from heat.

Beat yolks slightly; add hot mixture gradually, beating vigorously. Add ½ tsp. salt and few grains pepper. Fold in stiffly beaten egg whites, and spinach.

Pour into buttered shallow glass baking dish, 1½ quart capacity. Bake in pan of hot water in moderate oven, 325°F., about 35 min. Garnish with lemon wedge or grapefruit section. 5 to 6 servings.

TURNIP POTATO DUET

Cook 1 quart diced raw yellow turnip in boiling salted water about 15 min. Add 3½ cups diced raw potato; continue to cook until soft. Drain well; put through ricer. Add 2 tbsp. butter and ½ cup Sealtest milk. Season with salt and pepper. Reheat, stirring most of the time, until desired consistency. 6 servings.

FLUFFY TURNIPS

2 lbs. white turnips
2 tbsp. butter
2 tbsp. flour
½ cup Sealtest milk
Salt and pepper

Pare turnips. Cut in ½-inch cubes. Cook in covered pan in small amount boiling salted water until very tender. Drain. Mash, or beat with rotary beater, until smooth.

Melt butter in heavy saucepan. Add flour, mix until smooth. Add milk all at once. Cook, stirring constantly, until thickened.

Add turnips to cream sauce, and beat quickly with a fork or rotary beater until fluffy. Season with salt and pepper. Serve hot. 4 generous servings.

TOMATOES IN SAVORY SAUCE

2 tbsp. butter
3 medium tomatoes, peeled and halved
3 tbsp. sifted flour
1 tsp. sugar
1/8 tsp. dry mustard
3/4 cup Sealtest milk
Few drops Worcestershire sauce
Salt and pepper

Melt butter in frying pan. Fry tomatoes in butter until lightly browned and just tender. Remove all but two halves and keep warm.

Mash 2 halves of tomato remaining in pan. Blend flour with sugar and mustard and add to mashed tomato, stirring well. Add milk all at once. Cook, stirring constantly, until thickened. Season with Worcestershire sauce, salt and pepper. Pour over tomatoes. 2 servings.

NOTE: This makes a delicious main dish when tomatoes are placed on toast rounds and garnished with crisp bacon.

WHITE SAUCE — MEDIUM

(Cream Sauce)

2 tbsp. butter
2 tbsp. flour
1 cup Sealtest milk
1/4 tsp. salt
Dash pepper

Melt butter in heavy saucepan over low heat. Add flour; mix well. Pour in milk all at once and immediately stir vigorously over moderate heat until thickened. Season with salt and pepper. 1 cup.

WHITE SAUCE—THIN: Follow Medium White Sauce recipe above—but use only 1 tbsp. butter and 1 tbsp. flour.

WHITE SAUCE—THICK: Follow Medium White Sauce recipe above—but use 3 tbsp. butter and 3 tbsp. flour.

VERSATILE WHITE SAUCE USES

- Thin White Sauce . . . in cream soups
- Medium White Sauce . . . as a sauce for eggs, fish, meat and vegetables.
- Thick White Sauce . . . in souffles, croquettes

Salads

Salad is frequently served as a separate course in France—and no meal is considered complete without it. Whether you follow the French custom or serve your salads alongside the main dish, you'll find them as much fun to prepare as they are good to eat. Salads artistically arranged add a touch of glamour to a meal.

You'll find light taste-teasing salads in this chapter—and sturdy, man-sized ones that are packed solid with nutrition. The latter make fine hot-weather meals in themselves.

KINDS OF SALADS

There's a salad for any course on your menu.

FIRST COURSE SALADS are appetizers . . . greens with tart fruits and sherbet, meat tid-bits, fish, or any colorful tempting combination with highly seasoned dressing.

DINNER SALADS are complements to the meal . . . a bit of fruit, or vegetable, or the popular tossed greens with dressing.

SALAD PLATES are the main course . . . a whole meal almost, and include some protein food — cottage cheese, American cheese, chicken, meat, eggs or fish, and dressing.

DESSERT SALADS are the crowning glory of the meal . . . usually fruit—plain, jellied, or frozen—made lush with whipped cream dressing.

SALAD FIXIN'S

Need a salad idea? Here's a list from which to choose to create a simple or sophisticated salad.

VEGETABLES . . . asparagus, lima beans, green beans, waxed beans, beets, broccoli, cabbage, carrots, cauliflower, celery, chives, cucumber, mushrooms, onions, peas, peppers, pickles, potatoes, radishes, scallions, spinach, tomatoes.

FRUITS . . . apples, apricots, avocados, bananas, berries, cherries, dates, figs, grapefruit, grapes, melons, oranges, peaches, pears, pineapples, plums, prunes, raisins.

MISCELLANEOUS . . . American cheese, crabmeat, cream cheese, cottage cheese, chicken, eggs, ham, macaroni, meat loaf, pork, veal, beef, shrimp, lobster, salmon, sardines, tuna, turkey, cold cuts, nutmeats, olives.

GREENS . . . chicory, dandelion, endive, escarole, lettuce, romaine, young spinach, watercress.

DRESSINGS . . . French, cooked, mayonnaise, Thousand Island, sour cream, whipped cream, cottage cheese and variations of all of these.

ACCOMPANIMENTS . . . hot biscuits, brown bread, cheese straws, cheese crackers, toasted corn muffins, English muffins, toasted cheese sandwich, Melba toast, blueberry muffins, nut bread, potato chips, pretzels, hard or soft rolls, saltines, hot or cold sandwiches, toast.

HELPFUL POINTERS FOR MAKING SALADS

• Wash lettuce thoroughly, removing damaged leaves. Cut out core and let cold water run through the head to separate leaves easily and also to give additional cleaning. Drain on towel. Use outer leaves in tossed salads, inner leaves for lettuce cups. Store unused lettuce in hydrator or tightly covered pan in refrigerator.

• Prepare as many salad ingredients as you can in advance. Most ingredients taste better when cold.

• If cooked vegetables are used, such as cauliflower, green beans, carrots, mushrooms, etc., cook them only to the "crisp stage."

• Cut cooked chicken and other meats in large bite-size chunks.

• Prepare chicken and fish salads ahead of time; let stand in the refrigerator with the dressing to absorb and improve flavor.

• When *mixing* ingredients, mix lightly in large bowl to prevent crushing. Add dressing at the last minute for most salads. Add chopped raisins, dates and nuts to mixtures at last minute to prevent darkening.

NINETEEN INTRIGUING SALADS

Banana split with cottage cheese
Chicken, apple, celery and pecan (leave red skin on diced apple)
Chicken, ham and celery
Chicken salad—all white meat
Cooked peas, small cubes of American cheese and sliced pickle all mixed and moistened with mayonnaise
Cottage cheese mixed with shredded raw spinach or kale
Cottage cheese, watercress and grapefruit sections
Cubes of cold ham loaf in a lettuce cup with Russian dressing
Cubes or strips of ham mixed with sections of orange
Macaroni and tuna with tomato slices
Orange and grapefruit sections with sweet grapes and orange sherbet
Orange sections, avocado and cottage cheese
Sardine, sliced egg and tomato
Sliced egg with sour cream cole slaw
Sliced tongue with sour cream potato salad
Spoonfuls of cottage cheese in jellied lemon and ginger ale salad
String bean and cheese strips
Tomato rosette stuffed with cottage cheese egg salad
Two slices of orange with cottage cheese between, sandwich fashion

FRUIT AND COTTAGE CHEESE SALADS

AMBROSIA SALAD

1 cup orange sections
½ cup seedless grape halves
¼ cup chopped dates
1 cup Sealtest cottage cheese
¼ cup Sealtest sour cream
1 banana, sliced
Lettuce
¼ cup shredded coconut

Combine orange sections, grapes and dates; chill.

Press cheese through fine sieve. Add sour cream and banana. Mix gently but thoroughly. Fold chilled fruits into cheese mixture. Serve on crisp lettuce. Sprinkle each serving with coconut. 4 servings.

BANANA DESSERT SALAD

1 cup Sealtest cottage cheese
½ cup drained canned crushed pineapple
4 bananas, peeled
Lettuce
¼ cup chopped peanuts
½ cup Sealtest sour cream
2 tbsp. pineapple juice
8 maraschino cherries

Mix cottage cheese and pineapple. Cut bananas in half lengthwise and arrange on lettuce, allowing 2 halves to a serving. Put rounded spoonful of cheese mixture on each banana half. Sprinkle with chopped peanuts. Mix sour cream with pineapple juice and spoon a little over each cheese mound. Top with cherries. 4 servings.

BANANA SPLIT SALAD

Banana
Lettuce
Sealtest cottage cheese
Crushed strawberries
Sealtest sour cream
Chopped nuts
Whole strawberries

Peel banana and split lengthwise. Arrange, cut side up, on lettuce. Top with 2 generous spoonfuls (or scoops) of cottage cheese. Spoon crushed strawberries and then sour cream over each mound of cheese. Sprinkle with chopped nuts, and garnish with 2 whole berries. 1 serving.

BLUSHING PEAR

Put 2 canned pear halves together with generous layer of Sealtest cottage cheese sandwiched between. Dust a little paprika over one or both sides. Stick in short strip of green pepper for stem. Serve on crisp greens and garnish with Sealtest sour cream. 1 serving.

CRANBERRY PINEAPPLE SALAD

Arrange lettuce or other greens on salad plates. For each salad, place a canned pineapple ring on lettuce and then a round slice of canned or homemade cranberry jelly. Top each serving with large spoonful of Sealtest cottage cheese and garnish with sprig of mint.

FAN-TAN FRUIT SALAD

6 oranges, peeled and sectioned
2 grapefruit, peeled and sectioned
2 red apples, sliced without peeling
Lettuce
½ cup Sealtest cottage cheese
½ lb. sweet cherries, halved and pitted

Arrange alternate sections of orange, grapefruit and apple slices in fan shape on lettuce leaves.

Place small spoonful of cottage cheese on one-half of each cherry. Top with other half. Place filled cherries in center of salads. Serve with your favorite sour cream dressing. 4 servings.

FIG, ORANGE AND CHEESE SALAD

½ cup dried figs or dates, cut small
2 cups diced oranges, well-drained
¾ to 1 cup Sealtest cottage cheese
Mayonnaise or other salad dressing
Lettuce or other greens

Combine figs, oranges and cottage cheese. Mix very lightly. Serve on lettuce or other greens with mayonnaise or other salad dressing. If desired, sprinkle with chopped nuts. 6 servings.

FROZEN FRUIT SALAD

6 tbsp. sugar
¼ cup small wedges canned pineapple
½ cup strawberry wedges
⅓ cup Sealtest whipping cream
1½ tsp. lemon juice
1 cup Sealtest cottage cheese
Salad greens

Sprinkle sugar over pineapple and strawberries and mix well. Beat cream until stiff.

Add lemon juice to cottage cheese and beat with egg beater until smooth. Fold fruit and then cream into cottage cheese. Pour into 11" x 4" ice cube tray, sectioner removed. Freeze until firm but not too hard.

Cut into 12 pieces. Place in pairs on salad greens. If desired, garnish with pineapple wedges and strawberries. 6 servings.

GINGER PEAR SALAD

½ cup water
1 cup brown sugar
½ lemon, sliced
1 tsp. ground ginger
4 whole cloves
4 fresh ripe pears, pared, halved and cored
Lettuce
1½ cups Sealtest cottage cheese

Combine water, sugar, lemon, ginger and cloves in a saucepan. Bring to boil and boil 5 min. Add pear halves to syrup, cover and simmer until tender. (Turn pears in syrup occasionally during cooking time.) Cool, occasionally spooning syrup over pears. Chill.

Place drained pear halves, 2 per serving, on lettuce. Top with spoonfuls of cottage cheese. Serve with sour cream. 4 servings.

LONE STAR SALAD

1 medium avocado pear
1½ tsp. lime juice
1 cup Sealtest cottage cheese
Few grains salt
Lettuce or other greens
2 oranges, sectioned

Peel avocado and remove seed. Press pulp through a coarse sieve. Add lime juice. Fold in cottage cheese and mix together lightly. Season with salt. Chill.

Pile spoonfuls of avocado-cheese on lettuce or other greens. Garnish with orange sections. 4 generous servings.

ORANGE, ONION AND CHEESE SALAD

2 oranges, peeled
1 very large mild onion or 3 medium onions
$\frac{1}{3}$ to $\frac{1}{2}$ cup French dressing
Lettuce
1 cup Sealtest cottage cheese

Slice oranges and onions very thin. Separate onion into rings. Combine in shallow bowl. Pour dressing over top. Chill 1 hr. Arrange on lettuce. Top with spoonfuls of cheese. Serve with remaining dressing. 4 servings.

PRUNE WHEEL SALAD

2 apples
Salad greens
2 cups Sealtest cottage cheese
20 well-drained stewed prunes, pitted
5 maraschino cherries

Wash and core apples. Slice each into 8 thin rings. Arrange 3 rings overlapping in a triangular fashion on greens on each salad plate. Pile cheese to make a mound in center. Halve prunes; arrange 8 halves in circle around base of each mound. Top with cherry. 5 servings.

SOUTH SEA SALAD

1 medium pineapple
$\frac{1}{4}$ cup Sealtest sour cream
$\frac{1}{8}$ tsp. salt
$\frac{1}{2}$ cup sliced strawberries
1 cup Sealtest cottage cheese
$\frac{1}{2}$ cup shredded coconut

Cut pineapple (including top or crown) in quarters lengthwise. Cut out hard core. Cut inside flesh from the rind of each quarter, leaving the rind shells. Cut pineapple flesh in cubes. Add sour cream and salt; mix lightly.

Arrange pineapple mixture and strawberries in the 4 rind shells.

Drop small, rounded spoonfuls of cottage cheese in shredded coconut. Roll gently until completely coated. Place on top, and around salad. If desired, serve with additional sour cream and brown bread and butter sandwiches. 4 servings.

SUNBURST SALAD

4 oranges, sectioned
1 large grapefruit, sectioned
1 avocado
Romaine or other greens
2 cups Sealtest cottage cheese
Whole cooked cranberries
Sealtest sour cream

Arrange sections of orange and grapefruit and slices of avocado on romaine or other greens in fan shape. Top with spoonfuls of Sealtest cottage cheese. Garnish with whole cooked cranberries. Serve with Sealtest sour cream. 6 servings.

WALDORF CHEESE SALAD

¼ cup salad dressing
⅛ tsp. salt
2 cups diced apples
½ cup Sealtest cottage cheese
¼ cup raisins
Lettuce or other greens

Mix salad dressing and salt. Add apples and mix well. (Do not peel apples if skin is tender.) Add cottage cheese and raisins. Toss together lightly and serve on lettuce. 3 servings.

MEAT AND COTTAGE CHEESE SALADS

STUFFED TOMATO ROSETTES

1 large cucumber
2 cups Sealtest cottage cheese
⅓ cup sour cream
2 tsp. finely chopped onion
1 cup finely chopped dried beef
Salt and pepper
4 to 6 medium-sized tomatoes
Lettuce

Chop enough cucumber to make ½ cup. Slice remaining cucumber for garnishing. Mix cottage cheese, sour cream, onion, chopped cucumber and dried beef gently. Season with salt and pepper.

Wash or peel tomatoes; remove stem ends. Cut into 6 wedges as in a pie, leaving base uncut. Spread open slightly. Place on lettuce. Fill with cheese mixture. Garnish with sliced cucumber. 4 to 6 servings.

GOLDENROD SALAD

6 hard-cooked eggs
1 cup Sealtest cottage cheese
¼ cup liver paté
¾ tsp. lemon juice
¼ tsp. salt
Salad greens

Cut eggs in half lengthwise; remove yolks. Press 3 half-yolks through sieve.

Combine remaining yolks, cheese, liver paté, lemon juice and salt; mix well with fork; heap on egg whites. Arrange eggs on greens. Sprinkle sieved yolks over eggs. Serve with French dressing. 4 servings.

HAM'N CHEESE DOUBLE DECKERS

4 hard-cooked eggs, chopped fine
1½ cups Sealtest cottage cheese
1 tbsp. mayonnaise
2 tsp. prepared mustard
¼ tsp. salt
2 drops Tabasco
1 twelve-oz. can luncheon meat, sliced thin
Salad greens
Olive slices

Mix first 6 ingredients together lightly with fork. Spread on meat ces. Stack 2 slices together with cheese mixture in center and top. Place on salad greens; garnish with olive slices. 5 servings.

TUNA SPRING SALAD

2 tbsp. chopped olives
½ cup shredded carrot
½ cup chopped celery
¼ cup chopped parsley
1 small onion, finely chopped
1 tbsp. vinegar
1 cup Sealtest cottage cheese
¼ tsp. Worcestershire
1 seven-oz. can tuna
Salt and pepper
Lettuce

Mix olives, carrot, celery, parsley, onion and vinegar. Mix cottage cheese and Worcestershire.

Drain tuna. Break into large flakes with fork. Add vegetable and cheese mixtures. Toss lightly. Season with salt and pepper. Serve on lettuce. 4 servings.

COTTAGE TUNA TOMATOES

- 1 seven-oz. can tuna, well-drained
- 2/3 cup chopped celery
- 1 1/2 cups Sealtest cottage cheese
- 1 tsp. grated onion
- 1 tbsp. mayonnaise
- 3/4 tsp. salt
- Dash pepper
- 5 tomatoes, peeled and chilled
- Salad greens

Flake tuna. Add celery, cheese, onion, mayonnaise, salt and pepper. Mix lightly with fork.

Cut out stem end of each chilled peeled tomato. Place tomato upright. Cut into 8 wedges, as in a pie, but don't cut all the way through to bottom. Spread wedges apart gently; fill center with cheese-tuna mixture. Serve on greens. If desired, garnish with olive slices. 5 servings.

TV TRAY LUNCH

Cottage Tuna Tomatoes
Hot Popovers with Butter
Orange Sherbet — Brownies, page 138
Coffee with Cream — Milk

VEGETABLE AND COTTAGE CHEESE SALADS

COOL-AS-A-CUCUMBER SALAD

- 1 large cucumber
- 2 tbsp. chopped chives
- 1 cup Sealtest cottage cheese
- Watercress

Peel, and shred with coarse shredder, about three-fourths of cucumber (save rest to slice for garnishing).

Combine shredded cucumber, chives, and cottage cheese; mix well. Serve on a bed of watercress and garnish with cucumber slices. Serve with French dressing or sour cream, if desired. 3 or 4 servings.

CLOUDY DAY SUPPER

Cream of Tomato Soup
Cool-as-a-Cucumber Salad
Hot French Bread   Butter
Strawberry Shortcake
Milk   Coffee with Cream

CARROT CHEESE BOWL

Combine in salad bowl: a shredded head of lettuce, a small bunch of chicory cut in pieces, a bunch of watercress, 1 cup thin slices of carrot (fluted if desired). Toss together with French dressing. Top with generous spoonfuls of Sealtest cottage cheese; garnish with crisp lettuce leaves. 6 servings.

CARROT, APPLE AND CHEESE SALAD

2 cups shredded carrot
1 cup diced apple
1 cup Sealtest cottage cheese
Salt
Lettuce or other greens

Combine carrot, apple and cottage cheese. Toss together lightly. Season with salt. Serve on crisp lettuce leaves or other greens. 6 servings.

DRUM MAJOR SALAD

Sandwich Sealtest cottage cheese between two thick tomato slices; lace "drum" sides with thin strips green pepper. Arrange on greens. For drumsticks place stuffed olives on ends of carrot sticks.

STORYBOOK SUPPER

Chicken Alphabet Noodle Soup
Drum Major Salad
Peanut Butter Finger Sandwiches
Applesauce
Animal Crackers   Milk

FANFARE SALAD

5 tomatoes, peeled and chilled
2 cups Sealtest cottage cheese
Salad greens

Cut out stem end of each tomato. Place tomato upright; cut in 5 vertical slices (as in slicing bread), but do not cut all the way through to bottom. Spread apart gently; insert spoonfuls of cheese between tomato slices and serve on greens. If desired, garnish with cucumber slices. 5 servings.

MACARONI CHEESE RING

2 cups elbow macaroni
¼ cup French dressing
2 cups Sealtest cottage cheese
¼ cup diced pimiento
¼ cup diced green pepper
2 tbsp. finely chopped onion
2 tbsp. chopped parsley
Chicory or other greens

Cook macaroni according to pkg. directions. Drain well; cool. Add French dressing; mix well. Let stand few min. to marinate. Add remaining ingredients except greens. Mix gently but thoroughly. Press lightly into 9" ring. Chill several hrs. Loosen sides with knife. Turn out on chicory. Garnish with olives. 6 to 8 servings.

MERRY-GO-ROUND CHEESE SALAD

4 large tomatoes
Escarole or other salad greens
2 cups Sealtest cottage cheese
1 large cucumber, thinly sliced
Sour cream or other salad dressing

Wash tomatoes and remove stem ends. Place tomatoes upside down and cut each into 8 wedges (as in a pie) but don't cut all the way through to the bottom. Place on crisp escarole; press sections apart. Fill center of each tomato with generous scoop of cottage cheese.

Cut each cucumber slice from rind to center. Shape into small cones, or cornucopias, by overlapping the cut edges. Place cucumber cones between tomato wedges. Serve with sour cream or any desired salad dressing. 4 servings.

HEARTY SUMMER SLAW

2 cups shredded cabbage
1 one-lb. can grapefruit sections, well-drained and cut in ¾" pieces
⅓ cup thinly sliced radishes
1 tbsp. sugar
Dash pepper
2 cups Sealtest cottage cheese

Combine cabbage, radishes, grapefruit, sugar and pepper. Add cheese; fold in lightly. Serve on greens. 6 servings.

POTATO CHEESE SALAD RING

¼ cup French dressing
¼ cup mayonnaise
2 cups diced cooked potatoes
3 hard-cooked eggs, chopped
2 cups Sealtest cottage cheese
¼ cup diced pimiento
¼ cup diced green pepper
2 tbsp. finely chopped onion
2 tbsp. chopped parsley
1 to 1½ tsp. salt

Blend French dressing and mayonnaise; add potatoes and eggs; let stand few minutes. Add remaining ingredients. Mix gently but well. Press lightly into 9" ring mold. Chill several hrs. Loosen sides of salad from mold with knife and unmold on salad greens. Garnish with radishes, sliced olives. 6 to 8 servings.

SALAD BOWL

1 large head lettuce
1 bunch watercress
2 cucumbers
French dressing
1½ cups Sealtest cottage cheese
3 tomatoes

Reserve small leaves of lettuce; shred the rest. Combine shredded lettuce, watercress and sliced cucumbers in salad bowl; toss together with French dressing. Cover with slices of tomato topped with cottage cheese. Garnish with small lettuce leaves. 6 servings.

SOUP'N SALAD LUNCHEON

Cream of Corn and Pepper Soup
Salad Bowl
Parkerhouse Rolls Butter
Cherry Tarts a la Mode
Milk Coffee with Cream

TOMATO CHEESE ROSETTE

Peel tomato; remove stem end. Cut tomato in 6 wedges, leaving base uncut. Place on lettuce; spread open slightly. Fill center with ⅓ cup Sealtest cottage cheese. Garnish with cucumber slice.

VEGETABLE MEDLEY SALAD

1 large green pepper
5 scallions
5 radishes
3 stalks celery
1 large cucumber
3 medium carrots
Shredded lettuce
2 cups Sealtest cottage cheese
Sealtest sour cream, about 1 pt.

Wash and chill vegetables. Remove stem end and seeds from green pepper. Trim scallions and radishes. Scrape carrots. Peel cucumber. Cut all vegetables in chunks. Grind together in food chopper, using coarse blade.

Put generous mound of cottage cheese on shredded lettuce in center of salad plate. Make a ring of the mixed chopped vegetables around the cheese, then spoon on sour cream in another ring around the vegetables. Serve ice cold. 4 to 6 servings.

MOLDED SALADS WITH COTTAGE CHEESE

COTTAGE FRUIT SALAD

Something to perk up a homey meal

1 pkg. lemon or orange-flavored gelatin
1 cup hot water
2 tbsp. lemon juice
1½ cups Sealtest cottage cheese
1½ cups well-drained canned fruit cocktail

Dissolve gelatin in hot water. Add lemon juice. Chill until syrupy. Beat with egg beater until foamy. Add cheese; continue to beat with egg beater until well-blended. Fold in fruit. Pour into 1 qt. mold. Chill until set. Carefully run knife around edge to loosen. Unmold. Garnish with greens, bits of fruit. 6 servings.

CRANBERRY COTTAGE CHEESE SALAD

1 orange, pared and cubed
1½ cups cranberries
¼ cup sugar
1 cup hot water
1 pkg. lemon-flavored gelatin
¾ cup cold water
¼ cup finely chopped nuts
Lettuce or other greens
Sealtest cottage cheese

Grind orange and cranberries together in food grinder, using fine blade. Mix in sugar. Add hot water to gelatin and stir until dissolved. Add cold water. Chill until it begins to thicken.

Fold in cranberry mixture and nuts. Pour into individual molds. Chill until firm. Unmold on lettuce. Garnish with spoonfuls of cottage cheese. 6 servings.

EMERALD SALAD

1 pkg. lime-flavored gelatin
1 cup hot water
⅔ cup orange juice
1 cup orange sections
1 medium unpeeled apple, cut in thin strips
2 cups Sealtest cottage cheese
Lettuce or other greens

Dissolve gelatin in hot water. Add orange juice. Chill until thick and syrupy. Gently stir in orange sections and apple strips. Spoon into molds. Press a spoonful of cottage cheese down in center of each mold. Chill. When firm unmold in a circle on lettuce; pile more cottage cheese in center. Serve with sour cream or any other salad dressing desired. 6 to 8 servings.

JELLIED STUFFED PRUNES

1 pkg. lemon-flavored gelatin
1 cup hot water
¾ cup cold water
Salad greens
6 large pitted stewed dried prunes
¾ to 1 cup Sealtest cottage cheese

Dissolve gelatin in hot water. Add cold water. Pour into shallow square dish or pan. Chill until syrupy.

Stuff prunes with cottage cheese; press down into gelatin, spacing evenly, 1 to a portion. Chill until firm. Cut in squares; serve on greens. If desired, garnish with additional cheese. 6 servings.

JELLIED BEET AND COTTAGE CHEESE SALAD

1 pkg. lemon-flavored gelatin
1½ cups hot water
1 tbsp. horseradish
3 tbsp. vinegar
½ to 1 tsp. salt
1 cup finely chopped, cooked beets
⅓ cup finely chopped celery
1 cup Sealtest cottage cheese

Dissolve gelatin in hot water. Chill until syrupy.

Mix horseradish, vinegar and salt. Pour over beets and celery. Mix well. Combine gelatin and beet mixture; spoon into 6 individual molds. Press a spoonful of cottage cheese down into the center of each.

Chill until set. Unmold on lettuce or other greens. 6 servings.

KEY WEST SALAD

1 pkg. lime-flavored gelatin
1 cup hot water
1 medium avocado
1 cup Sealtest cottage cheese
1 tbsp. lemon juice
2 tbsp. mayonnaise
½ tsp. salt
½ cup diced orange sections
Salad greens

Dissolve gelatin in hot water. Chill until syrupy.

Mash half of the avocado (about ½ cupful). Cut the other half in small thin pieces (scant cupful).

Add cheese, mashed avocado, lemon juice, mayonnaise and salt to gelatin. Beat with egg beater until well-blended. Fold in orange sections and avocado pieces. Spoon into 1 qt. mold. Chill until set. Unmold on serving platter. Garnish with your favorite salad greens and if desired, with additional orange sections. 6 servings.

ALL-ON-ONE-PLATE LUNCHEON

Key West Salad
Thinly Sliced Cold Cuts
Brown Bread Sandwiches
Chocolate Milk Float

LAZY DAY SALAD LOAF

Just right for a foursome

- 1 envelope unflavored gelatine
- ½ cup tomato juice
- 1 cup Sealtest cottage cheese
- 1 cup ground cooked or canned ham
- ⅓ cup Sealtest sour cream
- 2 tbsp. catsup
- 2 tbsp. finely chopped green pepper
- Few grains pepper

Soften gelatine in tomato juice. Dissolve over boiling water. Combine remaining ingredients; add gelatine and mix well. Pour into small loaf dish, about 6" x 4" x 3". Chill several hours. Unmold. Slice. Serve on salad greens. 4 generous servings.

PORCH LUNCH

Lazy Day Salad Loaf
Tomato Stuffed with Cole Slaw
Sealtest Sour Cream Garnish
Potato Chips Olives
Pineapple Sundae
Milk

LEMON WALDORF SALAD LOAF

- 1 pkg. lemon-flavored gelatin
- 2 cups hot water
- 1 tsp. salt
- 1 tbsp. lemon juice
- 1 red apple, diced
- 1 cup Sealtest cottage cheese
- ¼ cup chopped walnuts

Dissolve gelatin in hot water; add salt and lemon juice. Cool.

Add diced apple to half the gelatin mixture. Pour into small loaf pan. Chill until almost set.

Add cottage cheese to remaining gelatin mixture; beat with rotary beater until blended. Stir in nuts. Pour over apple-gelatin mixture. Chill until set. Unmold on bed of chicory. Serve with sour cream dressing, if desired. 4 to 6 servings.

PEACH AND BERRY COTTAGE RING

1 pkg. lemon-flavored gelatin
1 cup hot water
¾ cup cold water
1 cup blueberries
8 to 10 peach slices
Lettuce
Sealtest cottage cheese

Dissolve gelatin in hot water. Add cold water; chill until syrupy; then spoon a little into bottom of ring mold. Stir in blueberries. Spoon remaining gelatin over top. Tuck in ring of sliced peaches around edge. Chill until firm. Unmold on lettuce or other greens. Fill center with cottage cheese. 6 generous servings.

SEAFOAM SALAD RINGS

2 cups Sealtest cottage cheese
½ to ¾ tsp. salt
1 tsp. sugar
1 tbsp. lemon juice
½ cup cream
1 envelope unflavored gelatine
¼ cup cold water
Lettuce or other salad greens
Fruit or vegetable salad

Combine cottage cheese, salt, sugar, lemon juice and cream.

Sprinkle gelatine over water. Let stand few min. until softened. Place over boiling water until dissolved. Stir into cheese mixture.

Pour into individual ring molds. Chill until firm. Unmold on lettuce or other greens. Fill center with fruit or vegetable salad. 6 servings.

ZESTY CHEESE ASPIC

1 envelope unflavored gelatine
¼ cup cold water
1 eight-oz. can tomato sauce
2 tsp. bottled horseradish
1 tbsp. catsup
2 drops Tabasco
1 cup Sealtest cottage cheese
Salad greens

Soften gelatine in cold water. Heat tomato sauce; add gelatine; stir until dissolved. Add horseradish, catsup, Tabasco and cheese; mix well. Spoon into small ring molds. Chill until set. Unmold on salad greens. If desired, fill each with mound of additional cottage cheese. 5 servings.

TOMATO-CHEESE ASPIC

1 envelope unflavored gelatine
¼ cup cold water
½ tsp. celery salt
½ tsp. salt
¼ tsp. sugar
2 cups tomato juice
½ tsp. Worcestershire sauce
Dash of Tabasco
2 tbsp. vinegar
2 tbsp. finely chopped chives
1 cup Sealtest cottage cheese

Sprinkle gelatine over water. Let stand few min. until softened. Add celery salt, salt and sugar to tomato juice. Heat until almost boiling; pour over gelatine, stirring until dissolved. Mix in Worcestershire, Tabasco, vinegar and chives. Pour into 6 individual molds; chill. When mixture begins to congeal, press a spoonful of cottage cheese in center of each mold. Chill until firm; unmold. 6 servings.

MISCELLANEOUS SALADS

CABBAGE CARROT SLAW

1 cup Sealtest sour cream
2 tsp. vinegar
½ to 1 tsp. salt
Few grains pepper
3 cups shredded cabbage, chilled
1½ cups grated carrots, chilled

Mix sour cream, vinegar, salt and pepper. Add cabbage and carrots. Toss together lightly. Serve on lettuce. 6 servings.
FOR VARIETY . . . add one of the following to the recipe above: chopped celery, chopped pickled beet, diced orange, sliced stuffed olives, small white grapes, thinly sliced radishes.

CREAM CHEESE CLOVERLEAVES

¾ lb. cream cheese
1½ tsp. grated onion
¼ tsp. garlic salt
⅛ tsp. salt
1¼ cups finely chopped celery
¾ cup finely sliced radishes
1 green pepper
1 tbsp. finely chopped parsley

Soften cream cheese with a spoon. Add onion, garlic salt, salt, celery and radishes; mix well. Slice stem end off pepper. Cut 5 or 6 rings about ¼" wide. Place each ring on bed of lettuce. Pile cream cheese mixture in center of each ring. Sprinkle with chopped parsley, and serve. 5 or 6 servings.

FROZEN PINEAPPLE SALAD

2 cups Sealtest sour cream
1 tbsp. lemon juice
¾ cup sugar
Lettuce or other greens
1 cup drained, sweetened crushed pineapple
¼ cup chopped maraschino cherries

Mix sour cream, lemon juice and sugar. Fold in pineapple and cherries.

Pour into freezing tray of refrigerator. Freeze, using directions given for your refrigerator. Cut into squares. Serve on lettuce or other greens. 6 servings.

FROZEN STRAWBERRY SALAD

2 cups Sealtest sour cream
1 tbsp. lemon juice
¾ cup sugar
1 cup crushed strawberries, slightly sweetened
Lettuce or other greens

Mix sour cream, lemon juice and sugar. Fold in strawberries. Pour into refrigerator tray. Freeze. Cut into squares. Serve on salad greens. 6 servings.

HEARTY SALAD

4 cups assorted crisp greens, shredded (lettuce, spinach, cabbage, escarole)
½ cup Sealtest sour cream
¼ lb. canned luncheon meat, julienne
1 tbsp. French dressing
Few grains pepper

Combine greens in salad bowl. Sprinkle meat on top.

Blend sour cream, French dressing, and pepper. If desired add a little salt. Toss greens and dressing lightly together. Serve immediately. 4 to 6 servings.

SALAD LUNCHEON

Cream of Corn Soup
Hearty Salad
Warm Buttered Rolls
Strawberry Shortcake
Iced Coffee with Cream Milk

HARVEST SALAD

1 cup coarsely shredded spinach
1 cup bite-size pieces raw cauliflower
⅓ cup grated carrot
¼ cup Sealtest sour cream
Salt and pepper

Mix spinach, cauliflower and carrot. Fold in sour cream lightly, just enough to mix. Season with salt and pepper. 4 servings.

HOLIDAY SALAD RING

2 one-lb. cans jellied cranberry sauce
2 envelopes unflavored gelatine
½ cup cold water
2 tbsp. lemon juice
6 tbsp. orange juice
Few grains salt
Lettuce or other greens
Turkey Ham Salad, recipe below

Whip cranberry sauce with rotary beater until smooth. Sprinkle gelatine over mixture of water, lemon and orange juice. Let stand 5 min. Dissolve over hot water.

Add gelatine mixture and salt to cranberry sauce. Stir until thoroughly blended. Pour into lightly buttered 1 qt. ring mold. Chill until firm.

Unmold on lettuce or other greens. Fill center of ring with Turkey Ham Salad. 6 generous servings.

TURKEY HAM SALAD

2 cups diced cooked turkey
1½ cups diced cooked ham
⅓ cup Sealtest sour cream
3 tbsp. mayonnaise
Salt and pepper
1 tbsp. capers

Mix ingredients together. 6 servings.

MERRY CHRISTMAS BUFFET

Hot Consomme
Holiday Salad Ring
Hot Buttered Cheese Biscuits
Christmas Cookies Ice Cream
Milk Coffee with Cream

LIME CUCUMBER SALAD

1 pkg. lime-flavored gelatin
1 cup hot water
¼ cup vinegar
1 tsp. salt
1 tsp. grated onion
1 cup Sealtest sour cream
1 medium cucumber, coarsely grated
Lettuce

Dissolve gelatin in hot water. Add vinegar, salt and onion. Chill until gelatin begins to thicken. Stir in sour cream and cucumber. Pour into 6 individual molds. Chill until firm. Unmold on lettuce. 6 servings.

PARADISE CHEESE SALAD

1 pkg. lemon-flavored gelatin
1 cup hot water
1 cup Sealtest sour cream
½ lb. cream cheese
1 cup canned crushed pineapple
Salad greens

Dissolve gelatin in hot water. Chill until syrupy. Beat in sour cream and mashed cream cheese with egg beater until smooth. Fold in pineapple. Pour into 1½ qt. mold. Chill; when firm unmold on salad greens. Garnish with orange sections or ring of drained crushed pineapple. 8 servings.

PINEAPPLE CARROT SLAW

3 cups finely shredded cabbage
¾ cup shredded carrot
¾ cup drained sweetened crushed pineapple
⅓ cup mayonnaise
2 tbsp. pineapple juice
Salt
Lettuce or other greens

Combine cabbage, carrot and pineapple. Thin mayonnaise with pineapple juice and add to cabbage mixture.

Toss together lightly. Season with salt; serve on lettuce or other greens. 4 to 6 servings.

SHRIMP AND RICE SALAD

1 cup raw white rice
1½ cups cooked or canned whole shrimp
½ cup Sealtest sour cream
Salt and pepper
Lettuce or other greens

Cook rice in boiling salted water until tender. Drain and chill.

Mix rice and shrimp lightly together. Add sour cream, and stir just enough to blend thoroughly. Season with salt and pepper. Serve on lettuce or other greens. 6 servings.

PEPPY POTATO SALAD

3 to 4 tbsp. French dressing
¾ cup Sealtest sour cream
3 cups cubed cooked potatoes
2 cubed hard-cooked eggs
Salt, pepper, onion salt
Stuffed olive slices
Salad greens

Blend French dressing and sour cream together lightly. Pour over potatoes and eggs; toss lightly. Season with salt, pepper and onion salt. Garnish with olive slices. Serve on greens, with Perky Dressing, recipe page 90. 6 servings.

SOUR CREAM POTATO SALAD

¼ cup Sealtest sour cream
¼ cup mayonnaise
3 cups diced, cooked potatoes
1 tsp. chopped chive
3 slices bacon, diced and fried
Salt and pepper
Lettuce, chicory or other greens

Blend sour cream and mayonnaise. Add to potatoes and mix well. Fold in chive and bacon. Season with salt and pepper. Serve on lettuce, chicory or other greens. 4 generous servings.

PICNIC MENU

Grilled Frankfurters
Toasted Rolls
Catsup Mustard Pickle Relish
Sour Cream Potato Salad
Tomato Slices Cucumber Circles
Buttered Corn on the Cob
Frosted Brownies
Buttermilk

SOUR CREAM SPINACH SALAD

1 lb. spinach, washed
½ to ¾ tsp. salt
Few grains pepper
2 hard-cooked eggs
¾ to 1 cup Sealtest sour cream
Lettuce or other greens

Chill and chop raw spinach coarsely. Add salt, pepper and chopped eggs to ½ cup sour cream. Just before serving, fold in spinach. Do not over mix. Serve on lettuce. Garnish with remaining sour cream. 6 servings.

STUFFED TOMATO SALAD

6 medium tomatoes
¾ to 1 cup Sealtest sour cream
Salt and pepper
1 cup shredded carrots
Lettuce or other greens
1 cup shredded cabbage

Peel tomatoes, and scoop out pulp. Dice pulp and drain. Season sour cream to taste with salt and pepper. Pour over cabbage and carrots. Add tomato pulp and toss together lightly. Fill tomatoes. Serve on lettuce, watercress or other greens. 6 servings.

TURKEY MOUSSE

1 envelope unflavored gelatine
1½ cups turkey or chicken stock
1½ cups leftover ground turkey or chicken
¼ tsp. curry powder
¼ cup mayonnaise
1 tsp. celery salt
2 tsp. grated onion
Salt and pepper
¾ cup whipping cream, whipped
Lettuce and salad dressing

Soften gelatine in ½ cup cold stock. Dissolve over hot water. Combine remaining stock, ground turkey, curry powder, mayonnaise, celery salt and onion. Add dissolved gelatine. Mix well. Season with salt and pepper. Chill until thick and syrupy. Beat until light and foamy. Fold in whipped cream.

Pour into fancy 1 qt. mold or loaf pan. Chill until firm. Unmold on serving platter. Serve with lettuce and salad dressing. If desired, garnish mousse with salted whipped cream (put on with pastry tube) and arrange 6 slices pineapple around base. Top each pineapple slice with turkey-shaped cut-out of canned jellied cranberry sauce. 6 servings.

TUNA-MACARONI SALAD

1 seven-oz. can tuna, flaked
½ cup chopped celery
⅓ cup diced green pepper
½ cup mayonnaise
1 eight-oz. pkg. elbow macaroni, cooked and chilled
½ cup buttermilk
½ tsp. prepared mustard
Salt and pepper

Combine tuna, celery and green pepper. Add to macaroni and mix lightly but thoroughly.

Blend mayonnaise, buttermilk and mustard. Fold into macaroni mixture. Season with salt and pepper. 6 generous servings.

SALAD PLATES

Salad plates are becoming more and more popular and are often almost complete meals. Men like them, especially if something substantial is added, such as a big scoop of cottage cheese and a cold slice of meat or two.

MAKE YOUR OWN SALAD PLATE

Place a bowl of cottage cheese in center of large platter. Arrange lettuce cups on the platter and fill with any of the fruits suggested below. Serve with a choice of dressings. Let guests help themselves.

Avocado slices
Fresh pineapple spears
Grapefruit and orange sections
Peach halves filled with blueberries
Melon balls
Pear halves filled with mint jelly
Pitted sweet cherries
Quartered bananas
Red plum halves
Strawberries

MIDSUMMER BUFFET

Frosty Jellied Consomme
Make Your Own Salad Plate
Hot Popovers Butter
Chocolate Cake a la Mode
Iced Coffee with Cream Milk

BOLOGNA ROLL-UPS SALAD PLATE

1 cup Sealtest cottage cheese
¼ cup chopped dill pickle
8 slices bologna
Cloves
Buttered hot rolls
Cole slaw
Watercress, radishes, olives

Mix cottage cheese and pickle lightly together. Place spoonful in center of each slice of bologna; spread to cover center third of slice. Bring edges of slice together and fasten with 2 cloves.

Arrange 2 roll-ups on each salad plate; add a buttered hot roll and a lettuce cup filled with cole slaw. Garnish with watercress, radishes, olives. 4 servings.

FRUIT AND SHERBET SALAD PLATE

Arrange 3 crisp lettuce cups on large salad plate. Fill one cup with sweet cherries. Fill second cup with mixture of honeydew melon and cantaloupe balls; garnish with sprinkling of blueberries. Fill third cup with orange slices and grapefruit sections; top with scoop of orange sherbet. Serve with a ham and cheese sandwich, and a chicken sandwich. 1 serving.

SUMMER FRUIT SALAD PLATE

Cantaloupe ring
Sealtest cottage cheese
Lettuce cups
Raspberries
Sweet cherry halves
Watermelon balls
Orange sections
Avocado slices
Apricot slices

Put cantaloupe ring in center of large luncheon plate. Top with generous scoop of cottage cheese. Arrange 3 lettuce cups around cantaloupe. Fill one cup with raspberries, one with cherry halves, and one with watermelon balls. Arrange orange sections, avocado and apricot slices fan-shape between the lettuce cups. 1 serving.

OTHER SALAD PLATE SUGGESTIONS

Each of the following combinations, attractively arranged on a large luncheon plate, may be served as a main dish.

Mixed orange sections and banana slices in lettuce cup
Sliced ham loaf Radishes
Toasted English muffin with jelly

* *

Two slices fresh or canned pineapple with cottage cheese or cream cheese in between, sandwich fashion, garnished with chicory
Pitted sweet cherries in lettuce cup
Chicken sandwich Olives

* *

Jellied peach half in lettuce cup
Sliced avocado and orange sections on watercress, garnished with strawberries
2 slices American cheese
Buttered hot small thin biscuits filled with bits of crisp bacon

* *

Melon balls and red raspberries in lettuce cup
Pear half in jellied ginger ale salad, on watercress
2 prunes stuffed with cottage cheese
Fig nut fingers, page 111

* *

Slice of pineapple topped with slice of orange, on lettuce
Shrimp salad in lettuce cup
Buttered slices California fruit loaf, page 93

* *

Ham'n cheese double deckers, page 67
Celery hearts Pickle fans
Potato chips

* *

Alternate slices of Swiss cheese, American cheese and boiled ham
Sour cream potato salad in lettuce cup
Sliced tomatoes Olives Triscuits

Stuffed tomato rosette, page 66
Sliced cold chicken
Radish roses Scallions
Buttered toasted corn muffin

* *

Tuna spring salad, page 67
French endive leaves stuffed with cottage cheese
Spiced peach
Buttered corn bacon squares, page 92

* *

2 fresh or canned pear halves topped with spoonfuls of cottage cheese or cream cheese, on lettuce
2 celery hearts stuffed with pimiento cheese spread
2 slices liverwurst Buttered date nut bread sandwich wedges

* *

Drained canned baked kidney beans in lettuce cup, garnished with sour cream
Alternate slices of tomato and fluted cucumber on watercress
2 halves deviled egg Pickle fans

* *

Tomato aspic cubes sprinkled with sieved cooked egg yolk, in lettuce cup
Ripe olives Cold cuts Carrot curls
Herb corn muffins, page 97

* *

Chicken salad in a roll
Cooked asparagus marinated in French dressing
Sliced tomatoes Watercress

* *

Sour cream Waldorf salad on lettuce
Orange sections alternated with grapefruit sections on lettuce
Olives Grilled American cheese sandwich

Salad Dressings

Sealtest sour cream makes a perfect salad dressing just as it comes from the container. You can put it on in generous gobs, as a topping—or toss it into the salad. Sour cream also makes a fine base for mixed dressings—and in this chapter we give you a variety of those.

There are fifteen different recipes; we'll let you decide which of them is the most delicious. Most likely, several of them will become favorites with your family.

As a general rule, it is best to dress your salad at the last minute —just before serving it.

CELERY SEED DRESSING

½ tsp. celery seed
¼ tsp. onion salt
½ tsp. dry mustard
½ tsp. tarragon vinegar
½ cup sour cream

Add celery seed, onion salt, mustard, and vinegar to sour cream. Mix gently but thoroughly. ½ cup.
SERVE WITH: mixed greens, egg salad, or sliced tomatoes.

CHILI DRESSING

Add 3 tbsp. chili sauce, 1 tbsp. chopped green pepper, 1 tbsp. drained chopped pimiento, pinch of salt to 1 cup sour cream. Fold in gently. 1¼ cups.
SERVE WITH: shrimp, tomato or meat salad.

COTTAGE CHEESE DRESSING

Fold ½ cup cottage cheese and pinch of salt gently into 1 cup sour cream. 1½ cups.
SERVE WITH: sliced tomatoes, tossed greens or fruit salad.

CREAMY CURRANT DRESSING

3 tbsp. currant jelly
½ cup sour cream

Whip jelly with fork until smooth. Add sour cream. Mix gently but thoroughly. About ⅔ cup.
SERVE WITH: fruit salad.

CREAMY MINT DRESSING

2 tbsp. finely chopped fresh mint leaves
1 tsp. sugar
1 tsp. lemon juice
1 cup sour cream

Add mint, sugar and lemon juice to sour cream; fold in gently but thoroughly. Chill for several hrs. or overnight before serving. 1 generous cup.
SERVE WITH: fruit salad, tomato slices or meat salad, especially lamb.

CUCUMBER DRESSING

Combine 2½ tsp. lemon juice, 1 cup sour cream and pinch of salt. Add 1 cup drained chopped cucumber; fold in gently; do not over mix. About 1½ cups.
SERVE WITH: fish salad, tomato aspic or wedges of lettuce.

CURRY DRESSING PIQUANT

1 tsp. curry powder
¼ tsp. salt
1 tsp. sugar
1 tbsp. horseradish
1 cup sour cream

Combine all ingredients. Fold together very gently. Chill for several hrs. or overnight before serving. 1 cup.
SERVE WITH: fish, fruit or meat salad.

To keep the rich, spoon-thick consistency of sour cream, do not stir too much in mixing.

DILL DRESSING

¼ cup very finely chopped dill pickle
1 tbsp. finely chopped parsley
1 cup sour cream

Add pickle and parsley to sour cream. Mix gently but thoroughly. About 1 cup.
SERVE WITH: cottage cheese, cucumber or fish salad.

GINGER-NUT DRESSING

2 tbsp. finely chopped candied ginger
¼ cup chopped nuts
1 tsp. honey
1 cup sour cream

Add ginger, nuts and honey to sour cream; fold in gently but well. Chill for several hrs. or overnight before serving. 1 generous cup.
SERVE WITH: fruit or poultry salad.

HORSERADISH DRESSING

Fold 2 tbsp. drained bottled horseradish and pinch of salt gently into 1 cup sour cream. 1 cup.
SERVE WITH: ham, tongue or shrimp salad.

OLIVE DRESSING

Fold 2 tbsp. chopped olives, ½ tsp. vinegar and pinch of salt gently into 1 cup sour cream. 1 cup.
SERVE WITH: tossed salad, cold cuts or lettuce.

PERKY DRESSING

Add 1 tbsp. French dressing to ½ cup sour cream; fold in lightly. ½ cup.
SERVE WITH: potato or other vegetable salad.

PIQUANT DRESSING

Fold ½ cup mayonnaise and pinch of salt gently into 1 cup sour cream. If desired, add ½ to 1 tsp. grated onion for a snappier dressing. 1⅓ cups.
SERVE WITH: chopped egg salad, tossed green salad or fruit.

SNAPPY DRESSING

1 cup cottage cheese
¼ lb. blue cheese, crumbled
Grated onion
Worcestershire sauce
Tabasco
½ to 1 cup sour cream

Combine cheeses; beat with electric mixer or hand rotary beater until smooth and blended. Season with grated onion, Worcestershire, Tabasco. Thin to desired consistency with sour cream. About 2 cups.
SERVE WITH: mixed greens, sliced tomatoes or vegetable salad.

TANGY TARTARE DRESSING

1 cup sour cream
¼ tsp. salt
½ cup India relish
¼ cup mayonnaise

Mix all ingredients together gently. Chill for several hrs. or overnight before serving. 1½ cups.
SERVE WITH: fish salad, egg salad, tomato slices, or lettuce.

Breads

You may have a terrific hand with souffles—and your casseroles may be the talk of the town but, let's face it, you haven't really arrived as a cook until your biscuits . . . your muffins . . . your bread specialties come out perfect every time!

A basket full of flaky hot biscuits or melt-in-your-mouth muffins can dress up even the simplest meal and turn it into something of a feast. Be sure to try Orange Tea Biscuits, page 92, or Herb Corn Muffins, page 97—and watch your guest reach for more!

BAKING POWDER BISCUITS

2 cups sifted flour
3 tsp. baking powder
1 tsp. salt
6 tbsp. butter
⅔ cup Sealtest milk

Combine flour, baking powder and salt in flour sifter. Sift into bowl. Cut in butter with pastry blender or 2 knives or rub in lightly with fingertips until it is in tiny particles. Mixture will resemble coarse meal.

Make a "well" in center of dry ingredients. Pour in milk all at once. Stir vigorously and quickly until dry ingredients are just moistened.

Turn out at once onto lightly floured board; knead *gently* with hands for a few seconds. Roll or pat lightly to about ½" thickness.

Dip biscuit cutter into bowl of flour. Tap it against bowl to remove excess flour. Cut straight through the dough (without twisting cutter). Re-flour cutter for each cutting.

Transfer biscuits with spatula to lightly buttered small shallow pan. Place close together for soft biscuits, 1" apart for crusty biscuits. Brush with milk.

Bake in very hot oven, 450°F., 12 to 15 min. or until golden brown. 12 medium biscuits or 20 small biscuits.

CHEESE BISCUITS: Stir 1 cup grated American cheese into dry ingredients.

CHEESE PINWHEELS: Roll the dough into rectangular sheet. Sprinkle with 1 cup grated cheese and roll up like a jelly roll. Cut crosswise into slices. Place on baking sheet.

ORANGE TEA BISCUITS: Add 2 tsp. grated orange rind to dry ingredients before adding butter. Press a small cube of sugar, dipped in orange juice, into each biscuit before baking.

CORN BACON SQUARES

Cut 6 slices of bacon in small pieces with scissors. Fry about half-done, stirring constantly. Drain well.

Prepare 1 pkg. corn muffin mix as directed on box. Spread batter in buttered pan, 8½" x 8½" x 1½". Sprinkle bacon over top. Bake in moderately hot oven, 375°F., about 20 min. 8 to 10 squares.

CALIFORNIA FRUIT LOAF

Cottage cheese, prunes and apricots deliciously blended—for a wonderful brunch bread—or for salad or tea-time sandwiches

¼ cup butter	**1½ cups sifted flour**
⅓ cup dark brown sugar	**1½ tsp. baking powder**
2 tsp. grated lemon rind	**½ tsp. soda**
2 tsp. grated orange rind	**½ tsp. salt**
1 egg, unbeaten	**½ cup chopped dried prunes**
1 cup Sealtest cottage cheese	**½ cup chopped dried apricots**

Cream together softened butter, sugar and rinds. Add egg; beat well. Stir in cheese.

Sift together flour, baking powder, soda and salt; add to first mixture along with fruits. Mix well. Mixture will be stiff. Pack in buttered loaf pan, 8½" x 4½" x 3". Bake in moderate oven, 350°F., about 1 hr. Cool. Wrap. Store in refrigerator. This loaf slices best after stored several hours. 1 loaf.

CARAMEL CHEESE ROLLS

A unique biscuit treat

1 cup Sealtest cottage cheese	**2 cups packaged biscuit mix**
¾ cup finely rolled vanilla wafer crumbs	**½ cup Sealtest milk**
	¼ cup melted butter
¼ cup dark brown sugar	**2 tbsp. sugar**

Mix cheese, crumbs and brown sugar together thoroughly with spoon.

Put biscuit mix in another bowl; add milk, butter and sugar; mix thoroughly with fork. Dough will be sticky, but do not add more mix. Roll out dough between 2 sheets of waxed paper into a 12" x 18" rectangle.

Remove top sheet of waxed paper; spread cheese-crumb mixture evenly over dough. Roll up tightly as for jelly roll (with the assistance of the bottom sheet of waxed paper). Cut gently in 1" slices; place cut side up in greased muffin pans. Brush tops with melted butter. Bake in hot oven, 425°F., about 15 min. Serve hot. 1 doz. rolls.

BLUEBERRY SCONES

2 cups sifted flour
3 tsp. baking powder
1 tsp. salt
2 tbsp. sugar
⅓ cup butter
⅓ cup buttermilk
1 egg
1 cup blueberries

Mix and sift flour, baking powder, salt and sugar. Cut in butter with 2 knives or pastry blender or rub in with fingertips.

Add buttermilk to egg (reserving 1 tbsp. unbeaten egg white). Beat until blended. Pour into dry ingredients all at once; stir quickly. Mix just enough to moisten ingredients. Lightly fold in blueberries.

Turn out on slightly floured board. Pat to ¼" to ½" thickness. Cut in squares, triangles or diamonds with floured knife. Brush with egg white diluted with 1 tsp. water. Sprinkle with granulated sugar. Bake on cookie sheet in hot oven, 425°F., 10 to 15 min. 15 to 20 medium scones.

SUNDAY SHOW-OFF BREAKFAST

Orange Slices
Fluffy Scrambled Eggs   Sausage Links
Blueberry Scones
Jam   Cottage Cheese
Milk   Coffee with Cream

FRENCH TOAST

2 eggs
1 cup Sealtest milk
Few grains salt
4 slices bread
Butter

Beat eggs slightly. Stir in milk and salt. Pour into flat shallow dish.

Dip each slice of bread into mixture, turning it and allowing time for both sides to take up liquid.

Fry slowly in butter until brown on both sides. Serve immediately with butter and maple syrup. 4 slices.

BUTTERMILK FRENCH TOAST: Substitute buttermilk for milk.

BAKED FRENCH TOAST

The oven takes over

3 eggs
3 tbsp. melted butter
1 cup Sealtest milk
½ tsp. salt
5 slices day-old bread

Beat eggs and butter together with an egg beater. Stir in milk and salt. Pour into flat shallow dish. Dip each slice of bread in mixture, turning and allowing time for both sides to take up liquid.

Bake on well-buttered cookie sheet in very hot oven, 450°F., 8 to 10 min. Turn slices and bake 5 min. longer. Serve immediately with butter and maple syrup. 5 slices.

SUMMER SUPPER

Baked French Toast   Buttered Fresh Asparagus
Sour Cream Spinach Salad, page 82
Fruit Cocktail with Sherbet
Milk   Iced Beverage

NUT BREAD

⅓ cup butter
½ cup sugar
1 egg, unbeaten
2 cups sifted flour
1 tsp. salt
3 tsp. baking powder
¾ cup pecans or other nuts, chopped fine
1 tsp. grated orange rind
1 cup Sealtest milk

Cream butter, add sugar gradually and cream thoroughly. Add egg; beat well.

Mix and sift flour, salt and baking powder. Stir in pecans and orange rind. Add to creamed mixture alternately with milk.

Pour into buttered medium loaf pan. Bake in moderate oven, 325°F., about 1¼ hrs. This loaf is better when made the day before serving. When cool, wrap in waxed paper. 1 loaf.

FIG NUT BREAD: Reduce pecans to ½ cup; reduce rind to ½ tsp. Add ¾ cup chopped dried figs to dry ingredients along with pecans and rind. 1 loaf.

MUFFINS

2 cups flour
3 tsp. baking powder
1 tsp. salt
2 tbsp. sugar
4 tbsp. butter or margarine
1 egg
1 cup Sealtest milk

Mix and sift flour, baking powder, salt and sugar. Cut in butter or margarine with two knives or rub in with fingertips.

Add egg to milk and beat slightly. Pour into dry ingredients all at once and stir quickly. Mix just long enough to moisten dry ingredients. The batter will not be smooth. Fill greased muffin pans about ⅔ full. Bake in a hot oven, 400°F., 20 to 25 min. 12 medium muffins.

BACON MUFFINS: Omit sugar. Add ½ cup chopped cooked bacon after cutting in shortening.

CHEESE MUFFINS: Omit sugar. Add ¾ cup grated cheese after cutting in the shortening.

JELLY MUFFINS: Put ½ the muffin mixture in bottom of 12 greased muffin pans. Place a little jelly in the center. Cover with remaining mixture.

NUT MUFFINS: Add ½ cup chopped nuts to dry ingredients after cutting in shortening.

RAISIN MUFFINS: Add ½ cup seedless raisins to dry ingredients after cutting in the shortening.

RICH MUFFINS: Increase the shortening to ½ cup.

DELUXE BUTTERMILK MUFFINS

2 cups sifted flour
3 tsp. baking powder
1 tsp. salt
2 tbsp. sugar
6 tbsp. butter
1 egg
1 cup Sealtest buttermilk

Mix and sift the dry ingredients. Cut in butter with 2 knives or pastry blender.

Add egg to buttermilk; beat slightly. Pour into dry ingredients all at once and stir quickly. Mix just enough to moisten.

Fill buttered muffin pans about ⅔ full. Bake in hot oven, 400°F., 20 to 25 min. 12 medium muffins.

BUTTERMILK BLUEBERRY MUFFINS

2 cups sifted flour
½ cup sugar
1 tsp. salt
¼ tsp. soda
2½ tsp. baking powder
1 egg, separated
¾ cup Sealtest buttermilk
¼ cup butter, melted
1 cup blueberries

Mix and sift flour, sugar, salt, soda and baking powder. Beat egg white until stiff.

Add egg yolk to buttermilk; blend well with fork; pour into dry ingredients; do not stir. Now add butter; stir quickly and vigorously just enough to moisten all dry ingredients.

Immediately fold in blueberries and egg white. Immediately spoon into well-buttered muffin pans, filling pans about ⅔ full. Bake in hot oven, 400°F., about 20 to 25 min. 15 medium muffins.

HERB CORN MUFFINS

2 cups packaged corn muffin mix
1 unbeaten egg
⅓ cup Sealtest sour cream
¼ tsp. ground thyme
½ tsp. salt
½ tsp. celery seed
2 tsp. grated onion

Combine all ingredients. Mix gently until well blended and dry ingredients are just moistened. Drop by spoonfuls into small, buttered muffin pans until ⅔ full. Bake according to pkg. directions until done. 12 small muffins.

SURPRISE MUFFINS

Prepare 1 pkg. corn muffin mix as directed on box. Fill buttered muffin pans ⅓ full; put a tsp. of orange marmalade or canned mincemeat in the center. Top with a little more batter so that pans are about half full. Bake as directed.

MELBA TOAST

A salad or soup accompaniment

Slice bread very thin. Cut slices in half, then spread out on baking sheet. Bake in slow oven, 300°F., 15 to 20 min. or until crisp and golden brown.

POPOVERS

1 cup sifted flour
½ tsp. salt
2 eggs
2 tsp. melted butter
1 cup Sealtest milk

Mix and sift together flour and salt. Beat eggs until foamy; add melted butter and milk, beating until well blended. Add sifted dry ingredients. Beat with rotary beater (electric or hand) for 1 min. or until smooth.

Pour into 6 well-greased custard cups, filling each about ½ full. Bake in hot oven, 425°F., 40 min. Open oven door and quickly stick the point of a sharp knife into the side of each popover (this makes popovers crisper). Bake 5 min. more and serve at once. 6 popovers.

FEATHERWEIGHT PANCAKES

Actually melt in your mouth

3 eggs, separated
¼ tsp. salt
¼ cup flour
¾ cup Sealtest cottage cheese

Heat griddle very slowly. Beat egg whites with egg beater until stiff but not dry.

Beat yolks with the same beater until light and lemon colored. Stir in salt, flour and cheese. Fold in whites.

Drop by small spoonfuls on hot lightly greased griddle. Bake until golden brown on both sides. Serve immediately with butter and maple syrup. Twelve 3″ pancakes. 4 servings.

SUNDAY BRUNCH

Orange Sections
Strawberry Garnish
Featherweight Pancakes
Maple Syrup Butter
Sausage Links
Milk Coffee with Cream

BLUEBERRY PANCAKES

1 cup sifted flour
1½ tsp. baking powder
1 tbsp. sugar
½ tsp. salt
¼ tsp. cinnamon
2 tbsp. melted butter
1 egg, separated
¾ cup Sealtest milk
¾ cup blueberries

Mix and sift flour, baking powder, sugar, salt and cinnamon.

Add melted butter to beaten egg yolk. Stir in milk. Add to dry ingredients, mixing just enough to moisten. Fold in stiffly beaten egg white. Add berries and mix lightly.

Bake on greased griddle. Serve with butter. 8 large pancakes.

SPOON BREAD

2 cups Sealtest milk
½ cup corn meal
(white or yellow)
1 tbsp. butter
1 tsp. salt
1 tsp. sugar
3 eggs, separated

Heat milk to scalding in a heavy saucepan. Add corn meal gradually, stirring constantly.

Add butter, salt and sugar. Stir until butter is melted. Cook over moderate heat, stirring constantly until thickened (about 10 to 15 min.).

Beat egg yolks until light. Add a small amount of the hot mixture to egg yolks; mix well. Combine egg mixture and remaining hot mixture, stirring until well blended. Beat egg whites until stiff but not dry; fold into corn meal mixture. Pour into a buttered 1 or 1½ qt. casserole or baking dish. Bake in moderately hot oven, 375°F., 45 min. 4 servings.

SOUTHERN LUNCHEON

Spoon Bread with Crispy Bacon Butter
Vegetable Medley Salad, page 72
Baked Apples a la Mode
Milk Coffee with Cream

BUTTERMILK WAFFLES

- 1 cup sifted flour
- 1 tbsp. sugar
- ¾ tsp. baking powder
- ¼ tsp. soda
- ½ tsp. salt
- 1 egg, separated
- ¾ cup Sealtest buttermilk
- ¼ cup butter, melted

Mix and sift flour, sugar, baking powder, soda and salt. Beat egg white until stiff.

Add egg yolk to buttermilk and beat with rotary beater until blended.

Make a well in dry ingredients. Pour in buttermilk and egg yolk mixture. Stir slightly. Pour in melted butter. Mix quickly just enough to moisten.

Fold in egg white. Bake on hot waffle iron. 3 waffles.

CORN MEAL WAFFLES

- ½ cup sifted flour
- 1 tsp. baking powder
- ½ tsp. salt
- 1 tbsp. sugar
- ½ cup corn meal
- ⅔ cup Sealtest milk
- ¼ cup melted butter
- 2 eggs, separated

Mix and sift flour, baking powder, salt and sugar. Add corn meal; stir in.

Add milk and butter to beaten egg yolks. Add to dry ingredients all at once; mix well. Fold in stiffly beaten egg whites.

Bake on hot waffle iron. Serve with butter and maple syrup. 3 large waffles.

WAFFLE TOAST

Delicious with cottage cheese

Remove crusts from bread. If desired, spread with butter. Bake in hot waffle iron until toasted.

Sandwiches

For unexpected visitors who drop in suddenly—for the buffet supper you plan to the last detail—for picnics, TV parties and informal receptions—for tea, lunch or brunch—for practically any occasion you can name, there are sandwiches that fill the bill admirably.

You may be addicted to the paper-thin variety that's a perennial favorite at English teas—or you may favor the hearty kind of sandwich which even growing boys consider adequate as a meal. In either case, you'll find a number of suggestions on the following pages.

KINDS OF SANDWICHES

CLOSED SANDWICH . . . two slices of buttered bread, or a buttered split roll, with your favorite filling . . . a meat, fish, poultry, cheese, egg, vegetable or even fruit combination, as light or hearty as you please.

OPEN FACE SANDWICH . . . just one slice of buttered bread or half a roll topped with a tempting filling for all to see.

TRIPLE DECKER SANDWICH . . . three slices of buttered bread (usually toasted) and two wholesome layers of filling . . . practically a whole meal by itself.

HOT MAIN COURSE SANDWICH . . . hot roast beef, chicken shortcake, grilled cheese, scrambled eggs, bacon, etc., served open face or closed.

PARTY SANDWICH . . . made with an extra special bread, an unusually tempting filling or cut in a special way . . . grand for buffet luncheons, teas, suppers or evening entertaining.

BREADS FOR SANDWICHES

Brown
Cheese bread
Corn bread
Cracked wheat
Date, orange or banana nut
Enriched white
Frankfurter rolls
French or Italian bread
Hamburger buns
Hard rolls
Pumpernickel
Raisin, cinnamon raisin
Rye
Whole wheat

GARNISHES

A crisp or carefully seasoned garnish can add color and bring out flavor when served with a sandwich.

Carrot strips
Celery hearts
Cole slaw or potato salad in small lettuce cups
Cucumber rings or strips
Green pepper rings
Pickled beets
Pickled onions
Plain, ripe or stuffed olives
Sliced or fan-shaped pickles
Sliced, quartered or stuffed eggs
Sliced radishes or radish roses
Spiced peaches
Sprigs of watercress or parsley

IDEAS FOR CUTTING AND SERVING SANDWICHES

With a sharp knife and a little imagination you can add to the attractiveness of a sandwich. Here are three ways to cut sandwiches to show them off.

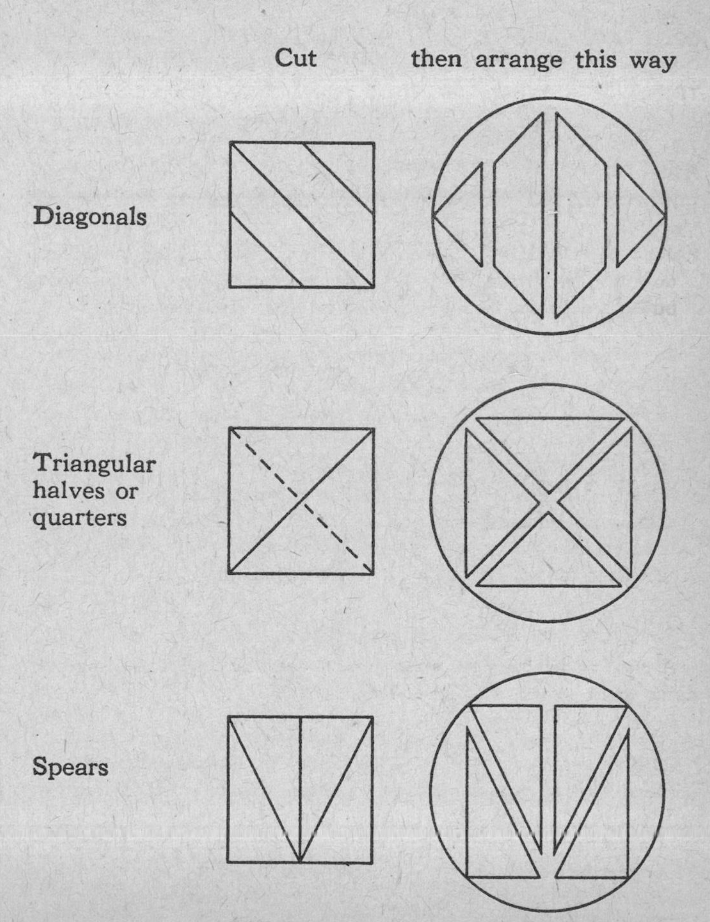

PANTRY SHELF SANDWICH FILLINGS

These 10 sandwich fillings are easily made with ready to serve cottage cheese, American cheese, sour cream—and items from your pantry shelf.

APRICOT CHEESE: Soak 1/4 cup dried apricots in water over night or until tender. Drain. Chop fine with knife or cut with wet kitchen scissors. Mix lightly with 1/2 cup cottage cheese. Season with salt. 3/4 cup. 2 to 3 sandwiches.

COCONUT AND CHEESE: Mix 1 cup shredded coconut and 1 cup cottage cheese. Season with a little salt, if desired. Especially good on thinly sliced brown bread. 1 1/4 cups. 5 sandwiches.

DATE AND CHEESE: Mix 1 cup finely chopped dates and 1 cup cottage cheese. Let stand awhile to blend flavors. About 1 1/2 cups. 5 to 6 sandwiches.

DATE, NUT AND CHEESE: Combine 1/4 cup chopped walnuts, 3/4 cup cottage cheese and 1/4 cup chopped dates; mix well. Let stand awhile to blend flavors. About 1 cup. 4 sandwiches.

DRIED BEEF AND CHEESE: Cut 2 oz. sliced dried beef into small pieces with scissors. Mix lightly with 1 cup cottage cheese. 1 cup. 4 sandwiches.

PEANUT CHEESE: Blend 1/4 cup peanut butter and 1/4 cup sour cream. Fold in 1 cup cottage cheese. 1 1/2 cups filling. 6 sandwiches.

PICKLE AND CHEESE: Add 2 tbsp. finely chopped sweet pickle or pickle relish to 2/3 cup shredded process American cheese. Stir in 1/4 cup sour cream, mixing until thoroughly blended. About 3/4 cup. 3 sandwiches.

PRUNE, NUT AND CHEESE: Soak 1 cup dried prunes over night or until tender. Drain. Pit and chop fine with knife or cut with wet kitchen scissors. Add 1/8 cup chopped nuts, 1 tsp. lemon juice and 1/2 cup cottage cheese; mix together lightly. (Omit nuts if desired.) Add a lettuce leaf when making sandwiches with this filling. 1 cup. 3 to 4 sandwiches.

RIPE OLIVE AND CHEESE: Combine 1/2 cup chopped ripe olives and 1 cup cottage cheese; mix well. 1 1/2 cups. 4 to 5 sandwiches.

TUNA-SOUR CREAM: Drain and finely flake one 7-oz. can tuna. Add 1/4 cup chopped celery and 2 tbsp. finely chopped onion. Stir in 6 tbsp. sour cream, mixing until well blended. About 1 1/4 cups. 4 to 5 sandwiches.

DELICIOUSLY DIFFERENT DOWN-TO-EARTH SANDWICHES

When ham on rye, lettuce and tomato, or peanut butter and jelly "go stale," try these different sandwiches to perk up interest.

BANANA CHEESE SANDWICH

Nibbling delight for a canasta party

Spread 12 slices of canned or homemade brown bread with 1 cup cottage cheese. Top half of them with thin slices banana. Put slices together. 6 sandwiches.

CANASTA PARTY
Banana Cheese Sandwiches
Assorted Nuts Pastel Mints
Tea Lemon

BANANA CREAM CHEESE YUMMY

Soften 4 oz. cream cheese to spreading consistency with ¼ cup sour cream. Spread on 6 slices whole wheat raisin bread, pumpernickel or rye. Arrange banana slices and chopped walnuts on 3 of them; top with remaining 3 slices. 3 sandwiches.

CHEESE, CUCUMBER AND ONION SANDWICH

Spread 8 slices of buttered bread generously with cottage cheese. Cover 4 of them with thin slices cucumber and thin slivers of onion; top with remaining slices. 4 sandwiches.

CUCUMBER CHEESE SANDWICH

Soften 4 oz. cream cheese to spreading consistency with ¼ cup sour cream. Add 1½ tbsp. finely chopped parsley and ½ tsp. onion salt; blend well. Spread on 6 slices of rye, pumpernickel or whole wheat bread. Arrange cucumber slices on 3 of them; top with remaining 3 slices. 3 sandwiches.

CHILI CHEESE BUNS

Combine 1 cup cottage cheese, ¼ cup finely chopped green pepper, and 3 tbsp. chili sauce. Mix until blended. Split 6 long finger buns almost through. Hollow out part of center; spread with butter. Fill with chili-cheese mixture. 6 buns.

DEVILED HAM AND CHEESE SANDWICH

Mix one 2¼-oz. can deviled ham with 2 tbsp. sweet pickle relish. Spread ham mixture on one slice of white or rye bread and cottage cheese on another slice; then put the 2 together. (You'll need about ⅔ cup cottage cheese.) 4 sandwiches.

EGG CREAM CHEESE SANDWICH

Mix well 2 oz. cream cheese, 2 coarsely chopped hard-cooked eggs, ¼ cup finely chopped stuffed olives and dash of Worcestershire sauce. Spread on 2 slices bread or 2 halves of split hard rolls; cover with 2 lightly buttered bread slices or remaining 2 roll halves. 2 sandwiches.

EGG SALAD SANDWICH

Mix 3 hard-cooked eggs, finely chopped, and 2 tbsp. finely chopped onion with ¼ cup sour cream. Season with salt and pepper. Spread between slices of buttered bread. 3 to 4 sandwiches.

TURKEY SALAD ROLL

A treat for Sunday supper

2 cups diced cooked turkey
1 cup diced celery
½ cup Sealtest sour cream
Salt and pepper
6 finger or frankfurter rolls
Butter
Lettuce

Put turkey and celery in a bowl. Add sour cream; toss together lightly. Season with salt and pepper. Chill until ready to serve.

Split rolls lengthwise, but not quite through. Spread with butter. (Rolls may be heated slightly in oven.)

Place a leaf of lettuce in each roll and fill with turkey salad. If desired, serve with a garnish of 2 or 3 orange slices in a lettuce cup. 6 servings.

TRIPLE DECKER SANDWICHES

Vary your noon-hour menu with triple decker sandwiches. A nourishing meal in themselves—and an ideal way to make left-overs seem like newcomers to the table.

GENERAL PROCEDURE

Toast 3 slices of bread and spread one side of each with butter. (Bread should be cut thin.)

Spread filling on first slice. Cover with lettuce and second slice of toast, buttered side down.

Then spread butter (or mayonnaise) on the *top* of this second slice.

Add second layer of filling.

Top with third slice of toast.

Stick in toothpicks to hold layers together.

Cut in triangles or other shapes.

NOTE:

Use mayonnaise wherever desired with any of the fillings.

Have fillings ready in advance. Work fast so that toast is still crisp and hot when served.

In the suggestions below, the first line represents the first layer; the second line represents the second layer.

- Sliced egg
  Sliced ham, thin slices tomato
- Sliced liverwurst, dill pickle
  Cottage cheese
- Sliced ham
  Peanut butter, pickle relish
- Sliced ham
  Swiss cheese, sliced tomato
- Crisp slices bacon
  American cheese, thin slices tomato
- Tuna salad
  Sliced egg sprinkled with India relish
- Sardines, boneless
  Egg salad, thin slices tomato
- Tongue, sliced
  Crisp bacon, thin slices tomato
- Chicken salad
  Crisp bacon, lettuce
- Salmon salad
  Sliced egg, sprinkled with chopped pimiento or pickle
- Sliced breast of chicken, lettuce
  Crisp bacon, thin slices tomato
  (regular club)

HOT MAIN COURSE SANDWICHES

Hot sandwiches make a satisfying easy-to-serve main course. Made with cheese or leftover meat and gravy, they can be economical as well as good to eat.

CHEESE SANDWICH BARBECUE

recipe page 42

PANCAKE SANDWICH

Spread your favorite hot sandwich filling between two thin pancakes. (Eat with fork.) This is especially good with hot roast beef and gravy.

TOASTED CHEESE

Toast triangles of bread on one side. Cover the other side with sliced American cheese. Place under low broiler heat until melted.

OPEN FACE SANDWICHES

Why not show off tempting sandwich fillings by serving them open face?

FOUR POINT SANDWICH

Mix 1 tbsp. crumbled blue cheese with ¼ cup cottage cheese. Mix a little chopped chives with a second ¼ cup of cottage cheese.

Pile each mixture on 2 triangles of buttered bread: whole wheat, white, light or dark rye. Arrange triangles alternately on a luncheon plate with points toward center; tuck tomato wedges in between. Nestle ½ hard-cooked egg in the center on greens. 1 serving.

RED BOW SANDWICH

Mix about ½ tbsp. sour cream and a few grains salt with ¼ cup cottage cheese. Pile on 2 buttered toast rounds. Top each round with 2 quarter-slices of tomato, points touching in center, and a dab of sour cream. Place on luncheon plate; garnish with 2 quarters of hard-cooked egg and 1 or 2 pickles. 1 serving.

SILVERY SARDINE SANDWICH

Blend 1 cup cottage cheese, ½ to 1 tsp. grated onion and a little salt and pepper.

Cut 2 or 3 frankfurter rolls in half lengthwise but not quite through; open up almost flat; toast and butter. Heap cottage cheese on rolls and place on luncheon plates. Top each with 4 silvery sardines and 2 pimiento strips. Garnish plate with radish roses on chicory or lettuce. 2 to 3 servings.

For 2 additional open face sandwiches see:

TURKEY SALAD ROLL, page 106
PUMPERNICKS, page 112

PARTY SANDWICHES

It's fun to serve party sandwiches that taste as delicious as they are pretty to look at. Besides serving to guests, pamper your family occasionally—especially at holiday time.

CALIFORNIA THREE DECKERS

Cut a round loaf of canned date nut bread in very thin slices. Put 3 slices together with cottage cheese between, 3-decker fashion. Cut into 4 to 6 wedges.

JAM BASKETS

Remove crusts from fresh bread; cut bread in thin slices. Spread with soft butter then with jam, jelly or marmalade. Beginning at one corner roll up diagonally and fasten with toothpick. Toast. These sandwiches add glamour to your tea table.

PUNCH PARTY

Strawberry Tantalizer, page 197
Fig Nut Fingers Jam Baskets
Mints

GARLAND SANDWICHES

Tinted cottage cheese makes the frosting

Cut sliced whole wheat or white bread in rounds with doughnut cutter. Spread half with butter. Put 2 rounds together with one of the tasty sandwich fillings below, or your favorite filling. Frost with tinted cottage cheese. Decorate with bits of pimiento, green pepper, watercress, chive.

TURKEY OLIVE FILLING: Mix 1 cup chopped cooked turkey, ¼ cup chopped celery, ¼ cup chopped ripe olives, ¼ cup mayonnaise, few drops Worcestershire, salt and pepper to taste. 10 fillings.

ANCHOVY EGG FILLING: Mix 4 chopped hard-cooked eggs, 1 to 2 tbsp. anchovy paste, 3 tbsp. mayonnaise, 3 tbsp. India relish. 10 fillings.

PARTY SANDWICH LOAF

A party loaf that rates an orchid

- 1 loaf unsliced bread
- Butter, slightly softened for spreading
- ¾ cup Sealtest cottage cheese
- ⅓ cup deviled ham
- ½ cup egg salad
- ¾ cup tuna salad
- ¾ cup chive Sealtest cottage cheese (cheese mixed with chopped chives)
- 3 to 4 pkgs. cream cheese
- ¼ to ⅓ cup cream or milk

Trim all crusts from bread; cut loaf into 6 lengthwise slices. Spread first slice with butter, then with cottage cheese. Spread next slice with butter. Place buttered side down on top of first slice. Spread butter on top of this second slice. Repeat procedure using deviled ham in second layer, egg salad in third, tuna salad in fourth and chive cottage cheese in last.

Soften cream cheese with spoon. Add cream or milk gradually, blending until soft and easy to spread. Frost loaf with cheese.

Chill thoroughly in refrigerator . . . several hours if possible. Garnish loaf with lettuce, radish roses and carrot curls. Cut into ½" slices with very sharp knife. If desired, use alternate slices of whole wheat and white bread. Other fillings may be used. 12 to 15 slices.

PARTY SANDWICH CAKE

Delectable conversation piece

2 pkgs. hot roll mix	2/3 cup mayonnaise
3 cans deviled ham, 2 1/4 oz. each	1 tsp. dry mustard
3/4 cup drained pickle relish	1 can grated tuna, 7 1/4 oz.
6 tbsp. softened butter	1/3 cup minced onion
2 jars pimiento cheese spread, 5 oz. each	1 1/2 lbs. cream cheese
4 hard-cooked eggs, chopped	Sealtest milk
	Green coloring

Make 1 large round loaf of bread with roll mix. Follow pkg. directions; bake in greased 9" spring form pan in moderately hot oven, 375°F., 30 min. Let cool in the pan.

Remove bottom crust; cut bread crosswise in 6 round slices about 1/2" thick. Cut off crusty edges from each slice with scissors.

Place bottom slice of bread on serving platter; spread with deviled ham. Top with second slice; cover with relish mixed with softened butter. Put on third slice; cover with pimiento cheese spread.

Put on fourth slice; spread with eggs mixed with 1/3 cup of the mayonnaise and the mustard. Put on fifth slice; spread with tuna mixed with onion and remaining 1/3 cup mayonnaise. Put on last slice.

Spread outside of "cake" with cream cheese that has been softened and mixed with a little milk, then tinted green with a little food coloring. Chill 3 hours or overnight.

If desired, decorate base of "cake" with parsley, radish roses, carrot curls, green and ripe olives; garnish top of "cake" with border of olives, cauliflowerettes and cooked shrimp stuck on with toothpicks; add a center bouquet of parsley and radish roses. One 9" cake.

FIG NUT FINGERS

Cut Fig Nut Bread, page 95, into thin slices. Put slices together with cottage cheese between. Cut each sandwich into fingers.

PINWHEELS

Remove crusts from loaf of fresh bread; cut bread in very thin slices lengthwise of loaf. Spread with cottage cheese, cream cheese, softened American cheese or with one of the Kraft cheese spreads. Place 4 stuffed olives in a row at one end. Beginning at this end, roll up as for jelly roll. Wrap in waxed paper and damp towel. Chill and slice.

PUMPERNICKS

Hearty delightfully different open-face sandwiches

First, prepare 3 sandwich spreads as follows:

SAVORY SALMON CHEESE: Combine one 3½-oz. can red salmon, drained and flaked, 1 tbsp. French dressing, ⅓ cup Sealtest cottage cheese, ⅓ cup finely chopped celery, 1 finely chopped pimiento, ⅛ tsp. salt.

DEVILED EGG CHEESE: Combine 3 finely chopped hard-cooked eggs, ¼ cup Sealtest cottage cheese, 1 tbsp. mayonnaise, 2 tsp. prepared mustard, ¼ tsp. salt.

SNAPPY COTTAGE CHEESE: Combine 1 cup Sealtest cottage cheese, 1 tsp. bottled horseradish, 1 tsp. parsley flakes, dash salt.

Now cut 4 large round crosswise slices of pumpernickel about ¼" thick. Butter. In the center of each slice spread a circle of Savory Salmon Cheese, ¼" to ½" deep. Next spread around that a ring of Deviled Egg Cheese, then another ring of Salmon Cheese and finally a ring of Snappy Cottage Cheese. Cut each slice in 6 to 8 wedges. 4 servings.

COMPANY LUNCHEON

Chicken Consomme

Pumpernicks

Grapefruit Avocado Salad French Dressing

Chocolate Nut Sundae Cookies

Milk Tea Coffee

Desserts

Desserts give that finishing touch to a meal that is so important; yet they complement the meal too. So top off a light meal with a hearty pie or scrumptious cake; ease off a heavy meal with a delectable Spanish cream or cooling sherbet.

Whether it's simple old-fashioned custard, sophisticated cheese cake or glamorous baked Alaska, make it so well that the memory lingers on.

(Note: A separate chapter. beginning on page 155, is devoted to ice cream.)

BANANA MARSHMALLOW CREAM

An airy fruit mold

32 marshmallows (about ½ lb.)
½ cup Sealtest light cream
½ cup finely chopped pecans
Juice of 1 lemon
1½ cups Sealtest whipping cream
1 banana, diced

Melt marshmallows in light cream over very low heat, stirring until smooth. Cool; add nuts. Mix lemon juice with diced banana; add to marshmallow mixture and blend well. Whip cream until stiff; fold into marshmallow mixture. Pour into a 1 qt. ring or pudding mold.

Chill 3 to 4 hrs. or overnight. When firm, unmold. If desired, garnish with banana slices and sweetened whipped cream. 6 to 8 servings.

BROWN AND WHITE PARFAIT

1 cup chilled drained stewed prunes
1 tbsp. lemon juice
1 cup Sealtest cottage cheese
½ cup Sealtest whipping cream

Pit prunes; cut in small pieces. Fold in lemon juice with fork. Beat cheese with rotary beater until curds are very fine. Fold in whipped cream. Fill parfait glasses with alternate spoonfuls cheese and prunes. 4 servings.

CHEESE BOWL

Mellow cheese served with tart fruit and crackers makes an elegant dessert

¾ cup sieved Sealtest cottage cheese
¼ lb. Roquefort cheese, sieved
1 tbsp. Sealtest sour cream
Few drops Worcestershire sauce
Crackers
Fruit

Mix cottage cheese, Roquefort cheese and sour cream just enough to blend. Add Worcestershire to taste.

Serve in bowl. Pass crackers and fruit. 1 generous cup. 6 servings.

CHOCOLATE CREAM CHARLOTTE

- 1 cup Sealtest whipping cream
- 3 tbsp. cocoa
- ¼ cup confectioners sugar
- 1 tsp. vanilla
- 6 lady fingers, separated

Combine cream, cocoa, sugar and vanilla in mixing bowl; chill. Just before serving, whip until stiff.

Arrange lady finger halves, end-up, in dessert dishes, 3 to a serving. Fill center with the chocolate whipped cream. 4 servings.

COTTAGE CHEESE DESSERT TOPPING

- 1 cup Sealtest cottage cheese
- 2 to 3 tbsp. Sealtest sour cream or sweet cream

Press cottage cheese through sieve. Add cream gradually and beat until fluffy. More cream may be added, depending upon the moistness of cottage cheese. Add few grains salt, if desired.

Serve on sour cherry tarts or pies, berry pies or cobblers, baked peaches, fruit salad desserts, upside-down cakes, gingerbread, fruit gelatine, etc. 8 to 10 servings.

COTTAGE DESSERT CREAM

- 1 cup Sealtest cottage cheese
- 2 eggs, separated
- ½ cup sugar
- ½ tsp. vanilla
- 1 tbsp. raspberry juice or 1 tbsp. orange juice and ¼ tsp. grated orange rind
- ¼ cup Sealtest whipping cream

Press cottage cheese through fine sieve. Add egg yolks, sugar, vanilla, juice and rind; beat with electric mixer or hand rotary beater until smooth and blended.

Beat egg whites until stiff but not dry. Whip cream. Fold egg whites and whipped cream into cheese mixture. Spoon mixture into dessert dishes. Chill for several hrs. 4 servings.

COTTAGE MAPLE CREME

For a very simple unique cottage cheese dessert that appeals to children, put a scoop of Sealtest cottage cheese in a dessert dish and dribble a spoonful of either maple syrup or chocolate syrup over it. Top with a spoonful of fluffy whipped cream.

COTTAGE MELBA

2 cups Sealtest cottage cheese
1 one-lb. can sliced peaches
Raspberry preserves
Whipped cream

Divide cheese among 5 or 6 dessert dishes. Spoon peaches and a little peach syrup over cheese. Top with spoonful of preserves and a generous dab of whipped cream. 5 to 6 servings.

CRANBERRY CREAM

1 cup canned jellied cranberry sauce
½ tsp. almond extract
1 cup Sealtest whipping cream
Cubed left-over cake

Beat cranberry sauce and almond extract together with fork. Fold in whipped cream. Pile on cubed cake. 4 to 5 servings.

FROZEN NEW ORLEANS COTTAGE CHEESE

1 cup Sealtest cottage cheese
1 tbsp. lemon juice
½ cup sugar
1 cup Sealtest sour cream or 1 cup Sealtest whipping cream
Fruit

Press cottage cheese through fine sieve. Add lemon juice and sugar; beat until smooth and blended. Add sour cream; mix well. Pour into refrigerator tray; freeze. (If sweet whipping cream is used, first whip until stiff and fold into cheese mixture after it has been partially frozen, and beaten.)

When mixture is frozen around edges about ½" from edge of tray, turn into chilled bowl and beat with cold rotary beater until smooth (not melted). Return to cold refrigerator tray; freeze until firm but not too hard.

Cut in squares and serve topped with fruit, such as raspberries, strawberries, pineapple or peaches. 4 to 5 servings.

HAWAIIAN DELIGHT

1 cup Sealtest cottage cheese
½ cup Sealtest whipping cream
¼ cup sugar
½ cup drained canned crushed pineapple
¼ tsp. almond extract

Press cottage cheese through fine sieve. Whip cream until stiff.

Add whipped cream, pineapple, sugar and almond extract to cheese; fold in gently but thoroughly. Chill. Spoon into dessert dishes. Serve 2 lady fingers with each portion. 4 servings.

STRAWBERRY FLUFF

2 tbsp. confectioners sugar
1½ cups Sealtest whipping cream
3 cups coarse angel cake crumbs
1½ cups crushed strawberries
½ cup toasted shredded coconut

Add sugar to cream; whip until stiff. Add cake crumbs, strawberries, and coconut. Fold in gently but thoroughly. Spoon into dessert dishes and chill for several hrs. before serving. 6 servings.
NOTE: To make large fluffy angel cake crumbs pull cake apart with fingers or fork.

STRAWBERRY MALLOW

1½ cups sliced strawberries
3 tbsp. sugar
½ lb. marshmallows
1 cup Sealtest whipping cream
1 tsp. vanilla

Mix strawberries with sugar. Chill.

Cut marshmallows in small pieces with wet kitchen scissors. Whip cream, add vanilla and fold in marshmallows.

Chill thoroughly. Just before serving gently combine with berries. 6 servings.

TAPIOCA CREAM PARFAIT

3 tbsp. quick-cooking tapioca
6 tbsp. sugar
¼ tsp. salt
1⅓ cups Sealtest milk
½ cup Sealtest whipping cream
2 cups raspberries

Mix tapioca, 4 tbsp. sugar and the salt in saucepan. Add milk gradually, mixing well. Cook, stirring constantly, until mixture comes to a boil, about 5 min. Remove from heat. Mixture will be thin. When cool, fold in whipped cream. Chill.

Crush raspberries slightly. Add remaining 2 tbsp. sugar. Arrange alternate layers of tapioca cream and raspberries in parfait glasses so that raspberries make top layer. 4 to 6 servings.

CUSTARDS

That delectable combination of eggs and milk, baked to velvety smoothness, is just as popular today as in the days of the crinoline.

BAKED CUSTARD

3 eggs
⅓ cup sugar
¼ tsp. salt
3 cups Sealtest milk, scalded
1 tsp. vanilla

Beat eggs slightly. Add sugar and salt. Mix well. Add milk gradually, stirring vigorously. Add vanilla. Pour into custard cups.

Place cups in baking pan; pour boiling water around them to almost height of custard. Bake in moderate oven, 350°F., 30 to 35 min. or until a silver knife inserted in the custard comes out clean.

Remove cups from water; cool on rack. Chill thoroughly. Serve in cups, or loosen around edge with paring knife, then turn out.

Serve custard plain or with a choice of toppings: chocolate sauce, maple syrup with pecans, fruit sauce, plain or whipped cream, praline sauce, page 178, toasted coconut. 6 servings.

LARGE CUSTARD: Add an extra egg to basic recipe above. Pour into 1½ qt. shallow casserole; bake in pan of hot water 30 to 35 min. or until inserted knife comes out clean.

CARAMEL CUSTARD: Melt ½ cup sugar in a heavy saucepan over moderate heat until light brown in color, stirring constantly. Remove from heat; add ½ cup boiling water, a few drops at a time, being careful not to let any syrup spatter on hands. Stir vigorously after each addition until blended and smooth.

Reduce milk in basic Baked Custard recipe to 2½ cups; decrease sugar to 2½ tbsp. Add caramel syrup to the scalded milk; mix well. (Bake 40 to 50 min. or until set.)

APRICOT CUSTARD: Place a drained canned apricot half in bottom of each custard cup, before pouring in custard.

MARSHMALLOW CUSTARD: Put one marshmallow in each custard cup before filling with custard mixture. When baked serve right side up. Marshmallow melts and forms interesting crust.

CREAM CUSTARD: Substitute 1 cup cream for 1 cup milk. Scald cream with milk.

BROWN TOP CUSTARD

A surprise variation of an old favorite

- 3 eggs
- 3 tbsp. sugar
- ⅛ tsp. salt
- 1½ cups Sealtest milk, scalded
- ½ tsp. vanilla

Beat 2 whole eggs and 1 yolk together with egg beater until blended. (Save 1 white for meringue.) Stir in sugar and salt. Add milk gradually, stirring vigorously. Add vanilla. Pour into custard cups, filling ¾ full.

Top with spoonful of Chocolate Meringue, recipe below. Push meringue down in custard with spoon to coat it. It will rise to surface. Bake in pan of hot water in moderate oven, 350°F., 40 to 50 min. Cool. 5 to 6 servings.

CHOCOLATE MERINGUE: Beat egg white until foamy. Gradually add 1½ tbsp. sugar; beat until stiff. Fold in melted ¼ square unsweetened chocolate and drop of vanilla, until well blended.

RICE AND RAISIN CUSTARD

- 2 eggs
- ⅓ cup sugar
- ¼ tsp. nutmeg
- ¼ tsp. salt
- ½ tsp. vanilla
- 2 cups Sealtest milk, scalded
- ½ cup raisins, washed and drained
- 1 cup cooked rice

Beat eggs slightly. Add sugar, nutmeg, salt and vanilla; beat until blended. Add hot milk gradually, stirring constantly. Stir in rice and raisins. Pour mixture into buttered 1 or 1½ qt. casserole or baking dish. Place in pan of hot water; bake in moderate oven, 350°F., 1 hr. or until set. 4 to 6 servings.

CARAMEL RICE AND RAISIN CUSTARD: Caramelize 1 cup sugar (melt in heavy skillet over low heat, stirring until light brown). Add ⅔ cup hot water carefully, to avoid spattering; cook to a syrup, stirring until smooth. Mix syrup with custard mixture in basic recipe above before stirring in rice and raisins.

CREME BRULEE

4 egg yolks
1/8 tsp. salt
1 1/2 cups Sealtest light cream, scalded in double boiler
1/3 cup brown sugar

Beat egg yolks well. Add salt and 1/2 the sugar. Mix well. Slowly add cream, stirring vigorously. Cook in double boiler over simmering water until mixture thickens slightly and coats spoon. Pour immediately into individual baking dishes. Cool. Chill several hrs.

Sieve remaining sugar over top. Brown sugar slowly under broiler. Watch carefully so that sugar does not scorch. Cool for short time. 4 servings.

FLOATING ISLAND DESSERT

2 eggs, separated
2 cups Sealtest milk
2 tsp. cornstarch
Dash of salt
3/4 cup sugar
1 tsp. vanilla

Beat egg yolks slightly. Add milk, beating until well blended.

Mix cornstarch, salt and 1/2 cup of the sugar in heavy saucepan. Add milk mixture gradually, stirring constantly. Cook over low heat, stirring constantly, until thickened and custard coats spoon. Cool slightly. Stir in vanilla. Pour into serving dishes. Chill.

Before serving, beat egg whites until stiff but not dry. Add 1/4 cup sugar gradually, beating well after each addition. Float a large fluff of egg white meringue on each serving of custard. 4 to 6 servings.

PUDDINGS

CHOC-COCONUT PUDDING

2 cups Sealtest chocolate drink
3 tbsp. cornstarch
Dash of salt
1 cup shredded coconut
1 tsp. vanilla

Add a little chocolate drink to cornstarch; mix to smooth paste in heavy saucepan. Add remaining chocolate drink, salt and coconut. Cook over low heat, stirring constantly, until thickened. Remove from heat; stir in vanilla. Cool, stirring occasionally. 4 servings.

BUTTERSCOTCH TRIFLE

Rich . . . but scrumptious

1 pkg. butterscotch pudding
1½ cups Sealtest milk
1¼ cups fine graham cracker crumbs
⅔ cup shredded coconut
¼ cup brown sugar
½ cup Sealtest whipping cream
⅓ cup melted butter

Prepare pudding according to pkg. directions using only 1½ cups milk. Stir in coconut. Cool.

Mix 1 cup graham cracker crumbs with sugar and butter. Press into bottom of 10" x 6" x 2" pan. Chill. Spread cooled pudding over crust. Chill several hrs. Cut in rectangles. Whip cream until almost stiff; fold in remaining ¼ cup crumbs; serve on rectangles. 6 to 8 servings.

FRENCH VANILLA CREAM PUDDING

1 pkg. vanilla pudding
1½ cups Sealtest milk
½ tsp. vanilla
1 cup Sealtest whipping cream

Empty contents of pkg. into saucepan. Add milk gradually, stirring until smooth. Cook over moderate heat, stirring constantly, until thickened. Remove from heat. Cool, stirring occasionally.

Add vanilla to cream and whip until stiff. Pour cooled pudding over whipped cream; fold in gently but thoroughly. Chill. Serve in individual dessert dishes. Garnish with orange wedges, if desired. 4 to 6 servings.

FRENCH CHOCOLATE CREAM PUDDING: Follow basic recipe above and add 3 squares unsweetened chocolate with milk.

FRENCH COFFEE CREAM PUDDING: Follow basic recipe above and add 1 tbsp. instant coffee powder.

FRENCH COCONUT CREAM PUDDING: Follow basic recipe above and fold in ½ cup moist shredded coconut before chilling.

FRENCH MAPLE CREAM PUDDING: Follow basic recipe above but substitute ½ cup maple syrup for ½ cup of the milk.

CHRISTMAS COTTAGE PUDDING

Make or buy your favorite plain cake; cut in 3" squares. Serve with Egg Nog Sauce, allowing about ½ cup per serving.

EGG NOG SAUCE

1 egg, separated
1 cup Sealtest egg nog*
½ cup Sealtest whipping cream
1½ tbsp. sugar

Combine egg yolk and 2 tbsp. egg nog in heavy saucepan. Blend well with fork. Stir in remaining egg nog. Cook over low heat, stirring constantly, until thickened. Cool. Fold in whipped cream.

Beat egg white until foamy. Add sugar; beat until stiff. Fold into egg nog mixture. Chill. Stir before serving. Also good on coffee gelatin, mixed fruits, Christmas pudding. 2½ cups sauce. 5 servings.

* Available at holiday time

MILKY CHOCOLATE BREAD PUDDING

2½ cups bread cubes
2½ cups Sealtest chocolate drink
3 tbsp. butter
2 eggs
⅓ to ½ cup sugar
¼ tsp. salt
¾ tsp. vanilla

Put bread cubes in buttered baking dish. Heat chocolate drink in double boiler. Add butter; stir until melted.

Beat eggs slightly; stir in sugar and salt. Add heated chocolate mixture gradually, stirring vigorously. Stir in vanilla; pour over bread cubes. Bake in pan of hot water in moderate oven, 350°F., for 30 to 40 min. or until a knife inserted comes out clean. 6 servings.

OLD FASHIONED BREAD PUDDINGS

2½ cups bread cubes
2 eggs
½ cup sugar
¼ tsp. salt
2¼ cups Sealtest milk, scalded
½ tsp. vanilla
Jelly
Whipped Sealtest cream

Put bread cubes in individual baking dishes.

Beat eggs slightly and add sugar and salt. Stir in milk gradually. Add vanilla. Pour over bread. Dot with jelly.

Bake in pan of hot water in moderate oven, 350°F., about 40 min. or until just set. Serve warm or cool. Top with spoonfuls of whipped cream. 6 servings.

SEAFOAMS

Refreshing lime puddings, light as sponge cake

- 2 tbsp. butter
- ¾ cup sugar
- 2 tsp. grated lime rind
- 3 eggs, separated
- 1 cup Sealtest cottage cheese
- 2 tbsp. flour
- ¼ tsp. salt
- ¼ cup FRESH lime juice

Cream softened butter, sugar and rind together. Beat egg whites until stiff.

Beat yolks and cheese together with egg beater until curds are very fine; add to butter mixture and blend well. Add flour, salt and lime juice; beat well with egg beater. Fold in egg whites.

Spoon into 6 buttered custard cups. Bake in pan of hot water in moderate oven, 325°F., 30 min. Cool. Turn out of cups if desired. 6 servings.

SUNSHINE SPONGE

Tempting, lemony, top-notch dessert

- 2 tbsp. butter
- ¾ cup sugar
- 2 tsp. grated lemon rind
- 3 eggs, separated
- 2 tbsp. flour
- ¼ tsp. salt
- ¼ cup FRESH lemon juice
- ¾ cup Sealtest milk

Cream softened butter, sugar and rind together. Beat in egg yolks. Add flour, salt, lemon juice; mix well. Stir in milk. Fold in stiffly beaten egg whites.

Pour into buttered deep 8″ glass layer cake pan. Bake in pan of hot water in moderate oven, 325°F., about 40 min. Cool. 5 to 6 servings.

VANILLA DESSERT SOUFFLE

A sweet souffle makes a glamorous dessert

- 1½ tbsp. butter
- 1½ tbsp. flour
- ½ cup Sealtest milk
- 3 eggs, separated
- ½ cup sugar
- 1½ tsp. vanilla
- ¼ tsp. cream of tartar

Make a thick white sauce with butter, flour and milk (see page 58). Beat yolks until thick and lemon-colored; gradually beat in sugar and vanilla. Add hot sauce gradually to beaten yolks, mixing thoroughly.

Add cream of tartar to whites; beat until stiff. Carefully fold in yolk mixture.

Pour into ungreased 1 or 1½ qt. baking dish. Set in pan of hot water. Bake in moderate oven, 350°F., about 45 min. Serve topped with whipped cream, custard or fruit sauce. 4 to 6 servings.

CHOCOLATE SOUFFLE: Follow basic recipe above, but melt 2 squares unsweetened chocolate in the white sauce.

COFFEE SOUFFLE: Follow basic recipe above and add 2 or 3 tbsp. instant coffee powder to white sauce.

MOLDED DESSERTS

COTTAGE CHEESE DESSERT RING

- 2 cups Sealtest cottage cheese
- 1 tbsp. sugar
- 2 tbsp. lemon juice
- ½ cup Sealtest whipping cream
- 1 envelope unflavored gelatine
- ¼ cup cold water
- Fruit
- Sweetened whipped cream

Combine cottage cheese, sugar, lemon juice and the ½ cup whipping cream. Beat with rotary beater until thoroughly blended and almost smooth.

Sprinkle gelatine over water. Let stand 5 min. or until softened. Dissolve over boiling water; add to cheese mixture, beating until well mixed. Pour into 1 qt. ring mold. Chill until firm.

Unmold on serving plate. Fill center with fruit (such as canned, fresh or frozen pineapple, peaches, strawberries, etc.). Garnish with whipped cream. 6 servings.

BANANA EGG NOG TRIFLE

Something gala for the yuletide season

1 envelope unflavored gelatine
⅓ cup cold water
2¼ cups Sealtest egg nog*
1 to 2 ripe bananas, sliced
One 7" sponge cake layer, homemade or bakers
½ cup Sealtest whipping cream
¼ tsp. almond flavoring

Soften gelatine in cold water. Dissolve over boiling water. Add to egg nog gradually, stirring rapidly. Pour over cake placed in 8" layer cake pan. Cake will float. Chill overnight.

Spoon into dessert dishes. Slice banana over top. (For variation top with spoonful of canned whole cranberry sauce.) Garnish with whipped cream flavored with almond. 5 to 6 servings.

EGG NOG BAVARIAN TORTE

16 lady fingers, about 3" long
2 envelopes unflavored gelatine
½ cup cold water
1 qt. Sealtest egg nog*
Sweetened whipped cream
Maraschino cherries

Separate lady fingers into halves. Line bottom and sides of 9" spring form pan with lady finger halves.

Soften gelatine in cold water. Dissolve over boiling water. Add to egg nog gradually, stirring rapidly. Chill until mixture is thickened and almost set. Beat with rotary beater until light and foamy. Pour into lady finger-lined pan. Chill until set, 2 or 3 hrs. or overnight. Unmold. Garnish with spoonfuls of whipped cream and top with maraschino cherries. 8 to 10 servings.

HOLIDAY EGG NOG BAVARIAN

1 envelope unflavored gelatine
¼ cup cold water
1½ cups Sealtest egg nog*
1 cup Sealtest whipping cream

Soften gelatine in cold water. Dissolve over boiling water. Add to egg nog gradually, stirring rapidly. Chill until thick and syrupy; beat until light and foamy.

Whip cream until stiff. Fold into gelatine mixture. Pour into 1 qt. mold. Chill until firm. Unmold and serve. 4 to 6 servings.

* Available at holiday time

BUTTERMILK STRAWBERRY WHIP

1 pkg. strawberry-flavored gelatin
1 cup hot water
1 cup Sealtest buttermilk
Sweetened whipped cream

Dissolve gelatin in hot water. Chill until almost set. Beat with rotary beater until light and foamy. Add buttermilk gradually, beating after each addition until well blended. Pour into 4 to 6 individual molds. Chill until set. Unmold and serve topped with whipped cream. 4 to 6 servings.

CHOCOLATE MOLDED DREAM

1 envelope unflavored gelatine
2½ cups Sealtest chocolate drink
1 pkg. chocolate pudding mix
⅓ cup finely chopped pecans or walnuts
Sealtest light or heavy cream

Soften gelatine in chocolate drink 5 min. Stir in pudding mix. Cook over boiling water, stirring constantly, until thickened. Pour into bowl. Cool slightly. Then chill until bowl is lukewarm to touch.

Beat pudding with egg beater until well-blended. Add nuts. Pour into 1 to 1¼ qt. mold or dish. Chill until firm. Unmold. If desired garnish with nut halves. Cut in squares or wedges; serve with plain cream. 6 servings.

MARSHMALLOW CREAM DREAM

1 envelope unflavored gelatine
½ cup cold water
½ cup sugar
1 tsp. vanilla
½ cup light corn syrup
½ to 1 cup macaroon or chocolate cookie crumbs or toasted shredded coconut
1 cup Sealtest whipping cream

Sprinkle gelatine over cold water; let stand until softened. Dissolve over boiling water. Add sugar; stir until dissolved.

Add gelatine mixture and vanilla to corn syrup, beating rapidly with rotary beater (electric or hand) until mixture is thick, white and holds its shape slightly.

Pour into 9" square pan that has been rinsed in cold water. Spread evenly. Let stand in cool place (not refrigerator) until set, about

1 hr. Cut in rectangles, about 1½" x 2", and remove from pan with wet spatula or knife.

Roll in crumbs or coconut. Arrange in dishes, about 4 to a serving. Pile sweetened whipped cream on top. 6 generous servings.

SPANISH CREAM

1 envelope unflavored gelatine
2 cups Sealtest milk
6 tbsp. sugar
⅛ tsp. salt
2 eggs, separated
1 tsp. vanilla

Sprinkle gelatine over milk in saucepan. Let stand 5 to 10 min. to soften. Add sugar and salt. Stir over low heat until gelatine and sugar dissolve (do not boil).

Beat egg yolks slightly. Add a little hot milk mixture, stirring constantly. Blend into hot mixture in saucepan. Cook over very low heat, stirring constantly, until mixture thickens and coats the spoon. Remove from heat; stir in vanilla. Chill until mixture begins to set.

Beat egg whites until stiff but not dry. Beat gelatine mixture until foamy, and fold into whites. Pour into 1 or 1½ qt. mold, or dessert dishes. Chill until firm. Unmold. Serve with canned fruit cocktail, if desired. 4 to 6 servings.

CHOCOLATE SPANISH CREAM: Add 1½ squares unsweetened chocolate, shaved, to milk after the gelatine is softened.

COFFEE SPANISH CREAM: Add 4 tsp. instant coffee powder to milk in Spanish Cream.

TART STRAWBERRY MOUSSE

2 cups washed, hulled strawberries
¼ cup sugar
1 tsp. grated lemon rind
1 envelope unflavored gelatine
¼ cup cold water
1 tbsp. lemon juice
½ cup orange juice
1 cup Sealtest sour cream

Mash strawberries. Add sugar and lemon rind. Soften gelatine in cold water. Dissolve over boiling water. Remove from heat. Add lemon and orange juice, mix well. Add to strawberry mixture; stir. Chill.

When almost set, whip with rotary beater until light and foamy. Fold in sour cream. Pour into 6 individual molds. Chill until firm. Unmold. If desired, top with sweetened whipped cream. 6 servings.

SHORTCAKES

BLUEBERRY ROLL

2 cups packaged biscuit mix
3 tbsp. sugar
½ tsp. nutmeg
1 egg
Sealtest whipping cream
1½ cups drained sweetened blueberries
Blueberry Sauce, recipe below

Combine biscuit mix, sugar and nutmeg; mix well. Beat egg; add enough cream to make ½ cup liquid; stir and add to dry ingredients; mix lightly. (If mixture is too dry, add a little more cream.) Pat out dough about ½" thick in rectangular shape, about 8" x 10", on well-floured board or waxed paper. Sprinkle blueberries over dough; roll up lengthwise. Bake on greased pan in hot oven, 400°F., 25 min. Serve warm with Blueberry Sauce and whipped cream. 4 to 6 servings.

BLUEBERRY SAUCE: Mix 2 tbsp. cornstarch and 1 tbsp. sugar with 1 cup juice drained from blueberries (add water to make 1 cup). Add ½ cup blueberries. Cook over low heat, stirring constantly, until thickened.

PINEAPPLE UPSIDE-DOWN SHORTCAKE

6 to 8 slices canned pineapple, quartered
¼ cup dark brown sugar
Few grains nutmeg
1½ cups sifted flour
2 tsp. baking powder
¾ tsp. salt
6 tbsp. butter
½ cup Sealtest milk

Place pineapple sections in buttered baking pan, 8" x 8" x 2". Sprinkle with brown sugar and nutmeg.

Mix and sift flour, baking powder and salt. Cut in butter with pastry blender or two knives. Add milk all at once. Mix until ingredients are just moistened.

Pat or roll dough to fit baking pan. Place on top of pineapple. Brush with milk and sprinkle with nutmeg. Bake in very hot oven, 450°F., 20 to 25 min. or until brown. Turn out of pan and serve warm. Top with whipped cream, if desired. 6 servings.

BLUEBERRY SHORTCAKE

With luscious cheese pastry

½ cup butter
½ lb. Old English cheese, grated
1½ cups sifted flour
1 qt. blueberries
Sugar
½ cup confectioners sugar
½ tsp. vanilla
1 pint Sealtest whipping cream

Stir butter until softened. Add cheese; mix with spoon or electric mixer until smooth and well blended. Stir in flour; shape into ball. Wrap in waxed paper; chill 1 hr.

Roll out ¼" thick on very well-floured board. Cut out twelve 3½" pastry rounds with large biscuit cutter. Prick well with fork. Bake on ungreased baking sheet in hot oven, 400°F., about 10 min. or until lightly browned.

Wash and lightly crush berries; sprinkle with a little granulated sugar.

Add confectioners sugar and vanilla to cream; beat with rotary beater until stiff. Arrange 6 pastry rounds on serving platter; top each with generous spoonful of whipped cream, then some berries and a second round. Spoon on more whipped cream and berries. 6 servings.

PRUNE-COT BUTTERMILK SHORTCAKES

1½ cups sifted flour
2¼ tsp. baking powder
¾ tsp. salt
⅓ cup butter
1 egg, slightly beaten
⅓ cup Sealtest buttermilk
1½ cups cooked and sweetened dried apricots, with juice
1½ cups cooked and sweetened dried prunes, pitted, with juice
Plain or whipped cream

Mix and sift flour, baking powder and salt. Cut in butter with pastry blender or 2 knives. Add egg and buttermilk all at once. Stir in vigorously and very quickly. Mix just long enough to moisten dry ingredients.

Turn out on floured board and knead lightly for a few seconds. Roll out to about ½" thickness. Cut into rounds. Bake on [illegible] baking sheet in very hot oven, 450°F., 12 to 15 min.

Cut or split biscuits crosswise. Place spoonfuls of [illegible] center and on top. Serve with cream. 6 servings.

OLD FASHIONED STRAWBERRY SHORTCAKE

2 cups sifted flour
3 tsp. baking powder
1 tsp. salt
6 tbsp. butter
1 egg, well beaten
⅓ cup Sealtest milk
Sweetened sliced strawberries
Whipped cream

Mix and sift dry ingredients. Cut in the 6 tbsp. butter with pastry blender or 2 knives. Add combined egg and milk. Mix quickly. Divide in half. Knead lightly on floured board. Roll to fit 9" cake pan.

Place one piece in buttered pan. Brush with butter. Cover with second piece. Brush with milk. Bake in moderately hot oven, 375°F., 20 to 25 min.

Separate layers. Spread bottom layer with butter. Put layers together with berries between and on top. Serve with cream. 6 servings.

SUNSHINE SPONGE SHORTCAKE

⅞ cup cake flour
1 tsp. baking powder
Dash of salt
2 eggs, separated
⅔ cup sugar
½ tsp. grated orange rind
¼ cup orange juice
1 qt. washed and hulled strawberries
½ cup confectioners sugar
1 pt. Sealtest whipping cream
Vanilla

Sift flour; measure. Add baking powder and salt. Sift together twice. Beat egg whites until stiff; gradually beat in ⅓ cup sugar.

Beat yolks until thick and lemon-colored. Add remaining ⅓ cup of sugar, and orange rind; beat until very thick. Stir in orange juice. Fold in whites. Fold in dry ingredients, sifting about ¼ cup at a time over the egg mixture. Be sure that batter is smooth.

Spread batter evenly in an 8" x 8" x 2" pan that has been greased, wax-paper lined and greased. Bake in moderate oven, 350°F., 20 to 25 min. Turn out on cake rack; remove paper; cool.

Slice strawberries. Whip cream with confectioners sugar and a little vanilla.

Split cake into 2 even layers. Cut a piece about 4" square out of center of top layer. Spoon half the strawberries over bottom layer. Cover berries with half the whipped cream. Top with second layer. Fill center with remaining strawberries and spoon whipped cream on cake around berry center. 6 to 8 servings.

CAKES

BANANA CREAM CAKE

A luscious dessert using homemade or bakers cake

Spread 1 plain layer of cake with sweetened whipped cream; cover with sliced bananas, then spread whipped cream over bananas. Place a second layer of cake on top; spread with whipped cream; decorate with red cherries.

BLUEBERRY PUFFS

1 pint blueberries
¼ cup butter
½ cup sugar
1 egg, separated
½ tsp. vanilla
1 cup sifted flour
¼ tsp. salt
1½ tsp. baking powder
⅓ cup Sealtest milk
Whipped cream

Put berries in 6 buttered custard cups. Cream butter. Add sugar gradually and cream well. Add egg yolk. Beat well. Add vanilla.

Mix and sift flour, salt and baking powder. Add alternately with milk to butter mixture. Fold in stiffly beaten egg white. Pour batter over berries. Bake in moderately hot oven, 375°F., 30 min. or until cake is done. Turn out into serving dishes and serve warm with whipped cream. 6 servings.

CHOCOLATE ICEBOX CAKE

3 cups Sealtest chocolate drink
3 to 4 tbsp. cornstarch
1 tsp. vanilla
Left-over cake (half a layer of sponge or white cake, or half of a 7″ angel cake)

Add chocolate drink gradually to cornstarch in heavy saucepan, stirring until smooth. Cook over low heat, stirring constantly, until thickened. Remove from heat; stir in vanilla.

Cut cake in ¼″ slices. Line bottom of waxed-paper-lined 9″ x 5″ x 3″ loaf pan with some of the cake slices. Pour in half the chocolate mixture. Arrange another layer of cake slices over the chocolate. Pour in remaining chocolate, then top with another layer of cake slices. Chill in refrigerator 3 hrs. or overnight. Serve with chocolate sauce or whipped cream. 4 to 6 servings.

CREAMY COCOA CAKE

½ cup cocoa
⅓ cup boiling water
⅔ cup Sealtest sour cream
⅔ cup butter
2 cups sifted cake flour
½ tsp. soda
1 tsp. salt
1½ tsp. baking powder
1⅔ cups sugar
3 eggs, unbeaten
1½ tsp. vanilla

Mix cocoa and boiling water together to form smooth paste. Cool slightly. Add sour cream and mix until thoroughly blended.

Stir butter until softened in mixing bowl. Sift dry ingredients together into the bowl. Add eggs, vanilla and half the cocoa mixture. Stir until all flour is dampened. Then beat 150 strokes by hand, or 1 min. in electric mixer at low speed. Scrape bowl and spoon or beater often during mixing. (Count only actual beating strokes or time.)

Add remaining half of cocoa mixture. Beat 300 strokes by hand or 2 min. in electric mixer at low speed, scraping bowl and spoon or beater often.

Pour batter into 2 deep 9" cake pans that have been greased, waxed-paper-lined, and greased again. Bake in moderate oven, 350°F., 30 min. or until cake just pulls away from sides of pans. Turn out on cake racks; remove paper; cool and frost with favorite frosting. Two 9" layers.

DARK MYSTERY CHOCOLATE CAKE

5 squares unsweetened chocolate
½ cup water
1 cup Sealtest sour cream
⅔ cup butter
2 cups sifted cake flour
1 tsp. soda
1 tsp. salt
1½ tsp. baking powder
1 cup granulated sugar
⅔ cup dark brown sugar
3 eggs, unbeaten
1½ tsp. vanilla

Cook chocolate and water over very low heat, stirring constantly, until chocolate is melted. Cool. Add sour cream. Mix until thoroughly blended.

Stir butter until softened in mixing bowl. Sift dry ingredients together into the bowl. Add eggs, vanilla and half the chocolate mixture. Stir until all the flour is dampened. Then beat 150 strokes by hand or 1 minute in electric mixer at low speed. Scrape bowl and spoon or beater often during mixing. (Count only actual beating strokes or beating time.)

Add remaining half of chocolate mixture. Beat 300 strokes by hand or 2 min. in electric mixer at low speed, scraping bowl and spoon or beater often.

Pour batter into 2 deep 9″ cake pans that have been greased, waxed-paper-lined and greased again. Bake in moderate oven, 350°F., 30 min. or until cake just pulls away from the sides of pans. Turn out on cake racks; remove paper and cool. Frost with favorite frosting. Two 9″ layers.

GOBLINS

Goblins, Sealtest ice cream and a dreamy drink make a wonderful party.

Make or buy your favorite small cup cakes. If homemade, and if you like, tint the batter orange before baking. Frost with confectioners sugar frosting; top with goblin heads.

GOBLIN HEADS: Melt 2 squares unsweetened chocolate and 2 tsp. butter together over simmering water without stirring. Remove from heat; stir just enough to blend. Dip in 24 marshmallows one at a time, turning each and spooning chocolate over top to coat evenly. Let harden on rack. Use dabs of frosting to make a goblin face on side of each coated marshmallow.

HATCHET CAKES

Prepare cake batter, using any recipe desired. Bake in buttered shallow pan or in round layers. Using paper pattern or cookie cutter, cut into hatchet shapes. Spread with boiled frosting or with butter frosting. Garnish with cherries.

HOLIDAY LOAF CAKE

Grease a 10″ x 5″ x 3″ loaf pan, line with waxed paper, regrease. Sprinkle ½ cup diced maraschino cherries and ⅓ cup diced citron over the bottom. Prepare Hungarian Cream Cake, next page. Pour over fruits. Bake in moderate oven, 325°F., 1 hr. 15 min. Turn out of pan onto cake rack. Cool. Frost with boiled frosting or butter cream frosting.

HUNGARIAN CREAM CAKE

2 cups sifted cake flour
2 tsp. baking powder
½ tsp. salt
2 eggs
1 tsp. almond extract
1½ tsp. vanilla
1¼ cups Sealtest whipping cream
1 cup sugar

Combine flour, baking powder and salt. Sift together 3 times.

Beat eggs with rotary beater until light and foamy. Add almond extract and vanilla. Add sugar gradually, beating well after each addition. Add dry ingredients alternately with cream, beating until just smooth after each addition. Pour into a greased square pan 8″ x 8″ x 2″.

Bake in a moderate oven, 350°F., 50 min. Turn out of pan on cake rack. Cool.

If desired, spread thin layer of sweetened, crushed strawberries over top of cake. Cover with sweetened, whipped cream and garnish with a few whole berries. One 8″ cake.

PEAR UPSIDE DOWN CAKE

6 tbsp. butter
½ cup brown sugar, firmly packed
1 to 2 winter pears
Maraschino cherries
½ cup granulated sugar
1 egg, unbeaten
½ tsp. vanilla
1 cup sifted cake flour
1½ tsp. baking powder
¼ tsp. salt
⅓ cup Sealtest milk
Plain or whipped cream

Melt 2 tbsp. of the butter in an 8″ square pan. Sprinkle brown sugar over butter.

Pare and core the pears. Cut crosswise in ½″ slices. Arrange on top of brown sugar. Place a cherry in center of each pear slice.

Cream remaining 4 tbsp. butter. Add ½ cup of granulated sugar gradually and cream thoroughly.

Add egg. Beat until fluffy. Add vanilla.

Mix and sift flour, baking powder and salt. Add to butter mixture alternately with milk. Pour batter over pears. Bake in moderately hot oven, 375°F., 25 to 30 min. Invert on serving plate. Serve with cream. 6 servings.

QUICK MOCHA CAKE

Add 2 tsp. instant coffee powder to contents of 1 pkg. white cake mix. Then prepare cake according to pkg. directions, using Sealtest chocolate drink in place of liquid called for on pkg. Bake according to directions. Frost with favorite frosting.

RAINBOW PARTY CAKE

Prepare cake batter, using any recipe desired.

Divide into 4 portions. Tint one portion a delicate yellow, one a delicate green and one a delicate pink. Leave fourth portion uncolored. Place alternate spoonfuls of each color in buttered layer cake pans. Bake.

Put layers together with fluffy boiled frosting. Serve with Sealtest ice cream.

For special occasions, use cake plate large enough so that a few flowers may be placed around the border of the dish for decoration. Green leafy sprays such as philodendron are also nice to use.

STRAWBERRY CREAM CARNIVAL CAKE

The ever-popular refrigerator cake with
a new shape and flavor combination

2 cups Sealtest whipping cream
½ cup confectioners sugar
1 tsp. vanilla
1½ cups crushed strawberries (1 pint)
27 chocolate wafers, 3" diameter

Line square pan, 9" x 9" x 1¾", with two strips of waxed paper cut to fit length and width of pan. Allow extra inches to be used as tabs to lift dessert out.

Add sugar and vanilla to cream; whip until stiff. Fold strawberries into cream gently but thoroughly.

Spread ¼ of strawberry-cream mixture evenly in bottom of pan. Cover with 9 chocolate wafers in 3 even rows. Fill pan with alternate layers of cream mixture and wafers, ending with cream. Chill in refrigerator 2 to 3 hrs. or overnight.

Invert on serving platter. Lift off pan; gently peel off waxed paper. If desired, garnish with ruffle of whipped cream, and whole strawberries. 8 to 10 servings.

SCRUMPTIOUS MINCEMEAT LAYER CAKE

2 bakers sponge cake layers, 7″ or 8″ diameter
1½ cups Sealtest whipping cream
¼ cup confectioners sugar
3 tbsp. sherry or rum
1 cup cooked or canned mincemeat

Split cake layers in half crosswise to make 4 layers. Whip cream until stiff, adding sugar and sherry while whipping. Put cake together with layer of whipped cream and layer of mincemeat between each cake layer.

Frost top and sides of cake with remaining whipped cream. Chill in refrigerator for several hrs. or overnight. If desired, decorate with red and green maraschino cherries. 8 to 12 servings.

STRAWBERRY FESTIVAL CAKE

For a "dessert-and-coffee party"

1 angel food loaf cake, about 12″ x 3½″ x 3″, bakers or homemade
2½ cups chilled Sealtest whipping cream
1 envelope unflavored gelatine
¼ cup cold water
6 tbsp. sugar
1½ cups mashed strawberries
Strawberry slices

Cut cake with sharp knife into 3 lengthwise layers. Whip the cream.

Soak gelatine in the water until softened. Dissolve over hot water. Add gelatine and sugar to mashed strawberries; mix well. Chill until thick and syrupy. Whip until light and foamy; add 2 cups of the whipped cream; fold in.

Spread most of this filling on two cake layers and a small amount on the third or top layer. Put layers together. Chill until filling is firm, about 1 to 3 hrs.

Frost cake with remaining whipped cream sweetened to taste. Garnish with strawberry slices. 10 to 12 servings.

FOR FAMILY SERVING: Fill and frost a round angel food ring cake, about 6″ in diameter, using ½ of recipe. 6 to 8 servings.

FLUFFY WHIPPED CREAM

Fluffy, delicious whipped cream adds the gourmet's touch to any dessert. Here are some suggestions for making lighter, more velvety whipped cream, quickly, effortlessly and without spattering.

Use a deep narrow bowl.

Chill cream, beater and bowl overnight if possible.

Beat cream quickly. Stop as soon as it holds its shape. Do not overbeat.

For sweetened flavored whipped cream, add sugar and flavoring after cream begins to thicken. Allow 2 to 3 tbsp. sugar and ¾ to 1 tsp. vanilla for ½ pint cream.

Whipping cream doubles in volume approximately. ½ pint yields 1 pint whipped.

COOKIES

ALMOND COOKIES

6 tbsp. butter
1⅓ cups dark brown sugar
1 tsp. vanilla
1 egg, separated
2 cups sifted flour
⅛ tsp. salt
⅛ tsp. soda
⅛ tsp. cinnamon
¼ lb. blanched almonds, coarsely chopped

Cream butter. Add sugar gradually; beat thoroughly. Add vanilla and egg yolk; beat until well-blended.

Mix and sift flour, salt, soda and cinnamon. Stir into butter mixture. Add almonds.

Beat egg white until stiff but not dry. Lightly fold into first mixture.

Divide dough in half; shape into two 1½" rolls. Wrap in waxed paper. Chill at least 3 hrs. Slice thin. Bake on buttered cookie sheet in moderately hot oven, 375°F., 10 to 15 min. 5 doz. cookies.

BROWNIES

- ½ cup butter
- 2 squares unsweetened chocolate
- 2 eggs
- 1 cup sugar
- ½ cup sifted flour
- ¼ tsp. baking powder
- ¼ tsp. salt
- 1 cup chopped nut meats
- 1 tsp. vanilla

Melt butter and chocolate together over boiling water.

Beat eggs well. Add sugar gradually and beat thoroughly with spoon. Add chocolate mixture. Beat well.

Mix and sift flour, baking powder and salt. Add nuts; stir into first mixture. Mix well. Add vanilla.

Bake in buttered pan, 8" x 8" x 2", in moderate oven, 350°F., about 25 min. Cut into squares while still warm. 9 squares.

BUTTERMILK OAT CRISPS

- 2 cups sifted flour
- ⅓ cup sugar
- 1 tsp. salt
- ½ tsp. baking soda
- 1 cup rolled oats, crumbled
- ½ cup Sealtest buttermilk
- ½ cup butter or margarine, melted

Sift flour, sugar, salt and soda into mixing bowl. Stir in oats. Add buttermilk and melted butter; stir until dry ingredients are just moistened. Knead dough lightly for a few seconds on well floured board. Roll out very thin (about ⅛" thick). Cut in strips about 2" x 4". (Sprinkle with salt or caraway seeds, if desired.) Bake on ungreased cookie sheet in hot oven, 400°F., about 8 min., or until golden brown. Serve hot with butter and jam, or cold with any variety of spreads. About 5 doz. crisps.

CHERRY DROPS

- ¼ cup butter
- ½ cup sugar
- 1 egg, unbeaten
- 1 cup sifted flour
- 1 tsp. baking powder
- ½ tsp. salt
- 3 tbsp. cream
- ½ tsp. vanilla
- 1½ cups drained maraschino cherries

Cream butter. Stir in sugar gradually, mixing until blended after each addition. Add egg and beat with spoon until fluffy.

In a second bowl, mix and sift flour, baking powder and salt. Add to first mixture alternately with cream. Add vanilla.

Dip cherries into batter, one at a time. (Pitted dates may be substituted for cherries.)

Place on well-buttered cookie sheet. Bake in moderately hot oven, 375°F., 10 to 12 min. 50 small cookies.

COTTAGE CHEESE BROWN EDGE COOKIES

- 1 cup sifted cake flour
- ½ tsp. baking powder
- ½ tsp. salt
- ¼ cup butter or margarine
- ¾ cup sugar
- 1 egg, unbeaten
- 1¼ tsp. lemon extract
- ½ cup Sealtest cottage cheese

Sift together flour, baking powder and salt.

Cream butter until light and fluffy. Add sugar gradually, beating well after each addition. Add egg and lemon extract. Beat with rotary beater until light and thoroughly blended. Add cheese, beating until smooth and blended. Add dry ingredients all at once, stirring just until well blended (do not overbeat).

Drop by teaspoonfuls, 3" apart, on greased cookie sheet. Bake in hot oven, 400°F., 10 to 15 min., until browned around edges. About 2½ doz. cookies.

COTTAGE CHEESE PASTRY COOKIES

Extra-special for gala occasions

Use basic recipe for Cottage Cheese Pastry, page 9.

COLORED SUGAR COOKIES: Roll pastry ⅛" thick. Cut with fancy cookie cutters. Sprinkle with colored sugar. Bake. ½ recipe makes about 3½ doz. cookies.

JELLY ROUNDS: Roll pastry ⅛" thick. Cut in 1¾" rounds. Cut center out of half of these. Place rounds without centers on top of plain rounds. Press together lightly. Bake. Fill centers with small amounts of jelly. ½ recipe makes about 2 doz. cookies.

FILLED PASTRY COOKIES: Roll pastry ⅛" thick. Cut in 1¾" rounds or squares. Dot half of these with jam. Top with remaining rounds. Moisten edges. Seal. Bake. Cool; sprinkle with confectioners sugar or decorate with frosting. 1 recipe makes about 3½ doz. cookies.

DELICIOUS BUTTER COOKIES

The ideal gift cookies

- ½ cup butter
- 1 cup sugar
- 1 egg, unbeaten
- ¾ tsp. vanilla
- 1½ cups sifted flour
- 2 tsp. baking powder
- ¼ tsp. salt

Cream butter; add sugar gradually; cream thoroughly. Add egg; beat well. Stir in vanilla.

Mix and sift flour, baking powder and salt. Add to first mixture; stir until blended. Chill ½ hr.

Roll out dough on floured board to ⅛″ thickness. Cut in various shapes with floured cookie cutters.

Bake on cookie sheet in moderately hot oven, 375°F., 8 to 10 min. 2½ to 3 doz. medium cookies.

CHRISTMAS COOKIES: Cut rolled cookie dough in Christmas shapes using cookie cutters or cardboard patterns. Make a hole in each cookie with a skewer while still warm. Decorate cookies with confectioners sugar frosting. Hang on the tree with colored ribbon or string.

CONFECTIONERS SUGAR FROSTING: Add a little milk to confectioners sugar (about 2 to 2½ tsp. milk for each ½ cup sugar). Add a few grains salt, a few drops vanilla. If desired, add a little coloring. Spread frosting on cookies with small spatula or knife. Or put on with decorating tube.

COLORED SUGAR: Rub one or more drops of coloring into a little granulated sugar. Sprinkle on cookies before baking.

SHORTBREAD COOKIES

- 1 cup butter
- ½ cup confectioners sugar
- 2½ cups sifted flour
- ¼ tsp. baking powder
- ¼ tsp. salt
- 3 tbsp. milk

Cream butter, add sugar and continue to cream until thoroughly blended.

Mix and sift flour, baking powder and salt. Add to butter mixture. Add milk. Mix just enough to moisten.

Roll out on floured board to about ¼″ thickness. Cut into 2″ squares; place on cookie sheet. Bake in moderate oven, 350°F., 20 to 25 min. or until browned. About 50 squares.

DATE SQUARES

1 cup sifted flour
¼ tsp. salt
⅛ tsp. soda
1 tsp. baking powder
1 cup brown sugar
½ cup butter
1½ cups rolled oats
3 cups pitted dates
1½ cups water
1½ cups sugar
1 tsp. vanilla

Mix and sift flour, salt, soda and baking powder. Stir in brown sugar. Work in butter with fingertips until well blended. Lightly stir in rolled oats. Press half of this mixture into bottom of a buttered baking pan, 11" x 7" x 1½".

Simmer dates, water and sugar in saucepan about 35 min. or until mixture thickens. Stir occasionally. Add vanilla. Pour over mixture in baking pan.

Sprinkle with remaining crumb mixture. Bake in a slow oven, 300°F., 30 min. Cool. Cut in squares. Forty 1½" squares.

HALLOWEEN LOLLYPOP COOKIES

1 cup sifted flour
1 tbsp. sugar
¼ tsp. baking soda
½ tsp. salt
½ cup butter
⅓ cup molasses
1 egg, unbeaten
¼ cup Sealtest buttermilk

Mix and sift the flour, sugar, baking soda and salt.

Cream the butter; add molasses a little at a time and stir until blended. Add egg and beat until fluffy. Add half of the flour mixture; mix well. Add buttermilk and stir in lightly. Add remaining flour mixture and mix until smooth.

Drop batter by small spoonfuls on buttered cookie sheet. Stick a toothpick in each cookie. Bake in hot oven, 400°F., 10 to 12 min. 50 small cookies.

TO FROST OR DECORATE: Moisten confectioners sugar with a little milk. Tint with any color desired. Spread on cookies or use to make eyes, nose and mouth.

FRUIT AND NUT BARS

Wholesome fruit snack

- ¼ cup soft butter
- ½ cup sugar
- ½ cup light corn syrup
- 1 egg
- ½ cup Sealtest milk
- 2 cups sifted flour
- 2 tsp. baking powder
- ½ tsp. salt
- 2 cups coarsely ground, dried fruits (apricots, mixed fruits, raisins, etc.)
- 1 cup chopped nuts

Mix butter, sugar, corn syrup and egg thoroughly. Beat in milk. Sift together flour, baking powder and salt; stir into first mixture. Mix in dried fruits and nuts.

Spread in greased, wax-paper-lined, and regreased 13" x 9" x 2½" baking pan. Bake in moderate oven, 350°F., 30 to 40 min.

Turn out of pan; remove paper. Cool; cut in 1" x 2" bars; sprinkle with confectioners sugar. About 4½ doz. bars.

MILK CHOCOLATE DROP COOKIES

For that after-school snack

- 1½ cups sifted flour
- 1½ tsp. baking powder
- ½ tsp. salt
- 1 square unsweetened chocolate
- 5 tbsp. butter
- ¾ cup sugar
- 1 egg
- 1 tsp. vanilla
- ½ cup Sealtest milk

Sift together flour, baking powder and salt; set aside. Melt chocolate and butter over hot water. Cool; pour into mixing bowl. Add sugar, egg and vanilla; beat thoroughly. Stir in flour mixture alternately with milk, only to blend.

Drop by teaspoonfuls on greased cookie sheet. Decorate with nuts or coconut. Bake in moderately hot oven, 375°F., 8 to 10 min. About 3 doz. cookies.

PUMPKIN COOKIES

Frost your favorite round chocolate cookies with an orange tinted confectioners sugar frosting, page 140, then add funny faces with chocolate frosting. With a heaping plate of chocolate ice cream, these are extra special!

CHEESE CAKES AND CHEESE PIES

Many a smart hostess follows the lead of exclusive restaurants and features a specialty of her house, like cheese cake.

Sophisticated and deliciously suave, the following cheese cake recipes are a little fussy to prepare, but well worth the time and effort. If you don't agree, we'll eat every last crumb!

CHEESE CAKE

1 six-oz. pkg. zwieback
¼ cup sugar
½ cup melted butter or margarine
4 cups Sealtest cottage cheese
4 tbsp. melted butter
4 eggs
¾ cup sugar
¼ cup cream
½ tsp. salt
¼ cup flour
¼ cup lemon juice
1½ tsp. grated lemon rind
½ tsp. grated orange rind

Roll zwieback into fine crumbs with rolling pin. Combine crumbs, ¼ cup sugar and ½ cup butter; mix thoroughly. Pack all but ⅓ cup of this mixture on bottom and sides of well-greased 9" spring form pan.

Press cheese through fine sieve or beat with electric mixer until smooth. Add 4 tbsp. butter, beating until blended. Add eggs one at a time, beating well after each addition with electric mixer or hand rotary beater. Add the ¾ cup sugar, and cream; beat well. Add remaining ingredients. Beat or stir until smooth and thoroughly blended.

Pour into crumb-lined 9" spring form pan. Sprinkle top of cake with remaining ⅓ cup crumbs. Bake in slow oven, 300°F., 1½ hrs. or until set. Cool. Run knife around edge of crust to loosen from pan. Remove spring form. One 9" cake.

COME-FOR-DESSERT MENU

Cheese Cake
Coffee with Cream
Mints Nuts Assorted Candies

PINT-SIZE CREAM CHEESE CAKE

½ six-oz. pkg. zwieback
¼ cup melted butter
¼ cup sugar
½ lb. cream cheese
2 eggs
½ cup sugar
¼ cup Sealtest sour cream
3 tbsp. flour
¾ tsp. grated lemon rind
1 tbsp. lemon juice

Roll zwieback into fine crumbs. Mix with butter and the ¼ cup sugar. Pack all but ¼ cup of this mixture on bottom and half way up sides of well-buttered 6-inch spring form pan.

Soften cheese with spoon; beat until fluffy. Add eggs one at a time; beat well after each addition until smooth. Add the ½ cup of sugar, then remaining ingredients. Beat until well blended. Pour into crumb-lined pan. Sprinkle remaining crumbs over top.

Bake in slow oven, 300°F., 1 hr. Cool on rack. Chill at least 3 hrs. 4 to 6 servings.

PINT-SIZE COTTAGE CHEESE CAKE

½ six-oz. pkg. zwieback
¼ cup butter, melted
¾ cup sugar
2 eggs
3 tbsp. flour
¼ tsp. salt
¼ cup Sealtest cream
1 tbsp. lemon juice
¾ tsp. grated lemon rind
1½ cups Sealtest cottage cheese, pressed through fine sieve

Roll zwieback into very fine crumbs. Mix with the butter and ¼ cup of the sugar. Pack all but ¼ cup of this mixture on bottom and sides of well-buttered 6″ spring form pan or 8″ pie pan.

Beat eggs until thick. Add remaining ½ cup sugar gradually, beating well. Add flour, salt, cream, lemon juice, rind and cheese. Mix lightly but thoroughly. Pour into pan. Sprinkle with remaining crumbs. Bake in slow oven, 300°F., 1 hr. Cool on rack. For a special party flourish, top with spoonfuls of Pineapple Topping, recipe below. 4 servings.

PINEAPPLE TOPPING: Mix 1 tbsp. cornstarch, 3 tbsp. sugar in saucepan. Stir in 1 cup canned sweetened crushed pineapple. Cook over moderate heat, stirring constantly, until thickened and clear. Cool slightly.

REFRIGERATOR PINEAPPLE CHEESE CAKE

1 six-oz. pkg. zwieback
¼ cup sugar
½ cup melted butter or margarine
2 envelopes unflavored gelatine
½ cup cold water
3 egg yolks
1 cup sugar
½ cup Sealtest milk
Dash of salt
4 cups Sealtest cottage cheese
1½ tsp. grated lemon rind
2 tbsp. lemon juice
3 egg whites, stiffly beaten
1 cup drained canned crushed pineapple
1 cup Sealtest whipping cream

Roll zwieback into fine crumbs with rolling pin. Combine crumbs, the ¼ cup sugar and the butter; mix thoroughly. Pack all but ⅓ cup of this mixture on bottom and sides of greased 9″ spring form pan.

Sprinkle gelatine over cold water. Let stand until softened, about 5 min.

Beat egg yolks slightly in top of double boiler. Add 1 cup sugar gradually, beating well with rotary beater. Stir in milk and salt. Cook over boiling water, stirring constantly, until slightly thickened and custard coats spoon. Stir in gelatine until dissolved. Cool slightly.

Press cheese through sieve or beat with electric mixer until smooth. Add lemon rind and juice; mix well. Add slightly cooled custard mixture, beating until thoroughly blended. Let cool until thickened and partially set. Beat with rotary beater (electric or hand) until light and foamy. Fold in egg whites, whipped cream, and pineapple.

Pour into crumb-lined pan. Sprinkle top with remaining crumbs. Chill 2 to 3 hrs. or until set. One large 9″ cake.

SURE-TO-PLEASE DINNER

Cranberry Cocktail
Broiled Chicken
Buttered Spinach Broiled Tomato
Celery Hearts and Olives
Refrigerator Pineapple Cheese Cake
Milk Coffee with Cream

APPLESAUCE CHEESE PIE

1½ cups fine gingersnap crumbs
5 tbsp. melted butter
2 cups Sealtest cottage cheese
2 eggs
½ cup sugar
¼ cup flour
2 tbsp. lemon juice
1 cup applesauce

Combine crumbs and butter. Mix thoroughly. Spread in 9″ pie pan. Press down firmly on bottom and sides of pan with fingers or back of a spoon.

Press cheese through fine sieve. Add eggs one at a time, beating well after each addition with electric mixer or hand rotary beater. Add sugar, flour, lemon juice and applesauce. Beat until smooth and thoroughly blended. Pour mixture into crumb-lined pan. Bake in moderate oven, 325°F., 1 hr., 10 min. or until set. Cool. One 9″ pie.

STRAWBERRY CHEESE PIE

½ six-oz. pkg. zwieback
2 tbsp. sugar
¼ cup melted butter or margarine
2 cups Sealtest cottage cheese
2 eggs
½ cup sugar
¼ cup Sealtest whipping cream
2 tbsp. flour
¾ tsp. grated lemon rind
1 tbsp. lemon juice
Strawberry Topping, recipe below

Roll zwieback into fine crumbs with rolling pin. Combine crumbs, the 2 tbsp. sugar and the butter; mix thoroughly. Pack on the bottom and sides of well-greased 9″ pie pan.

Press cottage cheese through fine sieve, or beat with electric mixer until smooth. Add eggs one at a time, beating well after each addition. Add sugar, cream, flour, lemon rind and juice. Beat until smooth and thoroughly blended. Pour into crumb-lined pan. Bake in a slow oven, 300°F., 1 hr. or until set. Cool. Cover with Strawberry Topping. One 9″ pie.

STRAWBERRY TOPPING: Mix ¼ cup sugar and 4 tsp. cornstarch in heavy saucepan. Add ½ cup water gradually, stirring until smooth. Cook over low heat, stirring constantly, until mixture thickens and becomes clear. Cool slightly. Add 1½ cups halved strawberries; mix gently but well.

DATE, NUT AND CHEESE PIE

- 1¼ cups fine graham cracker crumbs
- 5 tbsp. melted butter
- 2 cups Sealtest cottage cheese
- 2 eggs
- ½ cup sugar
- ¼ cup Sealtest milk
- 2 tbsp. flour
- ¾ tsp. grated lemon rind
- 1 tbsp. lemon juice
- 1 cup chopped dates
- 2 tbsp. chopped pecans

Mix crumbs and butter together thoroughly. Turn into 9" pie pan; press down firmly on bottom and sides of pan with fingers or back of spoon.

Press cheese through fine sieve or beat with electric mixer until smooth. Add eggs one at a time, beating well after each addition.

Add sugar, milk, flour, lemon rind and juice. Beat until smooth and thoroughly blended. Add dates and beat just enough to mix.

Pour into crumb-lined pan. Sprinkle with pecans. Bake in slow oven, 300°F., 1 hr. or until set. Cool. One 9" pie.

CHEESECAKE TARTLETS

Dainty tea-time nibblers with a surprise center

- 1 pkg. pastry mix or your favorite two crust pastry recipe
- ⅓ cup orange marmalade
- 1½ cups Sealtest cottage cheese
- 2 eggs
- ½ cup sugar
- 3 tbsp. flour
- ¼ tsp. salt
- ¼ cup Sealtest heavy cream
- 1 tbsp. lemon juice

Prepare pastry; roll out; cut in 3½" rounds. Fit into small muffin pans. Spoon a little marmalade in each.

Beat cheese with egg beater until smooth. Beat eggs until thick; add sugar gradually, beating well after each addition. Add flour, salt, cream, lemon juice and cheese. Mix lightly, but thoroughly Pour into pitcher, then into muffin pans filling to top. Bake in slow oven, 300°F., 1 hr. These little tartlets are delicious served warm from the oven. 20 tartlets.

PASTRIES

CHOCOLATE CHIP PIE

1 pkg. chocolate pudding
2 cups Sealtest chocolate drink
½ cup semi-sweet chocolate pieces, coarsely chopped
1 baked 8" Gingersnap Pie Shell, recipe below
Sweetened whipped Sealtest cream

Empty pkg. of pudding into saucepan. Add chocolate drink gradually, stirring until smooth. Cook over moderate heat, stirring constantly, until thickened. Remove from heat. Cool slightly. Add chocolate pieces; fold in. Pour into shell.

Chill until firm. Just before serving, top with cream. One 8" pie.

EIGHT-INCH GINGERSNAP PIE SHELL: Mix 1 cup of fine gingersnap crumbs and ¼ cup melted butter. Spread in 8" pie pan. Press down firmly on sides and bottom of pan with fingers or back of spoon. Bake in moderate oven, 350°F., 10 min. Cool. One 8" pie shell.

CREAMY LEMON PIE

With a tangy tempting soft filling that melts in your mouth

1 cup sugar
6 tbsp. cornstarch
¼ tsp. salt
2 cups Sealtest milk
2 tbsp. butter
1 egg, slightly beaten
½ cup fresh lemon juice
1 tsp. grated lemon rind
1 baked 8" Gingersnap Pie Shell, recipe above

Mix sugar, cornstarch and salt in top section of double boiler. Add milk gradually, mixing well. Cook over direct heat, stirring vigorously until thickened and beginning to bubble. Add butter; stir until melted. Remove from heat.

Add a little hot milk mixture gradually to egg, beating vigorously. Pour slowly back into remaining hot milk mixture, stirring constantly.

Add lemon juice and rind; stir vigorously until blended. Cook over simmering water 2 min. longer, stirring constantly. Cool slightly. Pour into shell. Cool. Chill thoroughly. If desired, top with whipped cream. 4 to 6 servings.

DEEP DISH PEACH PIE

4 cups sliced fresh peaches
½ cup sugar
3 tbsp. flour
½ tsp. cinnamon
⅛ tsp. salt
1 tsp. lemon juice
2 tbsp. butter
Pastry
Sealtest cream or ice cream

Place peaches in shallow baking dish, about 1½ qt. capacity.

Combine sugar, flour, cinnamon and salt. Sprinkle over peaches. Add lemon juice; dot with butter.

Cover with pastry rolled thin to fit the top. Cut gashes in pastry for steam to escape. Brush with milk. Bake in hot oven, 400°F., about 35 min. or until peaches are tender.

Serve warm with cream or ice cream. 4 to 5 servings.

FALL DINNER

Fruit Cup
Ham Tetrazzini, page 29 Baked Squash, page 56
Sliced Tomato Salad Creamy Mint Dressing, page 88
Deep Dish Peach Pie with Vanilla Ice Cream
Milk Coffee with Cream

PECAN PIE

1 unbaked 8" pie shell
1 cup pecan halves
3 eggs
1 cup dark corn syrup
⅓ cup sugar
⅛ tsp. salt
¼ cup melted butter
Whipped cream

Line pie shell with pecans. Beat eggs well. Add corn syrup, sugar, salt and butter. Mix and pour slowly into shell.

Bake in moderately hot oven, 375°F., on lower shelf about 40 min. Cool. Serve topped with spoonfuls of whipped cream. One 8" pie. 6 servings.

PUMPKIN PIE

1½ cups canned pumpkin	1½ tsp. cinnamon
⅓ cup brown sugar	1½ tsp. ginger
⅓ cup granulated sugar	2 eggs, slightly beaten
½ tsp. salt	½ cup Sealtest milk
1 tbsp. molasses	½ cup Sealtest cream
⅛ tsp. ground cloves	1 unbaked 9" pie shell

Combine pumpkin, sugars, salt, molasses and spices. Add eggs; stir in.

Scald milk and cream together in double boiler. Add to pumpkin mixture. Mix well. Pour into unbaked pie shell. Bake in very hot oven, 450°F., 10 min. Reduce heat to moderate, 350°F.; continue to bake 40 min. or until done.

Cool. If desired, top with pumpkin shapes cut from sliced cheese with cookie cutter. 6 servings.

BUTTERMILK LEMON TARTS

¼ cup sifted flour	2 eggs, separated
⅛ tsp. salt	1 tbsp. butter
½ cup sugar	3 tbsp. lemon juice
¼ cup water	4 baked tart shells
1 cup Sealtest buttermilk	3 tbsp. sugar

Mix flour, salt and ½ cup sugar in double boiler. Stir in water and buttermilk. Cook, stirring constantly, about 5 min. or until thickened. Cover and cook 10 min. longer.

Add a little of this mixture to the slightly beaten egg yolks. Mix well and return to double boiler. Cook a minute longer, stirring constantly. Add butter and lemon juice. Cool slightly and pour into tart shells.

Beat egg whites until stiff. Beat in the 3 tbsp. sugar and few grains salt quickly. Pile lightly on tarts; bake in moderate oven, 325°F., 12 to 15 min. 4 tarts.

CHERRY TARTS WITH COTTAGE CHEESE

- 1 No. 2 can sweetened pitted sour cherries
- ¼ cup sugar
- 5 tsp. cornstarch
- Few grains salt
- 2 tsp. butter
- 1 to 1½ cups Sealtest cottage cheese
- 6 baked tart shells

Drain cherries. Mix sugar, cornstarch and salt. Stir in cherry juice gradually. Cook until thickened and clear, stirring constantly. Add butter and cherries. Chill. When ready to serve, fill tart shells.

Garnish with spoonfuls of cottage cheese. If desired, cottage cheese may be pressed through sieve and beaten with a little cream and salt. 6 servings.

DELECTABLE SOUR CREAM RAISIN TARTS

- 1½ cups seedless raisins
- ¾ cup water
- 1 cup Sealtest sour cream
- ⅓ cup sugar
- ¼ tsp. salt
- 1 egg, slightly beaten
- 6 baked tart shells

Cook raisins in water in covered pan over moderate heat until puffy and water is all taken up. Add sour cream, sugar and salt. Mix well. Cook, stirring constantly, over moderate heat 5 to 10 min. or until mixture is moderately thick.

Add to egg gradually, stirring constantly. Return to heat. Cook 1 min. longer, stirring constantly. Cool. Fill tart shells. 6 servings.

PUMPKIN TARTS A LA MODE

- 1 cup canned pumpkin
- ⅓ cup sugar
- ¾ tsp. cinnamon
- ¼ tsp. ginger
- ⅛ tsp. cloves
- ¾ tsp. salt
- 1 cup milk
- 2 eggs, slightly beaten
- 6 unbaked tart shells, chilled
- Sealtest vanilla ice cream

Combine pumpkin, sugar, spices, salt, milk and eggs. Pour into tart shells. Bake in hot oven, 425°F., 8 min.

Reduce heat to moderate, 325°F. Bake 30 to 40 min. longer. Serve warm with spoonful of ice cream. 6 servings.

GLAZED FRUIT TARTS

- ⅓ cup sugar
- 1 tbsp. cornstarch
- ½ cup water
- 1 tbsp. lemon juice
- 1 pint strawberries
- 2 or 3 bananas
- Sweetened whipped cream, about 2 cups
- 6 baked tart shells

Mix sugar and cornstarch in saucepan. Add water gradually, stirring constantly. Add lemon juice. Cook over moderate heat, stirring constantly, until thickened and clear. Cool slightly.

Slice strawberries and bananas into tart shells. Spoon slightly cooled glaze over fruit, making sure that all pieces of fruit are covered. Cool. Top with whipped cream. 6 servings.

RED RASPBERRY TARTLETS

- Pastry
- 1½ cups red raspberries
- 6 tbsp. sugar
- 2 tbsp. butter
- Plain or whipped cream

Roll pastry out thin on board. Cut into 12 rounds with 3″ biscuit cutter.

Put 6 rounds on baking sheet. Pile berries in center of each. Sprinkle with sugar. Dot with butter.

Moisten edges with cold water. Top with remaining rounds. Press edges together with fork. Cut a few slits in the top to permit steam to escape. Brush with milk. Bake in a very hot oven, 450°F., about 15 min.

Cool. Serve with cream. 6 servings.

CREAM SPIRALS

Prepare ¼ Cottage Cheese Pastry recipe, page 9, (¼ cup butter or margarine, ½ cup flour and ¼ cup cottage cheese). Roll out pastry ⅛″ thick. Cut in strips 1″ wide and 18″ long. Make tubes (1¼″ diameter) of stiff brown paper. Wind a pastry strip around each tube, spiral fashion, with edges overlapping. Glaze as directed, page 9. Bake as directed, page 9. Remove paper tubes. Cool. Fill pastries with sweetened whipped cream. 7 spirals.

CONFECTIONS

CHOCOLATE MARSHMALLOW FUDGE

2 cups granulated sugar
2 squares unsweetened chocolate, cut fine
¾ cup Sealtest light cream
1 tbsp. light corn syrup
¼ tsp. salt
¼ lb. (16) marshmallows, quartered
¾ tsp. vanilla

Combine sugar, chocolate, cream, corn syrup and salt in a heavy saucepan. Cook over low heat, stirring constantly, until sugar dissolves and mixture boils. Continue cooking, without stirring, to 234° to 236°F., or until fudge forms soft ball when a little is dropped in cold water. Remove from heat; add vanilla.

Cool to lukewarm (110°F.); then beat until mixture begins to thicken and lose its gloss. Arrange marshmallows on bottom of greased 8" or 9" pan. Pour and spread beaten fudge over marshmallows. When cold, cut in squares. Ten 2" pieces.

CHOCOLATE CREAM FUDGE

1 cup granulated sugar
1 cup dark brown sugar
1 cup Sealtest whipping cream
Dash of salt
2 squares unsweetened chocolate, cut fine
1 tsp. cornstarch
1 tsp. water
1 tsp. vanilla

Combine sugars, cream, chocolate and salt in heavy saucepan. Mix well. Place over low heat and bring slowly to a boil, stirring constantly.

Mix cornstarch with water to a smooth paste and add to fudge as it boils, stirring just to mix. Continue cooking, without stirring, to 238° to 240°F. or until fudge forms soft ball when a little is dropped in cold water. Remove from heat; add vanilla.

Cool until bottom of pan is just slightly warm to the touch. Beat until fudge is thick and creamy and begins to lose its glossy appearance. Quickly pour into a buttered 8" or 9" pan. Cut in squares. About sixteen 2" pieces.

CREOLE PRALINES

1 cup dark brown sugar
1½ cups Sealtest whipping cream
1 cup granulated sugar
2 cups shredded coconut or chopped pecans
Dash of salt

Combine sugars, cream and salt in heavy saucepan; bring to a boil slowly, stirring only until sugar dissolves. Continue cooking to 238° to 240°F. or until mixture forms soft ball when a little is dropped in cold water.

Cool to lukewarm, 90° to 110°F. Beat until mixture starts to thicken. Stir in coconut. Drop from teaspoon onto waxed paper. Or spread in buttered 8" square pan and when firm, cut into squares. About 1½ lbs. pralines.

FRUIT BALLS

½ cup pitted dried prunes
½ cup dried apricots
½ cup raisins
½ cup nutmeats
Confectioners sugar

Put prunes, apricots and raisins in colander. Rinse well; drain well.

Put fruit and nutmeats through food grinder. Shape into small balls. Roll in confectioners sugar.

For a holiday gift, wrap in waxed paper and tie with colored ribbon. 15 to 20 small balls.

CANDIED WALNUTS

1½ cups granulated sugar
½ cup Sealtest sour cream
1 tsp. vanilla
2½ cups walnut halves

Bring sugar and sour cream to boil in heavy saucepan, stirring constantly. Cook to soft-ball stage, 236° to 238°F. Remove from heat. Add vanilla; beat until mixture begins to thicken.

Add nuts; stir until well coated. Turn out on greased cookie sheet; separate in individual pieces. About 1⅛ lbs. nuts.

Ice Cream

There are those who insist that ice cream, pure and simple, is the perfect food—and that to cover it with a sauce or incorporate it into a pie comes under the heading of gilding the lily.

If you're intrigued by the tremendous versatility of ice cream, the next 30 pages are just for you! They'll give you ideas for every type of meal—for breakfast, lunch or supper from family dinner to formal banquet.

ALASKAS

Elegant, glamorous baked Alaska is simple as A B C if you'll rigidly follow these 3 musts:

a. the ice cream must be very hard
b. the ice cream must be sealed in with a fluffy egg meringue
c. the oven must be piping hot

The result—out of this world eating!

BAKED ALASKA CAKE

Exciting and mysterious

4 egg whites
6 tbsp. sugar
1/4 tsp. salt
1/2 tsp. vanilla
1 qt. hard Sealtest chocolate ice cream
One 9" cake layer

Beat egg whites until stiff but not dry. Add sugar and salt gradually; beat in quickly but thoroughly. Add vanilla.

Place cake on cookie sheet or heat proof platter. Pile ice cream on cake, leaving 3/4" around edge uncovered. Quickly spread meringue over entire surface of ice cream.

Bake in very hot oven, 450°F., about 3 min. or until just delicately browned. Or if desired, brown under the broiler. Serve immediately. 6 to 8 servings.

BAKED ALASKA TARTS

For two

1 1/2 tbsp. currant jelly
2 baked tart shells
1 egg white
1 1/2 tbsp. sugar
Few grains salt
1/8 tsp. vanilla
1/2 to 3/4 pint hard Sealtest vanilla ice cream

Spread jelly in bottom of tart shells. Beat egg white until stiff but not dry. Add sugar and salt gradually; beat in quickly, but thoroughly. Add vanilla.

Fill tarts with ice cream. Quickly spread meringue over entire surface of ice cream.

Bake in very hot oven, 450° F., about 3 min. or until just delicately browned. Serve immediately. 2 servings.

BIRTHDAY ALASKA

One 6″ to 8″ square cake layer
Currant jelly
4 egg whites
6 tbsp. sugar
¼ tsp. salt
½ tsp. vanilla
½ half-gallon pkg. hard Sealtest strawberry ice cream

Place cake on cookie sheet or heat-proof platter. Spread with jelly.

Beat egg whites until stiff but not dry. Add sugar and salt gradually; beat in quickly but thoroughly. Add vanilla.

Place ice cream on jelly covered cake. Quickly spread meringue over the entire surface of the ice cream. Bake in a very hot oven, 450°F., about 3 min. or until just delicately browned. Serve immediately. 6 to 8 servings.

ORANGE ALASKA

Beautiful and frosty

2 large chilled oranges, halved
2 egg whites
3 tbsp. sugar
Few grains salt
1 to 1½ pints hard Sealtest vanilla ice cream
¼ tsp. vanilla

Scoop out orange pulp, making clean hollow shells. Cut a thin slice from bottom of each shell to make it stand steady. Place on cookie sheet.

Beat egg whites until stiff but not dry. Add sugar and salt gradually; beat in quickly but thoroughly. Add vanilla.

Fill shells with ice cream. Cover ice cream *completely* with meringue. If desired sprinkle with a little green sugar (rub a bit of green coloring into a little granulated sugar). Bake in very hot oven, 450°F., about 3 min. or until just delicately browned. Serve immediately on paper doily. 4 servings.

NOTE: For an interesting variation, put a few orange sections in the orange shells; then top with ice cream.

GRAPEFRUIT ALASKA: Substitute small grapefruit shells for orange shells.

SMALL FRY FAVORITES

In any form ice cream is small fry fare. For party and special occasions, ice cream can be easily and quickly made into story-book souvenirs to delight any youngster.

BLACK WITCH

Sealtest vanilla ice cream	Raisins
Cookie or cake	Maraschino cherry
Licorice strips	Ice cream cone

Place a round ball of vanilla ice cream on a round cookie or piece of cake. Press raisins into ice cream to form eyes and nose, cherry to form mouth. Fringe licorice with scissors and use as hair. Top with ice cream cone for hat.

BROWN BEANIE

Scoop 2 round dips of Sealtest ice cream into ice cream cone or paper cup. Quickly invert just the very top in warm chocolate coating. To make coating, melt 1/4 cup semi-sweet chocolate pieces and 1 tsp. of butter together over simmering water. Do not stir until soft. Blend in 1 1/2 tbsp. milk. Remove from heat; pour into small bowl. 6 toppings.

CANDY CANDLE

Insert a striped candy stick into the center of a ball of your favorite Sealtest ice cream. For the handle poke candy circle or large gum drop into side.

CIRCUS WAGON

Cut small square of Sealtest vanilla ice cream from pkg.; place small chocolate wafer "wheel" at each corner. Top with a few animal crackers. Put border of whipped cream around top for "fence", using spoon or pastry tube. Add a few gum drops for color.

FUNNY FACE

Frost cup cakes with chocolate icing. Decorate the tops with Indian corn candy to make faces. Serve with Sealtest ice cream.

DING DONG BELL

Fine for the 4th of July

Pack Sealtest vanilla ice cream solidly in custard cup. Return to freezer section of refrigerator or home freezer until very firm. Run sharp knife around inside of cup; unmold ice cream on its side. Place red maraschino cherry (with stem) at base of "bell" for "clapper." Put another cherry at top for "hanger." Sprinkle with colored sugar.

EASTER EGG NEST

Cut a square slice of Sealtest chocolate ice cream from pkg. Nest a few jelly beans on center of slice; ring jelly beans with coconut.

HUMPTY DUMPTY

Fill a pastry tube with whipped cream or frosting; make a hat, collar and face on a large candy egg. Serve on Sealtest ice cream.

JOLLY ICE CREAM SANTA

Sprinkle green-tinted or white coconut on serving plate to make Santa's collar. Put a generous scoop of Sealtest strawberry ice cream in center of coconut. Use semi-sweet chocolate pieces for eyes, and maraschino cherry for nose. Set an ice cream cone, with tip broken off, on top for a hat. Make Santa's beard and hat trimmings of sweetened whipped cream put through decorating tube.

JOLLY SANTA'S SLEIGH

Sprinkle coconut on serving plate for snow. Put 2 candy canes parallel on plate for sleigh runners (hold round ends up); top with a slice of Sealtest ice cream. Make sleigh's edges with sweetened whipped cream put through a decorating tube; build back edge up higher. Sprinkle cream with green sugar. Fill sleigh with candy.

LOLLY-MIKE

Fill colored cup cone with Sealtest vanilla or chocolate ice cream. Insert lollipop for microphone.

PARTY CLOWN

Youngsters of all ages enjoy these jolly clowns for dessert.

Invert filled ice cream cone on a chocolate wafer or round piece of cake. Stick in raisins or chocolate bits for eyes and nose, a bit of cherry for mouth.

PARTY POPS

Cut 1½" to 2" squares from ½ gal. pkg. Sealtest vanilla ice cream. Insert wooden spoon in each and put in freezer until spoon holds. Dip lower end in chocolate syrup and then in finely chopped peanuts. Serve on paper plates.

PINK ICE CREAM SANDWICH

Place a slice of firm Sealtest strawberry ice cream (cut from ½ gal. pkg.) between 2 graham crackers.

ROCKET SPRAY

July Fourth special

Take a slice of Sealtest vanilla ice cream and from it cut a round portion, using a large biscuit cutter or glass. Stick blueberries atop 10 red toothpicks; insert in center of ice cream, spray-fashion.

SNOW BALL

Pour 3 to 4 tbsp. chocolate sauce into dessert dish. Dip a ball of Sealtest chocolate ice cream with spoon or scoop and quickly roll in shredded coconut; place in center of chocolate sauce.

SPACE PLANET

Form a large ball of Sealtest ice cream; cut in half with sharp knife. To make planet put halves back together with a large flat cookie between. For axis, push a piece of striped candy stick into each "pole".

SPRING BASKET

Fill a Mary Ann cake cup with 6 or 7 melonball scoops of various flavors of Sealtest ice cream. Make basket handle from an orange slice rind moistened in orange juice and dipped in sugar.

SPOOKY ICE CREAM CUP

Wash orange and cut off top. Carefully scoop out the pulp using first a sharp knife, then a spoon. Cut out eyes, nose and mouth, as for a jack-o-lantern. Fill orange shell with Sealtest vanilla or chocolate ice cream. Replace top for hat. Serve with cookies.

SWEET FIRECRACKER

Turn out contents of half-gallon pkg. of Sealtest vanilla ice cream on cutting board. Cut in eighths (first in half lengthwise, then in fourths crosswise). Place each piece of ice cream on its long side on a blue dessert plate or Fourth of July paper party plate.

Decorate ice cream as a firecracker: sprinkle red colored sugar in diagonal stripes over the top; stick in piece of red maraschino cherry for "fuse". (To make red colored sugar, rub a little red coloring into granulated sugar.)

PARFAITS

Parfaits are elegant, wonderful party fare made by alternating layers of ice cream, whipped cream, crushed fruit or rich colorful syrups, and usually served in tall, slender glasses. If you don't have regular parfait glasses, use any pretty, slender glasses. One quart of ice cream will make 4 to 6 medium parfaits.

BLACK & WHITE

Fill parfait glass with alternate layers of Sealtest chocolate ice cream and stiffly whipped cream, ending with cream. Top with a soft chocolate mint pattie.

BLUEBERRY PEACHIE

Fill parfait glass with alternate layers of Sealtest peach ice cream and Blueberry Topping, page 174. Top with whipped cream.

FLUFFY WHIPPED CREAM: See Page 137 for directions for making perfect whipped cream.

CHERRY PARFAIT

For a Washington's Birthday dinner

Fill parfait glass with alternate layers of Cherry Sauce, page 176, and Sealtest vanilla ice cream. Garnish with whipped cream. Top with a cherry.

CHOCOLATE MARSHMALLOW PARFAIT

Fill parfait glass with alternate layers of Sealtest chocolate ice cream and marshmallow sauce, ending with sauce. If desired, sprinkle with slivered Brazil nuts.

CONCORD COOL-OFF

- 2½ cups Concord grapes (measure after taking from bunch)
- ¼ cup sugar
- Few grains salt
- 1½ tsp. cornstarch
- 1 tbsp. lemon juice
- 1 tsp. butter
- Sealtest vanilla ice cream
- Whipped cream

Separate grape skins from pulp. Reserve skins. Cook pulp slowly in pan until soft. Put skins and pulp through coarse sieve.

Mix sugar, salt and cornstarch. Add to grape mixture. Cook over moderate heat until thickened, stirring constantly.

Add lemon juice and butter. Chill. Fill parfait glasses with alternate layers of grape mixture and ice cream. Garnish with whipped cream. If desired, top each parfait with a whole grape. 6 servings.

CRANBERRY PARFAIT

Fill parfait glass with alternate layers of cranberry sauce and Sealtest vanilla ice cream. Top with whipped cream and a bit of cranberry sauce.

CURRANT TEMPTER

Fill parfait glass with alternate layers of Currant Topping, page 175, and Sealtest vanilla ice cream. Top with whipped cream. Garnish with chocolate dipped almonds.

CHOCOLATE DIPPED ALMONDS: Dip just about a third of each almond in semi-sweet chocolate pieces melted over hot water. Let cool on waxed paper.

FROSTY RAINBOW SKYROCKET

Use the tallest slender glass you can find for this

Sealtest vanilla ice cream	**Pineapple sauce, page 177**
Melba Sauce, page 177	**Sweetened sliced fresh peaches**

Whipped cream

Fill parfait glass with alternate layers of ice cream and a variety of colorful sauces. One suggested combination: Melba Sauce, Pineapple Sauce and sweetened sliced peaches. Top with whipped cream and a whole raspberry.

HIGHLAND TREAT

Fill parfait glass with alternate layers of butterscotch sauce and Sealtest butter pecan or butter almond ice cream. Garnish with whipped cream.

MINTED MAGIC

Beat ¾ cup of green mint jelly lightly with a fork to break it up. Fold in ¼ cup whipped cream. Fill parfait glasses with alternate layers of Sealtest vanilla ice cream and jelly mixture, allowing 1 qt. ice cream for 6 parfaits. If desired, top with whipped cream. Decorate with peppermint candies. 6 servings.

MOCHA FUDGE MARVELOUS

Fill parfait glass with alternate layers of Mocha Fudge Sauce, page 177, and Sealtest coffee ice cream. Top with whipped cream.

PARFAIT MELBA

Fill parfait glass with alternate layers of Sealtest vanilla or peach ice cream and Melba Sauce, page 177. Top with whipped cream; sprinkle with toasted almonds.

PARFAIT ROYALE

Fill parfait glass with alternate spoonfuls of whipped cream and royale ice cream (vanilla ice cream marbled with strawberry, raspberry, butterscotch or chocolate, etc.). Use a tablespoon or teaspoon to dip the ice cream carefully to preserve the attractive marbled effect. Garnish with whipped cream.

PINEAPPLE PARFAIT

Fill parfait glass with alternate layers of pineapple sauce and Sealtest vanilla ice cream. Top with whipped cream. Garnish with Fruit Kabob.

FRUIT KABOB FOR BEAUTIFUL GARNISH: String 2 strawberries and a pineapple chunk on a toothpick.

RASPBERRY REFRESHER

- 1/3 cup currant jelly
- 1 cup raspberries
- 1/2 cup whipping cream
- Sealtest vanilla ice cream

Beat jelly with fork; fold in raspberries and whipped cream (reserve a few berries and a little whipped cream to garnish the top).

Fill parfait glasses with alternate layers of ice cream and the raspberry mixture. 6 servings.

SHERBET PARFAIT

Fill parfait glass with alternate layers of Sealtest sherbet and ice cream. Garnish with whipped cream and a maraschino cherry.

SOME INTERESTING FLAVOR COMBINATIONS: Vanilla ice cream with orange sherbet . . . . banana ice cream with lemon sherbet . . . . strawberry ice cream with pineapple sherbet . . . . peach ice cream with lime sherbet . . . . butter pecan ice cream with raspberry sherbet.

SHERBET FRUIT CUPS

Sherbet is as versatile as ice cream and adds refreshing delight to salad plates, cakes or pies and elegance to hot or cold meats. In fruit cups, sherbets add cool refreshment.

FROSTY SHERBET BASKET

Cut small oranges in half and carefully scoop out the pulp using first a sharp knife, then a spoon. The edges of the orange shells may be scalloped with scissors, if desired. Fill shells with Sealtest lemon sherbet or any other favorite flavor. Garnish with sprigs of mint. Serve as a dessert or as accompaniment to roast lamb or other meat.

BROILED ORANGES WITH SHERBET

3 large or 6 medium oranges
¼ cup brown sugar
6 tsp. butter
Sealtest lime or orange sherbet

Cut oranges in half and remove any seeds. Cut out center membrane with scissors. Cut around each section with sharp knife.

Sprinkle with brown sugar. Dot with butter. Brown slowly under broiler until sections of orange puff up. Serve warm with a scoop of sherbet. 6 servings.

CANTALOUPE PINEAPPLE SHERBET CUP

1½ cups diced cantaloupe
½ cup Pineapple Sauce, pg. 177
2 tbsp. lime juice
Sealtest sherbet, any flavor

Combine cantaloupe and pineapple sauce. Add lime juice. Chill thoroughly. Serve in sherbet cups and garnish with spoonfuls of sherbet. 6 servings.

MELON BALLS

1 cup blueberries
1 cup honeydew melon balls
1 cup cantaloupe balls
2 tbsp. lemon juice
1 pint Sealtest orange or lemon sherbet

Combine fruit and lemon juice. Chill. Place in sherbet cups. Put a scoop of sherbet on each serving. 6 servings.

ORANGE AVOCADO CUP

1½ cups avocado balls
1½ cups orange sections
Sealtest orange sherbet, or any other flavor

Combine avocado and orange sections. Chill. Place in sherbet cups; put a scoop of orange sherbet or any other flavor desired on each serving. 6 servings.

PINEAPPLE SHERBET POTPOURRI

Arrange orange sections, grapefruit sections and halved strawberries in sherbet glasses. Put pineapple sherbet in the center and garnish with sprigs of mint.

PEACHES A LA SHERBET

2 cups sweetened sliced peaches
1 pint Sealtest sherbet, any flavor

Put peaches in dessert dishes. Top with scoops of sherbet. 4 servings.

SHERBET AMBROSIA

1½ cups orange sections
1 cup sliced bananas
½ cup toasted shredded coconut
Sealtest orange sherbet

Mix oranges and bananas. Put in dessert dishes. Sprinkle with coconut; place a large scoop of sherbet on each. 6 servings.

SUNDAE GLAMOUR

Your favorite flavor of ice cream with a special sauce or fruit becomes a super-duper sundae.

ALOHA SUNDAE

Serve crushed pineapple over Sealtest strawberry ice cream. Garnish with whipped cream and a cherry.

BANANA SPLIT

Cut a banana in half lengthwise; place on plate; top with a scoop of chocolate, a scoop of vanilla and a scoop of strawberry ice cream.

Spoon Pineapple Sauce, page 177, over the chocolate, chocolate sauce over the vanilla, and sweetened sliced fresh strawberries over the strawberry. If desired, top with fluffy whipped cream, maraschino cherries and chopped or whole nuts.

BLACK AND WHITE SUNDAE

Pour chocolate sauce over a scoop of chocolate and a scoop of vanilla ice cream. Top with whipped cream and chopped nuts.

BLACK NIGHT

Pour chocolate sauce over Sealtest chocolate ice cream. Top with walnuts.

BROILED PEACH COUPE

8 small canned peach halves — **Sealtest vanilla ice cream**

Place peach halves in shallow baking pan, cut side up. Broil slowly until golden brown, about 5 min. Serve warm topped with ice cream. 4 servings.

BROWNIE SUNDAE

Sealtest vanilla ice cream — **Brownies, page 138**
Chocolate sauce

Place a generous serving of ice cream on each warm brownie square. Top with hot or cold chocolate sauce.

BUTTERSCOTCH GOOBER

Spoon Peanut Butterscotch, page 178, over Sealtest vanilla ice cream. Top with one whole peanut.

BUTTERSCOTCH NUT SUNDAE

Pour butterscotch sauce over Sealtest chocolate or coffee ice cream. Top with chopped nuts.

BUTTERSCOTCH SURPRISE

First pour butterscotch sauce and then marshmallow sauce over Sealtest vanilla ice cream. Garnish with chopped nuts.

CARAMEL NUT SUNDAE

½ cup chopped nut meats — **1 cup Quick Caramel Sauce, page 175**
Sealtest vanilla ice cream

Fold nuts into sauce; serve on ice cream. 8 to 10 servings.

CARNIVAL SUNDAE

Pour thawed frozen concentrated grape juice over a portion of Sealtest ice cream. Then spoon on a little chilled canned fruit cocktail. Top with fluffy whipped cream.

CHOCOLATE MAPLE SUNDAE

Pour chocolate sauce over a portion of Sealtest vanilla ice cream. Top with a generous spoonful of chopped walnuts mixed with a little maple syrup, then some whipped cream.

CHRISTMAS SUNDAE

Delicious with a tray of holiday goodies

1 pint cranberries, about ½ lb.
1 cup sugar
½ cup water
Sealtest vanilla ice cream

Mix cranberries, sugar and water in saucepan. Stir over moderate heat 1 to 2 min.

Bring to a boil, stirring occasionally. Cover pan and cook over low heat about 10 min.

Remove from heat. Let stand covered 20 min. Pour into refrigerator dish. Chill. Spoon over ice cream. 6 servings.

COFFEE PRALINE SUNDAE

Serve Praline Sauce, page 178, over Sealtest coffee ice cream. Garnish with whipped cream.

COFFEE SUPREME

Pour chocolate syrup over Sealtest coffee ice cream. Top with whipped cream and a maraschino cherry.

FROSTED GREEN GRAPE SUNDAE

A sparkling gem of a sundae

Remove small green seedless grapes from stems. Dip into Sealtest heavy cream, then into sifted confectioners sugar. Dry on rack or on waxed paper. Serve on any flavor of Sealtest ice cream desired.

DUSTY ROAD

Pour chocolate sauce over Sealtest vanilla ice cream. Sprinkle lightly with malted milk powder, top with whipped cream and a maraschino cherry.

FRUIT MERINGUES

Place a generous spoonful of Sealtest vanilla or strawberry ice cream on each Meringue Shell. Top with Pineapple Sauce, page 177. Or use peach ice cream topped with sweetened sliced fresh peaches.

MERINGUE SHELLS

- 1/8 tsp. salt
- 4 egg whites
- 1 cup sugar
- 1/2 tsp. vinegar
- 3/4 tsp. vanilla or almond extract

Add salt to egg whites. Beat until stiff but not dry. Add sugar gradually, beating well after each addition.

Add vinegar and vanilla. Beat thoroughly. Drop by heaping tablespoonfuls onto a cookie sheet covered with waxed paper. Lightly make a depression in center of each mound with back of spoon.

Bake in very slow oven, 250°F., about 50 min. Remove meringues with spatula. Cool. 12 large shells.

GINGERBREAD SUNDAE

- 6 squares warm gingerbread, homemade or bakers
- Sealtest vanilla ice cream
- Warm chocolate sauce

Top gingerbread with spoonfuls of ice cream. Serve with chocolate sauce. For an interesting variation, split the squares of gingerbread and toast them. 6 servings.

GINGER TREAT

Scoop out large balls of Sealtest vanilla ice cream. Quickly roll in gingersnap crumbs. Serve immediately. For a special treat, serve with chocolate sauce. To make crumbs, roll gingersnap cookies with rolling pin. Allow 3/4 to 1 cup crumbs for each pint of ice cream.

HONEY CAKE SUNDAE

Sealtest vanilla ice cream
4 squares sponge cake, homemade or bought
2 bananas, thinly sliced
⅓ cup diced canned pineapple
⅓ cup honey, warmed

Place a generous serving of ice cream on each piece of sponge cake. Mix bananas and pineapple together lightly and spoon over ice cream. Pour warm honey over each serving. 4 servings.

HONEY OF A SUNDAE

Dribble honey over Sealtest ice cream, using about 2 tbsp. for each serving. Top with whipped cream and a whole maraschino cherry.

HOT FUDGE SUNDAE

Pour hot fudge sauce over Sealtest chocolate ice cream. Top with slivered almonds and a maraschino cherry.

JAM DANDY

Spoon cherry preserves over Sealtest orange sherbet.

MAPLE CHANTILLY

⅓ cup maple syrup
½ cup whipping cream
Sealtest vanilla ice cream

Thicken maple syrup by cooking until it boils down to about ¼ cup. Cool. Whip the cream. Gently fold in about half the syrup. Spoon over the ice cream. Dribble the remaining thickened maple syrup over the top of the cream as an extra garnish. 1 generous cup topping. 6 servings.

MAPLE CHOCOLATE SUNDAE

Pour maple syrup over Sealtest chocolate ice cream. Top with whipped cream and a maraschino cherry.

MARASCHINO CHERRY SUNDAE

Spoon 6 to 8 whole maraschino cherries over a dish of Sealtest chocolate ice cream, then a little of the maraschino cherry juice.

MARSHMALLOW GOOBER

Spoon marshmallow sauce over Sealtest chocolate ice cream. Top with generous serving of Goober Sauce, page 176. Garnish with one whole peanut.

ORANGE BLOSSOM

Spoon warm marmalade over Sealtest vanilla ice cream.

PEACH FLIP

Fill the hollows of fresh or canned peach halves with Sealtest vanilla ice cream. Garnish with chopped maraschino cherries.

PEACH MELBA

Spoon sweetened sliced peaches over Sealtest vanilla ice cream. Top with velvety smooth Melba Sauce, page 177.

PEACH TREAT

Serve Sealtest peach ice cream on cake. Top with sweetened sliced peaches and a dab of whipped cream.

PEANUT BALLS

Sealtest vanilla ice cream
Chopped peanuts
Chocolate sauce

Scoop large balls of ice cream. Quickly roll in peanuts. Serve immediately topped with chocolate sauce.

PINEAPPLE GLOW

Canned sweetened crushed pineapple
Sealtest vanilla ice cream

Spoon pineapple over ice cream. If desired, top with fluffy whipped cream and a red maraschino cherry.

POPCORN DIXIE

Alternate layers of Sealtest vanilla ice cream, chocolate syrup and popcorn in paper cup. Top with popcorn.

PRETZEL CRUNCH

Pour chocolate sauce over Sealtest vanilla ice cream. Top with crumbled crunchy pretzels.

RAINBOW ALLURE

Place 4 small scoops of Sealtest ice cream of different flavors in each dish, such as chocolate ice cream, strawberry ice cream, lemon sherbet and black raspberry ice cream. Top with crushed maraschino cherries.

SAUCY SUNDAE

Spoon slightly warm applesauce over generous scoop of Sealtest vanilla ice cream. Yummie.

SCOT-MALLOW SUNDAE

Combine equal amounts of butterscotch sauce and marshmallow sauce; mix well. Pour over a portion of Sealtest chocolate or vanilla ice cream. Top with chopped salted peanuts.

SOUTHERN BELLE

- Sealtest orange sherbet
- 6 slices canned pineapple
- 1 cup marshmallow sauce
- Maraschino cherries

Put a generous spoonful of orange sherbet on each slice of pineapple. Top with marshmallow sauce and a maraschino cherry. 6 servings.

STRAWBERRY SUNDAE

Spoon sliced strawberries over Sealtest strawberry ice cream. Top with whipped cream.

STRAWBERRY TRIFLE

Top squares of homemade or bought cake with spoonfuls of Sealtest vanilla or strawberry ice cream. Spoon sweetened crushed strawberries over all. Top with fluffy whipped cream.

SUNDAE BUFFET

Fill large dessert bowl with scoops of several different flavors of Sealtest ice cream (must be hard). Garnish with sliced fresh peaches, fresh pineapple wedges, whole sweet cherries with stems and any other fresh fruit in season. In separate bowls offer a choice of chocolate sauce, butterscotch sauce, coconut, chopped nuts and whipped cream—to satisfy the whims of every guest.

SUNDAE TARTS

Fill homemade or bakers tart shells with Sealtest butter pecan ice cream. Top with chocolate sauce and whipped cream.

WHATSIT SUNDAE

Make your own

It's fun and so easy for you and your guests to make sundaes at home. Serve Sealtest ice cream in a large bowl; surround with an attractive assortment of toppings to suit the occasion. Let guests help themselves. The following sauces are suggested: sweetened berries, pineapple or other fruits, fruit preserves, butterscotch sauce, caramel sauce, chocolate sauce, nuts, toasted coconut, whipped cream.

TOPPINGS

Tempting ice cream toppings, easy to make and store until needed, help the busy homemaker add glamour and deliciousness to ice cream.

JIFFY-QUICK TOPPINGS

Almond, pecans or walnuts, chopped or whole
Crushed hard candy, especially peppermint
Crushed macaroons
Fresh, canned or frozen fruits
Frosted animal crackers
Gum drops
Jams, jellies, preserves
Malted milk powder
Maraschino cherries, whole or chopped
Semi-sweet chocolate pieces
Slivered unsweetened chocolate
Toasted coconut
Whipped cream

BANANA CREAM

½ cup mashed banana
½ cup whipped cream
1 tsp. confectioners sugar
½ tsp. vanilla

Combine all ingredients; mix well. Serve immediately on Sealtest ice cream with a generous sprinkle of chopped nuts. ⅔ cup. 4 servings.

BING CHERRY SAUCE

2 tbsp. sugar
1 tbsp. cornstarch
Few grains salt
½ cup syrup from canned Bing cherries
¼ cup orange juice
1 tsp. butter
Few drops almond extract
1¼ cups canned Bing cherries, drained

Combine sugar, cornstarch and salt in saucepan; mix well. Stir in cherry syrup and orange juice gradually. Cook until thickened and clear, stirring constantly. Stir in butter and extract. Fold in cherries. Cool. About 1½ cups. 5 to 6 servings.

BLUEBERRY TOPPING

½ cup sugar
⅛ tsp. nutmeg
½ tbsp. cornstarch
Few grains salt
½ cup cold water
2 cups blueberries
1 to 2 tsp. lemon juice

Mix sugar, nutmeg, cornstarch and salt in saucepan. Stir in water gradually to make a smooth mixture. Add blueberries.

Cook over low to moderate heat until sauce is thickened and clear, stirring constantly.

Stir in lemon juice. Cool. About 1¾ cups. 6 to 8 servings.

BUTTERSCOTCH SAUCE

¾ cup brown sugar
2 tbsp. butter
½ cup light corn syrup
⅓ cup cream
Few grains salt

Place sugar, butter and corn syrup in a heavy saucepan. Cook over very low heat without stirring to 234°F. or until a soft ball forms when a little of the mixture is dropped in cold water.

Cool slightly. Stir in cream; add salt. Serve warm or cold. This sauce thickens on standing. Thin with 1 or 2 tbsp. milk or cream. 1¼ cups. 6 to 10 servings.

CALIFORNIA TOPPING

- ⅓ cup water
- Few grains salt
- ⅓ cup sugar
- ½ cup finely chopped pitted dates
- ½ cup diced orange sections

Pour water into saucepan. Add salt, sugar, dates and oranges; blend. Bring to a boil over moderate heat, stirring occasionally. Simmer for 5 min., stirring occasionally. Chill. 1 generous cup.

CARAMEL SAUCE

- ¾ cup light corn syrup
- 3 tbsp. cream
- 3 tbsp. milk
- Few grains salt

Cook corn syrup in heavy saucepan over moderate heat without stirring until light brown. Reduce heat slightly; add cream and milk slowly, mixing until smooth after each addition. Add salt. 6 servings.

QUICK CARAMEL SAUCE

- ½ lb. Kraft caramels
- ½ cup Sealtest cream

Place unwrapped caramels in double boiler. Cook, stirring occasionally, until they begin to melt; add cream and mix well. Continue to cook until sauce is smooth.

Serve warm or cold. If sauce gets too thick on standing, add a little cream; mix well. 1¼ cups. 6 to 10 servings.

CURRANT TOPPING

- 2 cups fresh red currants
- ¼ cup water
- ½ cup sugar
- 2 tsp. flour

Combine currants and water in pan. Cook over low heat, stirring occasionally for 5 min. or until soft. Put through fine sieve.

Mix sugar, flour and ⅛ tsp. salt. Add to currants. Cook over low heat, stirring occasionally, for 5 min. or until thickened. Chill. About 1 cup. 4 to 6 servings.

CHERRY SAUCE

¼ cup sugar
1 tbsp. cornstarch
Few grains salt
¾ cup canned cherry juice
1¼ cups drained canned sweetened sour cherries
2 tsp. butter

Mix sugar, cornstarch and salt. Stir in cherry juice gradually.

Cook until thickened and clear, stirring constantly. Add cherries and butter. Serve warm or cold. 6 servings.

CHOCOLATE SAUCE

3 squares unsweetened chocolate
½ cup Sealtest milk
¾ cup sugar
1 tbsp. butter
Few grains salt
¾ tsp. vanilla

Cook chocolate and milk together over low heat, stirring constantly until smooth.

Add sugar, butter and salt. Continue to cook over moderate heat, stirring constantly for 3 to 5 min. or until slightly thickened.

Remove from heat. Add vanilla. Serve hot or cold. This sauce thickens on standing. Thin with a little milk or cream. Generous 1¼ cups. 6 to 10 servings.

CREAMY CHOCOLATE SAUCE: Substitute cream for milk. Increase the amount of butter to 3 tbsp.

MEXICAN CHOCOLATE SAUCE: When serving Chocolate Sauce sprinkle generously with salted peanuts.

GOOBER SAUCE

Gradually stir ¾ cup Sealtest heavy cream into ¼ cup creamy peanut butter. Blend thoroughly. 1 cup. 5 to 6 servings.

MAPLE NUT SAUCE

1 cup maple syrup
½ cup chopped walnuts

Cook syrup over low heat until it thickens slightly, 220°F. Cool.

Serve on ice cream with a generous sprinkle of nuts. ¾ cup. 4 to 6 servings.

MARSHMALLOW SAUCE

¼ lb. marshmallows
¼ cup milk

Combine marshmallows and milk in a double boiler. Heat, stirring occasionally until marshmallows are melted. Remove from heat. Serve warm. ¾ cup. 4 to 6 servings.

MELBA SAUCE

1 twelve-oz. pkg. frozen sweetened red raspberries, thawed
1 tbsp. cornstarch
3 tbsp. cold water
2¼ tsp. lemon juice

Press berries through fine sieve. Blend cornstarch and water until smooth; add to berries. Cook in heavy saucepan, stirring constantly, until thickened and clear. Add lemon juice; stir in. Chill. 1 cup. 6 to 8 servings.

MOCHA FUDGE SAUCE

3 squares unsweetened chocolate
½ cup strong coffee
¼ cup milk
⅔ cup sugar
1 tbsp. butter
Few grains salt
½ tsp. vanilla

Cook chocolate, coffee and milk together over low heat, stirring constantly until smooth.

Add sugar, butter and salt. Continue to cook over moderate heat, stirring constantly 3 to 5 min. or until slightly thickened.

Remove from heat. Add vanilla. Serve warm or cold. About 1½ cups. 8 to 12 servings.

PINEAPPLE SAUCE

1 cup canned sweetened crushed pineapple
1 tbsp. cornstarch
2 tbsp. lemon or lime juice

Drain pineapple. Add juice gradually to cornstarch in heavy saucepan making a smooth mixture.

Cook, stirring constantly until thickened and clear. Remove from heat.

Add pineapple. Add lemon or lime juice. Cool. About 1 cup. 4 to 6 servings.

PEANUT BUTTERSCOTCH

Mix equal parts of crunchy peanut butter and butterscotch sauce, bought or homemade. If necessary thin with a little milk, blending in a small amount at a time.

PINEAPPLE MINT SAUCE

Beat 2 tbsp. of green mint jelly lightly with fork to break it up. Fold in ½ cup drained canned crushed pineapple. Chill. When serving top with maraschino cherry. ½ cup. 3 servings.

PRALINE SAUCE

1 cup sugar
¾ cup boiling water
Few grains salt
½ tsp. vanilla
¼ cup chopped pecans

Melt sugar in heavy pan over moderate heat until light brown, stirring constantly. Remove from heat. Add boiling water a few drops at a time, being careful not to let any syrup spatter on hands. Stir vigorously until blended after each addition.

Cook until moderately thick, 218°F. Add salt. Cool. Add vanilla and nuts. 1 cup. 6 to 8 servings.

TOFFEE TOPPING

2 tbsp. brown sugar
¼ cup granulated sugar
2 tbsp. light corn syrup
2 tbsp. dark corn syrup
⅛ tsp. salt
2 tbsp. butter
½ cup Sealtest whipping cream
1 tsp. rum extract
½ cup chopped walnuts

Combine sugars, syrups and salt in a heavy saucepan. Cook over low heat without stirring to 234°F. or until a soft ball forms when a little of the mixture is dropped in cold water. Stir in butter, then cream and extract. Cool; fold in nuts. Chill. About 1½ cups. 6 servings.

FROSTY TRICKS AND TREATS

Here are some ice cream answers to that question, "What can I serve that's a little different?"

BALLOT BOX

Turn out contents of half-gallon pkg. Sealtest chocolate ice cream on serving platter. Make a "slot" in the center and write "Ballot Box" above it, using stiffly whipped cream put through pastry tube. Decorate around top and base and down corner edges with fluting of whipped cream. Place cookie donkeys and elephants on top and sides.

COOKIE DONKEYS AND ELEPHANTS: Prepare Delicious Butter Cookie dough, page 140. Roll out. Cut in donkey and elephant shapes, using cookie cutters or cardboard patterns. Frost with Confectioners Sugar Frosting, page 140. Tint a little of the frosting to make the eyes.

BIRTHDAY CAKE QUICKIE

Just turn out contents of a half-gallon pkg. of Sealtest ice cream onto a serving platter and write "Happy Birthday" on it, using whipped cream put through a pastry tube. Decorate around top and base and down corner edges with fluting of whipped cream. Put ring of cup cakes around the base; stick candle in each.

CANDLE MAGIC

Cut a slice of Sealtest ice cream from a half gallon package. Remove a strip 1" wide from the slice and save for "candle." Place slice flat on dessert plate; cut out a small square in center of slice for base of "candle." Now place the 1" wide strip upright in the square. Make a handle by adding a small ring-shaped candy or cracker.

Quickly dip small sugar cube in lemon extract; set on top of "candle." Light immediately with match to set aflame.

DOUGHNUT SPLIT

Split doughnut in half; toast under broiler. Top with scoops of Sealtest ice cream. If desired, add your favorite sauce.

BIRTHDAY ICE CREAM RING

¼ cup butter
½ cup sugar
1 egg, unbeaten
½ tsp. vanilla
1 cup sifted cake flour
1½ tsp. baking powder
¼ tsp. salt
⅓ cup milk
Sealtest vanilla or strawberry ice cream

Cream butter, add sugar gradually and cream thoroughly. Add egg and beat until fluffy. Add vanilla.

Mix and sift flour, baking powder and salt; add to first mixture alternately with milk.

Pour into well-buttered ring mold, about 8½" x 2½". Bake in moderate oven, 350°F., 20 to 25 min. Turn out of pan. Frost when cool. Fill center with ice cream. 6 servings.

STRAWBERRY FROSTING

1½ cups sifted confectioners sugar
½ cup strawberry preserves
2 tbsp. melted butter

Mix sugar and preserves until smooth and creamy.

Add butter and mix well. If frosting seems thin, add a little more confectioners sugar. About ¾ cup frosting . . . enough for birthday cake ring above.

CRISPIE ICE CREAM PIE

¾ cup semi-sweet chocolate pieces
1½ tbsp. butter
1¾ cups crispie rice cereal
Sealtest ice cream, any flavor

Melt chocolate and butter in double boiler. Remove from heat; add cereal and toss together quickly but thoroughly. Press on sides and bottom of buttered 9" pie pan. Let stand at room temperature.

When ready to serve fill with ice cream. If desired, garnish with whipped cream. Serve immediately. 6 to 8 servings.

FROZEN ECLAIRS

Cut off the tops of eclair shells, homemade or bought. Fill with Sealtest ice cream and put tops back on. Serve with chocolate sauce, and lots of whipped cream.

CHOCOLATE WAFFLES A LA MODE

¼ cup butter
1 square unsweetened chocolate
1 egg
½ cup granulated sugar
¼ cup sifted flour
⅛ tsp. baking powder
⅛ tsp. salt
½ cup chopped nut meats
½ tsp. vanilla
Sealtest vanilla ice cream

Melt butter and chocolate over boiling water. Beat egg well, add sugar gradually and beat thoroughly. Add butter and chocolate. Beat well.

Mix and sift the flour, baking powder and salt. Add nuts and stir into first mixture. Mix well. Add vanilla.

Bake on hot waffle iron. Take out in sections. (The waffles will be quite soft at first.)

Serve warm with ice cream. 1½ to 2 large waffles or 6 to 8 sections. 6 to 8 servings.

QUICK WAFFLES A LA MODE

Buy waffles ready made; reheat. Or make waffles from package mix. Top a quarter or half waffle with spoonfuls of Sealtest ice cream. Dribble your favorite syrup over this; garnish with a red maraschino cherry.

EGG NOG PARFAIT PIE

1 cup finely rolled gingersnap crumbs
¼ cup melted butter
1 pkg. lemon-flavored gelatin
1 cup hot water
½ pt. Sealtest vanilla ice cream
1¼ cups Sealtest egg nog*
¾ tsp. rum flavoring

Mix crumbs and butter. Spread in 9" pie pan; press down firmly on bottom and sides of pan with back of spoon. Bake in moderate oven, 350°F., 10 min. Cool.

Dissolve gelatin in hot water. Add ice cream, a spoonful at a time, stirring until melted. Chill until thickened but not set (about 8 min.). Add egg nog and flavoring; beat with egg beater until light and fluffy. Pour into pie shell; chill until firm, about 3 hrs. If desired garnish with spoonfuls of whipped cream topped with bits of maraschino cherry. 6 servings.

* Available at holiday time

FIRE BALL

Sealtest strawberry ice cream
Shredded coconut
Sugar cube
Peppermint or lemon extract

Dip a ball of ice cream with a spoon or scoop and quickly roll in coconut.

Soak a small sugar cube in lemon extract. Set on top of ice cream ball. Put a lighted match to sugar cube to produce a flame.

FLAMING DUET

Sealtest coffee ice cream
Sealtest chocolate ice cream
Chocolate sauce
2 small sugar cubes
Lemon extract

Scoop a ball of coffee ice cream and a ball of chocolate ice cream onto a dessert plate. Spoon chocolate sauce down the sides of the ice cream.

Dip sugar cubes in lemon extract for just a second. Put one cube on each ball of ice cream. Place a lighted match to sugar cubes. Serve at once.

FLOWER POTS

Especially nice for May Day

2 qts. Sealtest vanilla ice cream
1/8 lb. slivered sweet chocolate

Press ice cream lightly into chilled custard cups. Sprinkle the chocolate over the top. Insert a small flower in each cup, first wrapping its stem in waxed paper. Real or artificial flowers may be used. 8 to 10 flower pots.

FRUIT BASKETS

1 square sponge cake
Sealtest ice cream or whipped cream
Mixed sweetened fresh fruits (sliced peaches, bananas, orange sections, cubed pineapple, berries, etc.)

Cut cake in squares. Scoop out center of each square. Fill with mixed fruit; top with ice cream or whipped cream.

HALLOWEEN PRANKS

Place a scoop of Sealtest chocolate ice cream on orange tinted layer cake. Use pieces of marshmallow to make a face on the ice cream.

Cut witches, jack-o-lanterns, cornstalks, etc. out of black or orange paper. Paste each on end of toothpick. Stick toothpick in center of dish of ice cream.

ICE CREAM HAWAIIAN

1 medium pineapple
1½ cups sliced strawberries
½ to ¾ cup sugar
Sealtest strawberry ice cream

Remove ends from pineapple. Cut pineapple in 6 round slices. Remove the core and almost all of the pineapple from each slice leaving the thin rind rings.

Dice the pineapple, add the crushed strawberries and sugar and mix well. Add more sugar if desired. Chill.

Arrange the rind rings on a platter and fill with the ice cream. Garnish with the top or crown of the pineapple cut in half lengthwise. Serve with the strawberry pineapple mixture. 6 servings.

ICE CREAM COTTAGE PUDDING

Lemony and delicious

Cut a homemade or bakers layer of cake in individual portions. Then slice through the middle, sandwich fashion. Place Sealtest vanilla ice cream between the halves and serve with Lemon Sauce.

LEMON SAUCE

⅔ cup sugar
2½ tbsp. cornstarch
⅛ tsp. salt
2 cups boiling water
5 tbsp. lemon juice
2 tsp. grated lemon rind
1½ tbsp. butter

Mix sugar, cornstarch and salt; stir in boiling water. Cook, stirring constantly, until thickened and clear. Remove from heat.

Stir in lemon juice, rind and butter. Cool slightly. 6 servings.

ICE CREAM AT BREAKFAST

Start the day with a flourish by serving fresh strawberries, sliced peaches or sliced bananas topped with a generous scoop of Sealtest ice cream.

And if hot cereal's your dish, ice cream over hot oatmeal is a real taste thrill.

MINCE-APPLES A LA MODE

6 medium baking apples
Sugar
1¼ cups mincemeat
Sealtest vanilla ice cream

Wash and core apples. Pare about 1″ of skin from stem end. Sprinkle the inside lightly with sugar. Place in shallow baking dish. Stuff apples with mincemeat. Add just enough water to cover bottom of dish. Cover dish.

Bake in hot oven, 400°F., 30 to 40 min. or until apples are soft. Pour off liquid; boil until thick and pour over apples. Cool. Serve with ice cream. 6 servings.

PARTY ICE CREAM

Place spoonfuls of Sealtest ice cream on dessert plate. Top with any decoration desired such as flower, flag, etc. by inserting in gum drop in middle of ice cream.

SNOW CAP SPLIT

Place two generous scoops Sealtest vanilla ice cream in a dessert dish. Surround with crushed raspberries and 4 banana spears (quartered banana) pointing upward. Dribble a spoonful of marshmallow sauce down the side of each banana spear. Pile whipped cream high in the center and sprinkle with chopped nuts. Top with a maraschino cherry with stem.

STRAWBERRY ICE CREAM PUFFS

Cut off tops of homemade or bought cream puffs. Fill with Sealtest strawberry ice cream; replace tops. Sprinkle lightly with confectioners sugar. If desired serve with sweetened sliced strawberries.

CHOCOLATE ICE CREAM DREAMS: Fill puffs with Sealtest chocolate ice cream; top with warm chocolate sauce, and whipped cream.

CREAM PUFFS

- ½ cup water
- ¼ cup butter
- ½ cup sifted flour
- 2 eggs

Heat water and butter to boiling point in saucepan. Mix in flour all at once. Stir constantly until mixture leaves sides of pan and forms into a ball, about 1 min. Remove from heat. Cool about 5 min.

Beat in eggs one at a time, beating until smooth after each addition. Whip mixture until velvety. Drop by spoonfuls in mounds several inches apart on lightly greased baking sheet. Bake in hot oven, 400°F., about 30 to 35 min.

Cool puffs on rack. 6 medium puffs.

STRAWBERRY PARFAIT PIE

- 1 pkg. lemon-flavored gelatin
- 1¼ cups hot water
- 1½ cups sliced fresh strawberries
- One 9" baked pie shell
- 1 pint Sealtest strawberry ice cream

Dissolve gelatin in hot water. Add ice cream, a spoonful at a time, stirring until melted. Chill until thickened but not set, 15 to 20 min.

Fold in drained berries. Turn into pie shell. Chill until firm. If desired, garnish with spoonfuls of whipped cream topped with sliced strawberries. One 9" pie. 6 servings.

TAHITI SPECIAL

Place 2 generous scoops of Sealtest vanilla ice cream in dessert dish. Spoon strawberry and pineapple sauces over this. Top with slices of banana. Garnish with shredded coconut, plain or toasted.

Beverages

Dairy products combine with a surprising variety of refreshing, delicious beverages. Perhaps your family already has its favorite ice cream or milk drink; perhaps you've already discovered that buttermilk gives a wonderful, tangy flavor to fruit juices; that chocolate drink can be party fare as in Choc-Orange Float, page 190.

In any case, you'll find it worth your while to try some of the following. You may discover a new family favorite!

DREAMY ICE CREAM DRINKS

APRICOT FIZZ

1 No. 2½ can apricot halves
Carbonated water
1 pint Sealtest vanilla ice cream

Press apricots through a sieve and stir until juice and pulp are well mixed. Put ice cream in glasses, pour in the apricot mixture and stir lightly again. Fill glasses with carbonated water. 6 servings.

COLA COOLER

For each serving, fill glass ⅔ full with a cola drink and top with spoonful of Sealtest vanilla ice cream. Do not stir.

CURRANT DELIGHT

Currants are seasonal but make a heavenly summer beverage when available.

¾ cup sugar
3 cups fresh red currants (measure after removed from bunch)
3½ cups water
1 pint Sealtest vanilla ice cream

Combine sugar, currants and 1 cup of water in a saucepan. Cook, stirring occasionally for 3 to 5 min. or until currants are soft. Press through a sieve. Add the remaining 2½ cups of water. Chill. Put ice cream in glasses and fill with currant juice. 6 servings.

FROSTED CUSTARD

Prepare one recipe of Custard Cream Smoothie, page 198. When ready to serve, beat well with rotary beater; stir in ½ pint Sealtest vanilla or coffee ice cream. 6 servings.

HONOLULU PUNCH

⅔ cup chilled pineapple juice
1 generous spoonful Sealtest vanilla ice cream

Combine pineapple juice and ice cream. Beat to a froth with rotary beater. 1 serving.

PEACH GINGER FRAPPE

¾ cup sliced peaches
Sugar
½ pint Sealtest peach or vanilla ice cream
Ginger ale

Mash peaches with a fork and add sugar to taste. Place in 6 glasses and add the ice cream. Fill glasses with ginger ale. 6 servings.

SPARKLING ROOT BEER

Quickly mix ½ cup chilled root beer and one tbsp. milk in a tall glass. Add a generous scoop of Sealtest vanilla or chocolate ice cream. Fill glass with root beer. 1 serving.

STRAWBERRY DELUXE

Put 2 tbsp. strawberry jam and 2 or 3 generous spoonfuls of Sealtest vanilla ice cream in a tall glass. Slowly fill glass with chilled ginger ale. 1 serving.

VANILLA SODA

2 tbsp. Vanilla Syrup
2 tbsp. cream
Carbonated water
Sealtest vanilla ice cream

Pour Vanilla Syrup in large glass. Add cream and stir well.

Fill glass ⅔ full with carbonated water and stir lightly to mix. Add gently 1 or 2 generous spoonfuls of ice cream and serve immediately. 1 serving.

VANILLA SYRUP: Add a little vanilla flavoring to light corn syrup.

CHOCOLATE SODA

2 tbsp. Chocolate Sauce, pg. 176
2 tbsp. cream
Carbonated water
Sealtest vanilla ice cream

Pour Chocolate Sauce into large glass. Add cream and stir well.

Fill glass ⅔ full with carbonated water and stir lightly to mix. Add gently 1 or 2 generous spoonfuls of ice cream. Serve immediately. 1 serving.

STRAWBERRY SODA

2 tbsp. sugar
½ cup crushed fresh strawberries
½ cup Sealtest cream
2 seven-oz. bottles of ginger ale or carbonated water
1 pint Sealtest vanilla ice cream

Mix sugar with strawberries. Pour 2 tbsp. crushed berries into each 10-oz. glass. Add 2 tbsp. of cream and stir well.

Fill each glass ⅔ full with ginger ale; stir to mix. Add 1 or 2 spoonfuls of ice cream. Top with whipped cream and a whole berry. 4 servings.

CARAMEL SODA

2 tbsp. Quick Caramel Sauce, page 175
2 tbsp. cream
Carbonated water
Sealtest vanilla ice cream

Pour Caramel Sauce in large glass. Add cream and stir well.

Fill glass ⅔ full with carbonated water and stir lightly to mix.

Add gently 1 or 2 generous spoonfuls of ice cream. Serve immediately. 1 serving.

LEMON SODA

2 tbsp. Lemon Syrup
2 tbsp. heavy cream
Carbonated water
Sealtest vanilla ice cream

Pour Lemon Syrup in large glass. Add cream and stir well. Fill glass ⅔ full with carbonated water and stir lightly to mix.

Add gently 1 or 2 generous spoonfuls ice cream. Serve immediately. 1 serving.

LEMON SYRUP

¼ cup lemon juice
¾ cup light corn syrup
1 tsp. lemon extract

Combine ingredients and mix well. Chill. 1 cup syrup. 8 servings.

FLAVORFUL CHOCOLATE DRINKS

BANANA CHOCOLATE COOLER

Peel and mash 1 medium banana. Add 2 cups Sealtest chocolate drink. Beat well with egg beater. Serve ice cold garnished with whipped cream. 2 to 3 servings.

CHOCOLATE MALTED

Serve extra milk to the family with this wonderful concoction.

3 to 4 heaping tsp. chocolate-flavored malted milk powder
1 spoonful vanilla ice cream, optional
1 cup cold Sealtest milk

Place malted milk powder in glass. Add 3 tsp. milk; mix to smooth paste. Add remaining milk and the ice cream; stir until blended. 1 serving.

CHOC-ORANGE FLOAT

For a special treat, fill a glass ⅔ full with ice-cold Sealtest chocolate drink; then add a generous scoop of Sealtest orange sherbet or ice. 1 serving.

CHOC-ORANGE FROSTED: Fill glass ⅔ full with Sealtest chocolate drink; pour into mixing bowl. Add scoop of Sealtest sherbet; beat with egg beater or electric mixer. Return to glass. 1 serving.

COFFEE CHOCOLATE

1 pint Sealtest coffee ice cream
3 cups Sealtest chocolate drink
Whipped cream

Add one half of ice cream to chocolate drink. Mix well with spoon or beater until melted. Pour into glasses. Top with remaining ice cream, then whipped cream. 4 servings.

HOT SPICED CHOCOLATE TODDY

Mix 2 cups piping hot Sealtest chocolate drink with ⅛ tsp. grated nutmeg and dash of ground clove. Top with spoonful of whipped cream. 2 servings.

MOCHA FLIP

Mix 1½ tsp. instant coffee with 1 tbsp. sugar. Add 2 eggs and beat with egg beater until well mixed. Add 2 cups Sealtest chocolate drink gradually, beating well. Serve cold. 2 servings.

SUPER CHOCOLATE MALTED MILK

Place 3 heaping tsp. of sweetened chocolate-flavored malted milk powder in a glass. Add 3 tsp. chocolate drink. Mix to a smooth paste. Fill with cold Sealtest chocolate drink, stirring until well blended.

If a mixer or shaker is used, pour chocolate drink into glass to measure; pour into container; then add malted milk powder and mix until well blended. 1 serving.

CHOCOLATE MALTED FLOAT: Add a scoop of Sealtest chocolate ice cream to recipe above.

TAFFY MINT COOLER

2 cups Sealtest chocolate drink, ice-cold
2 tbsp. molasses
½ tsp. peppermint flavoring

Mix chocolate drink, molasses and flavoring together thoroughly. Pour into cold glasses and serve immediately. 2 servings.

FROSTY SHERBET DRINKS

CRANBERRY PUNCH

Combine 1 cup ginger ale and 3 cups canned cranberry juice. Pour into glasses and float scoop of Sealtest lemon or orange sherbet in each glass. 4 glasses or 8 punch cups.

BLUEBERRY LEMON FIZZ

1 cup blueberries
½ cup water
¼ cup sugar
½ pint Sealtest lemon sherbet
Carbonated water

Combine blueberries, water and sugar in saucepan. Cook 3 to 5 min. or until blueberries are soft, stirring occasionally.

Press through sieve. Chill. Put lemon sherbet in 6 glasses. Add blueberry mixture. Fill glasses with carbonated water. 6 servings.

FROSTY LEMONADE

½ cup sugar
3½ cups water
¾ cup lemon juice
1 pint Sealtest lemon sherbet
Fresh mint

Combine sugar and ½ cup of the water in a pan. Cover and boil 1 min. Chill.

Add lemon juice and remaining 3 cups water.

Put sherbet in glasses and fill with lemonade. Garnish with mint. 6 servings.

GRAPE FRAPPE

1 cup fresh or canned orange juice, chilled
2 cups grape juice, chilled
2 cups ginger ale, chilled
1 pint Sealtest orange sherbet

Mix orange juice, grape juice and ginger ale. Pour into glasses. Float generous spoonful of sherbet in each glass. 6 servings.

MINTED APRICOT FREEZE

2 cups canned apricot juice
4 mint leaves, crushed
Sealtest orange or lemon sherbet

Combine apricot juice and mint leaves. Chill. Strain to remove mint leaves. Pour apricot juice into chilled glasses and float a scoop of sherbet in each. 6 servings.

ORANGE COLA

For each serving fill glass 2/3 full with a cola drink. Top with a generous spoonful of Sealtest orange sherbet.

ORANGE JULEP

1 pint Sealtest orange sherbet — **Fresh mint**
1 qt. ginger ale — **Orange slices**
Maraschino cherries

Put orange sherbet in glasses and fill with ginger ale. Garnish with sprigs of mint, orange slices cut in half and the cherries. 6 servings.

LEMON JULEP: Substitute lemon sherbet in recipe above. Garnish with mint and lemon slices.

ORANGE SHRUB

Add 1 pint Sealtest orange sherbet or ice to 1½ qts. Sealtest milk. Beat with rotary beater until blended. Pour into tall glasses. Float spoonful of sherbet or ice on top. Or for a new look, hook sherbet on the edge of glass.

For a very special occasion garnish with sprigs of Crystallized Mint Leaves, below, and a maraschino cherry. 6 servings.

CRYSTALLIZED MINT LEAVES

Wash about 12 small sprigs of fresh mint, and drain on paper towel. Blend 2 drops peppermint flavoring with ¼ cup granulated sugar in bowl. Beat 1 egg white until it holds a peak.

Now, coat each mint leaf with egg white, using brush or finger. Next, coat each sprig with sugar. (Hold sprig over sugar bowl and spoon sugar over it repeatedly until well-coated.) Dry sprigs on waxed paper on wire rack on cookie sheet in slow oven, 225°F., with door open, about 15 min.

NOTE: This garnish is also especially good for cold meat platters, and it adds a touch of glamour to summer salad plates.

HOLIDAY EGG NOG DRINKS

That wonderful happy holiday season of fun and hospitality is the traditional time for Sealtest Egg Nog . . . always ready to serve . . . always smoothly delicious. If perchance you have some left over, here are a couple of suggestions for using it.

BANANA NOG

1 ripe banana
½ cup cold milk
½ cup cold Sealtest egg nog*

Slice banana into deep bowl. Beat with egg beater until smooth and creamy. Add milk and egg nog; beat until well mixed. 1 generous serving.

FROSTED FLIP

¾ cup Sealtest egg nog*
Sealtest vanilla ice cream

Combine egg nog and generous spoonful of ice cream in a bowl. Beat with rotary beater until blended. Pour into glass. If desired, top with whipped cream and sprinkle with a little crushed peppermint candy. 1 serving.

STRAWBERRY NOG FROSTED FLOAT

½ cup Sealtest egg nog*
½ cup milk
Sealtest strawberry ice cream
Finely chopped maraschino cherry

Combine egg nog, milk and ⅓ cup of ice cream in a bowl. Beat with egg beater until blended. Pour into tall glass. Top with generous spoonful ice cream; sprinkle with a little cherry. 1 generous serving.

* Available at holiday time

Here are two homemade egg nog recipes well worth the effort when prepared egg nog is not available.

HONEY EGG NOG FLIP

3 tbsp. honey
Few grains salt
6 eggs
4½ cups Sealtest milk
¾ tsp. vanilla
Nutmeg
Sealtest vanilla ice cream

Add honey and salt to eggs and beat well with rotary beater. Stir in milk and vanilla. Sprinkle with nutmeg. Float a spoonful of ice cream on top of each serving. 6 servings.

PINEAPPLE EGG NOG

3 eggs, separated
3 tbsp. sugar
½ cup crushed pineapple
½ cup Sealtest cream
1 cup Sealtest milk
Whipped cream

Beat egg yolks until light and foamy. Add sugar and beat well. Add pineapple, cream and milk; stir to blend. Beat egg whites until stiff; fold into pineapple mixture. Pour into punch cups. Garnish with whipped cream and pineapple. 4 to 6 servings.

For 5 additional Sealtest Egg Nog recipes see:
CHRISTMAS COTTAGE PUDDING, page 122
BANANA EGG NOG TRIFLE, page 125
EGG NOG BAVARIAN TORTE, page 125
HOLIDAY EGG NOG BAVARIAN, page 125
EGG NOG PARFAIT PIE, page 181

REFRESHING MILK DRINKS

BANANA MILK SHAKE

1 ripe banana
1 cup cold Sealtest milk

Slice banana into a bowl; beat with egg beater or electric mixer until smooth and creamy. Add milk; mix well. Serve immediately. 1 generous serving.

MOCHA COOLER

2½ cups Sealtest milk, scalded
1 pint Sealtest chocolate ice cream
2½ cups hot coffee

Mix milk and hot coffee. Chill. Add half of ice cream to coffee mixture. Beat with rotary beater until smooth.

Pour into glasses and float remaining ice cream on top. If desired, garnish with whipped cream. Serve immediately. 6 to 8 servings.

MOLASSES SMOOTHIE

Pour ¾ cup Sealtest milk into a glass. Stir in 1 tbsp. molasses, then a generous spoonful of Sealtest vanilla ice cream. For sophistication, add a drop of peppermint flavoring. 1 serving.

PINK CONFECTION

Add 1 heaping spoonful, about ⅓ pkg., raspberry-flavored rennet dessert powder to a glass of cold Sealtest milk. Stir until dissolved. Serve at once. 1 serving.

PRUNE COOLER

Combine 1 cup Sealtest milk, ½ pint Sealtest vanilla ice cream and 1½ cups bottled prune juice. Beat until frothy. Float spoonful of ice cream on top. 3 servings.

RASPBERRY FREEZE

1 pint red raspberries
3½ cups Sealtest milk
2 tbsp. sugar
Few grains salt
1 pint Sealtest vanilla ice cream
Whipped cream

Crush berries and add to milk. Put through sieve and press out all of the juice. Stir in sugar and salt.

Place ice cream in 6 glasses or in pitcher and pour in raspberry milk. Top with whipped cream. 6 servings.

PURPLE COW

Gradually add 2 to 3 tbsp. frozen concentrated grape juice to ¾ of an 8 oz. glass of cold Sealtest milk, stirring constantly and briskly. (Always pour juice into milk.) Serve immediately. 1 serving.

RASPBERRY QUENCHER

- ½ cup finely sieved raspberries
- 1 pint Sealtest vanilla ice cream
- 1½ cups cold milk
- Sugar
- ½ cup sweetened whipped cream

Add sieved raspberries to half of ice cream. Beat with rotary beater until smooth, creamy and well blended. Add milk all at once. Continue beating until blended and frothy. Sweeten with sugar. Pour into four 8 oz. glasses. Top with remaining ice cream and garnish with sweetened whipped cream. 4 servings.

SPARKLING MILK

Fill glass generously half full with Sealtest milk. Slowly fill with ice cold ginger ale. 1 serving.

STRAWBERRY TANTALIZER

- 1 pint strawberries
- ⅓ to ½ cup sugar
- 2 cups Sealtest milk
- ½ pint Sealtest vanilla or strawberry ice cream
- Whipped cream

Clean and sieve berries, reserving 4 for garnish. Mix in sugar. Chill. Add milk and ice cream. Stir until ice cream is partially melted. Pour into glasses. Garnish with whipped cream and berries. 4 servings.

TROPICAL MALTED

- 3 bananas
- ½ pint Sealtest vanilla ice cream
- ½ cup chocolate flavored malted milk powder
- 5 cups Sealtest milk

Press bananas through sieve. Combine ingredients and shake well in covered jar. Or beat with rotary beater. 6 servings.

HEAVENLY CREAM DRINKS

CREAMY BANANA SHAKE

4 ripe bananas
3 cups cold Sealtest milk
½ cup Sealtest cream
2 tsp. vanilla

Peel bananas. Break in pieces and place in a bowl. Beat with rotary beater until smooth.

Add milk, cream and vanilla. Continue to beat until well mixed. 4 generous servings.

BANANA MILK FLOAT: Float a scoop of Sealtest vanilla ice cream in each portion.

CUSTARD CREAM SMOOTHIE

3 eggs
¼ cup sugar
¼ tsp. salt
3 cups Sealtest milk
½ tsp. vanilla or almond flavoring
1 cup Sealtest cream

Beat eggs slightly. Stir in sugar and salt. Add milk and cream. Cook in double boiler, stirring constantly until mixture coats spoon.

Remove from heat. Add vanilla. Chill.

Just before serving, beat well with rotary beater. If desired, top with whipped cream and garnish with berries in season. As a special treat, stir in ½ pint Sealtest vanilla or coffee ice cream just before serving. 6 servings.

RASPBERRY SPARKLE

1⅓ cups sweetened raspberries (or sweetened stewed rhubarb)
¾ cup Sealtest whipping cream
2 seven-oz. bottles carbonated water

Press raspberries through a fine sieve; stir until juice and pulp are mixed. Put ⅓ cup raspberry puree and 3 tbsp. cream in each 10 oz. glass. Stir to blend. Slowly fill glasses with chilled carbonated water; stir lightly. 4 servings.

TANGY BUTTERMILK DRINKS

APRICOT HALF'N HALF

Mix equal parts of Sealtest buttermilk and apricot nectar or juice. Sweeten to taste with sugar.

BUTTERMILK EGG NOG

Beat 3 eggs until frothy. Add ½ cup sugar gradually, beating well. Add 1½ tsp. vanilla and 3 cups Sealtest buttermilk; beat until blended. Serve sprinkled with nutmeg. About 1 qt.

BUTTERMILK FRUIT SMOOTHIES

For a deliciously cooling and healthful treat, mix one 6 oz. can quick-frozen fruit juice concentrate with 3 parts (measure in the can) of "ice-cold" Sealtest buttermilk instead of water. Any of the frozen juices *(orange, grape, tangerine, grapefruit, tomato, lemon, cranberry,* or *orange and grapefruit)* make delicious combinations—so take your choice.

CHOCOLATE FROSTED DELUXE

Mix 2 cups Sealtest buttermilk, 2 cups Sealtest chocolate drink and about 2 tbsp. sugar. Add 1 pint of Sealtest chocolate ice cream. Beat until smooth and frothy. Serve immediately. 6 servings. Or combine 1 qt. buttermilk, ½ cup chocolate syrup, and 1 pint of chocolate ice cream. Beat until smooth; serve immediately. 6 servings.

CREAMY BUTTERMILK FIZZ

Mix equal parts of Sealtest buttermilk and cream soda. Serve ice cold in tall glasses.

DREAMY COFFEE FROST

Combine 2 cups Sealtest buttermilk, 2 cups cold coffee, 1 tbsp. sugar and 1 pint Sealtest coffee ice cream. Beat until smooth and frothy. Serve immediately. 6 generous servings.

GRAPE FREEZE

Mix 2 cups Sealtest buttermilk with 2 cups grape juice. Pour into serving glasses. Float spoonfuls of Sealtest vanilla ice cream in each glass. (A pint of ice cream will do for 6.) 6 servings.

PINEAPPLE BUTTERMILK PICK-UP

- 1 No. 2 can pineapple juice, chilled
- 1 qt. Sealtest buttermilk

Combine pineapple juice and buttermilk. Mix well. 6 servings.

PRUNE FLOAT

Mix 2 cups of Sealtest buttermilk with 2 cups of prune juice. Add sugar to taste. Pour into serving glasses. Float spoonfuls of Sealtest vanilla ice cream in each serving. (A pint of ice cream will do for 6.) 6 servings.

SAUCY BUTTERMILK

- 1 qt. Sealtest buttermilk
- 2 cups applesauce, chilled

Combine buttermilk and applesauce. Mix well. Add sugar if desired. 6 servings.

STRAWBERRY BUTTERMILK FANCY

- 1 qt. Sealtest buttermilk, chilled
- 2 cups sweetened crushed strawberries

Combine buttermilk and strawberries. Mix well. 6 servings.

VEGETABLE COCKTAIL

Mix 1½ cups vegetable juice cocktail (V-8 or similar juice) with 1½ cups Sealtest buttermilk. Add a dash of Tabasco sauce. Season to taste with salt. 6 servings.

Sour Cream and Yogurt

Here are two popular Sealtest dairy products that give a gourmet flourish to any dish they grace. Their luscious smoothness and tantalizing piquancy make them especially appealing. SOUR CREAM can be used with a lavish hand, for it usually contains the same or less butterfat as light or coffee cream. YOGURT, like sour cream, has been used extensively in Europe and is now enjoying the popularity in this country it well deserves. Made from milk, yogurt has a custard-like consistency that can be eaten by spoon. It has the high food value of milk plus a stimulating digestive quality that is beneficial.

SOUR CREAM

To make it easy to find our Sealtest sour cream recipes, we are listing them here separately.

MAIN DISHES page

Beef Stroganoff 24
Beets in Sour Sauce .. 53
Blintzes 42
Cheese Noodle Casserole 42
Elegant Veal Birds ... 31
Escalloped Eggplant and Tomato 54
Julienne Veal Stew ... 32
Potato Puff Souffle ... 55
Veal Noodle Casserole . 32

SALADS

Banana Split 62
Cabbage Carrot Slaw .. 77
Frozen Pineapple 78
Frozen Strawberry 78
Harvest 79
Hearty 78
Lime Cucumber 80
Paradise Cheese 80
Peppy Potato 81
Shrimp and Rice 80
Sour Cream Potato 81
Sour Cream Spinach .. 82
Stuffed Tomato 82
Turkey Ham 79

page

SALAD DRESSINGS ... 87

SANDWICHES

Banana Cream Cheese . 105
Cucumber Cheese 105
Egg Salad 106
Red Bow 108
Turkey Salad Roll 106

SANDWICH FILLINGS

Peanut Cheese 104
Pickle and Cheese 104
Tuna Sour Cream 104

DESSERTS

Creamy Cocoa Cake ... 132
Dark Mystery Chocolate Cake 132
Raisin Tarts 151
Frozen New Orleans Cottage Cheese 116
Pint-Size Cream Cheese Cake 144
Tart Strawberry Mousse 127

MISCELLANEOUS

Appetizer Cheese Cake 8
Candied Walnuts 154
Fluffy Cottage Cheese . 12
Sour Cream Potato Soup 19

YOGURT

Here are some new tempting ways to use Sealtest yogurt.

CHILLED YOGURT SOUPS

Combine 1 can condensed soup (cream of tomato, celery, or chicken) and 1 half-pint Sealtest yogurt. Blend thoroughly. Chill. Pour into soup dishes. Garnish with chopped parsley or chives. 4 servings.

ORANGE WALDORF SALAD

1 large unpeeled red apple, diced
2 oranges, peeled and cut in sections
½ cup diced celery
½ cup Sweet-Sour Fruit Dressing, recipe below
Lettuce or other greens
¼ cup chopped nuts
Grated orange rind

Mix diced apple, orange sections, and celery in a bowl. Moisten with dressing. Serve on lettuce or other greens on individual plates or in salad bowl. Sprinkle with nuts and rind. 4 servings.

SWEET-SOUR FRUIT DRESSING

1 cup Sealtest cottage cheese
1 half-pint Sealtest yogurt
1 tbsp. sugar
1 tbsp. mayonnaise
¼ cup frozen orange juice concentrate
Pinch of salt

Press cottage cheese through fine sieve. Add remaining ingredients. Beat with rotary beater until fluffy. About 1½ cups dressing.

YOGURT THOUSAND ISLAND DRESSING

1 half-pint Sealtest yogurt
3 tbsp. finely chopped celery
1 tbsp. finely chopped olives
¼ tsp. grated onion
¼ tsp. salt
¼ cup chili sauce
1 hard-cooked egg, finely chopped

Mix all ingredients together gently but thoroughly. Chill for several hrs. or overnight before serving. About 1½ cups.
SERVE WITH: fish, egg, or tomato salad or on lettuce wedges.

STRAWBERRY-YOGURT MILK SHAKE

3 tbsp. strawberry jam
1 half-pint Sealtest yogurt
Sealtest vanilla or strawberry ice cream
½ cup milk

Combine jam, yogurt and milk. Add ice cream; beat with a mixer or rotary beater until smooth and frothy. Serve immediately. 3 servings.

YOGURT-FRUIT REFRESHERS

Combine 3 tbsp. or more thawed frozen concentrated fruit juice (orange, grape, limeade or lemonade) with 1 half-pint chilled Sealtest yogurt. Blend thoroughly. 1 to 2 servings.

LEMON-YOGURT MERINGUE PIE

- **2 cups sugar**
- **6 tbsp. cornstarch**
- **⅛ tsp. salt**
- **1½ cups Sealtest yogurt**
- **½ cup lemon juice**
- **1 tsp. grated lemon rind**
- **1 baked 9″ pastry shell or crumb crust**
- **3 egg yolks, well beaten**

Mix sugar, cornstarch, salt, yogurt, lemon juice and lemon rind in a heavy saucepan. Cook over moderate heat, stirring constantly, until mixture boils and thickens. Continue cooking, stirring constantly, over lowered heat for 2 to 3 min. Stir a little of the hot mixture into beaten egg yolks. Add to remaining hot mixture, mixing well. Continue cooking, stirring constantly, for 2 min. Cool slightly, stirring occasionally, and pour into baked pastry shell.

Spread top with meringue. Bake in moderate oven, 325°F., about 15 min. or until golden brown. One 9″ pie.

MERINGUE: Beat 3 egg whites until stiff. Gradually beat in 6 tbsp. sugar.

GOLDEN YOGURT FROSTING

Extra good with chocolate cake

- **2 cups sugar**
- **5 tbsp. cornstarch**
- **⅛ tsp. salt**
- **1 tsp. grated orange rind**
- **½ cup orange juice**
- **1½ cups Sealtest yogurt**
- **3 tbsp. butter**

Mix sugar, cornstarch, salt and orange rind in heavy saucepan. Gradually stir in orange juice and yogurt, mixing until smoothly blended. Cook over moderate heat, stirring constantly, until mixture thickens and comes to a boil. Lower heat and continue cooking, stirring constantly, for about 5 min. Remove from heat; add butter; stir until melted. Cool. Enough to fill and frost two 8″ layers.

LIME SPONGE

1 cup hot water
1 pkg. lime-flavored gelatin
1 half-pint Sealtest yogurt

Add hot water to gelatin; stir until completely dissolved. Chill until almost set and quivery. Whip with egg beater or electric mixer until very light and foamy, using highest speed. Add yogurt gradually, beating constantly. Pour into dessert dishes. Chill until set. 6 servings.

YOGURT OAT CRISPS

2 cups sifted flour
⅓ cup sugar
1 tsp. salt
½ tsp. baking soda
1 cup quick-cooking rolled oats, crumbled
½ cup butter or margarine, melted
½ cup Sealtest yogurt

Sift flour, sugar, salt and soda into mixing bowl. Stir in oats. Add yogurt and butter; stir until dry ingredients are just moistened.

Knead dough lightly for a few seconds on well-floured board. Roll out very thin (about ⅛" thick). Cut in strips about 2" x 4". Sprinkle with salt, or sugar and cinnamon, if desired. Bake on ungreased cookie sheet in hot oven, 400°F., about 8 min., or until golden brown. About 5 doz. crisps.

YOGURT GRAHAM BREAD

2 cups sifted graham flour
¼ cup sugar
½ tsp. salt
¾ tsp. soda
½ tsp. baking powder
¼ cup melted butter
1 half-pint Sealtest yogurt
¼ cup molasses

Combine flour, sugar, salt, soda and baking powder; mix thoroughly. Add melted butter, yogurt and molasses to dry ingredients. Stir until well mixed, but do not overbeat.

Pour batter into greased loaf pan, 9" x 5" x 3". Bake in moderately hot oven, 375°F., about 50 min. 1 loaf.

Helpful Information

We all know there's more to preparing a meal than placing food on the table. A happy homemaker performs her many duties well and enjoys doing them. She has a well-equipped kitchen, a well-stocked larder, and she knows the importance of following a recipe carefully.

In this chapter we offer helpful pointers on what makes a good cook and how to measure ingredients properly.

WHAT MAKES A GOOD COOK

Are you just removing price tags from pots and pans and getting the feel of your new kitchen or are you an experienced homemaker completely at home in your fully equipped, well organized kitchen? Regardless, we're sure you want to be a good cook, so here are a few simple basic pointers.

PLANNING. Try to acquire the habit of planning meals at least one day ahead—better still two or three days ahead, but keep plans flexible enough to adjust to any last minute emergency that may come up. Today's reliable refrigerators and freezers make it possible to store food for considerable periods of time.

After planning comes **MARKETING.** A shopping list is a must. Don't be lured by spot sales unless they fit into your over-all plans. A wise shopper will always take advantage of good buys but only when they fit into her plans. Foods that are plentiful and in season are usually the best buys and are at their peak in flavor. Learn to read labels . . . . they can aid you in many ways as to content, servings, method of preparation.

Now you come to the main job, the actual cooking. Master a few **BASIC RECIPES** and learn to use them with variations. Before you start any cooking, read your recipe carefully and check your ingredients. Be sure to follow directions as written, and if you are trying a new recipe for the first time it is important to follow it accurately in every detail.

In the testing kitchens maintained by many large food companies, recipes are developed specifically to help you use their products to the best advantage. These recipes are tested over and over again for just the right ingredients, the correct cooking time and the right utensils until perfect results are attained and only then are they made available to you. By following their directions carefully you are benefiting from the experience of experts.

And now—your food is all prepared, ready to serve; but it doesn't end there. Every well-cooked meal deserves an attractive table with a friendly atmosphere. Crisp clean linens, pretty table settings and a relaxed hostess are almost as important as well-cooked food—for they transform mere eating into gracious dining—the happy reward of a good cook and hostess.

HOW TO MEASURE

ALWAYS USE LEVEL MEASUREMENTS

Few grains	=	very light sprinkling
3 teaspoons	=	1 tablespoon
4 tablespoons	=	¼ cup
5⅓ tablespoons	=	⅓ cup
16 tablespoons	=	1 cup
2 cups	=	1 pint
4 cups	=	1 quart
4 quarts	=	1 gallon
8 quarts	=	1 peck
4 pecks	=	1 bushel
16 ounces	=	1 pound

TO MEASURE LIQUIDS

Use a cup that has a space above the 1 cup line. This will prevent spilling and avoid the tendency to skimp in measuring liquids. Place on a level surface at eye level, if possible.

TO MEASURE DRY MATERIALS

For 1 cupful, use a cup that has the cup line right at the rim. Fill container lightly, using a spoon or scoop. Do not shake down. Level off with a knife.

Flour should be sifted once before measuring.

Brown sugar is an exception to the rule and should be packed tightly into the container.

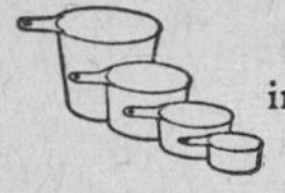

For fractions of a cup, use the measures that come in nests of four—1 cup, ½ cup, ⅓ cup and ¼ cup.

To measure spoonfuls, use standard measuring spoons which come in sets of four—1 tablespoon, 1 teaspoon, ½ teaspoon and ¼ teaspoon.

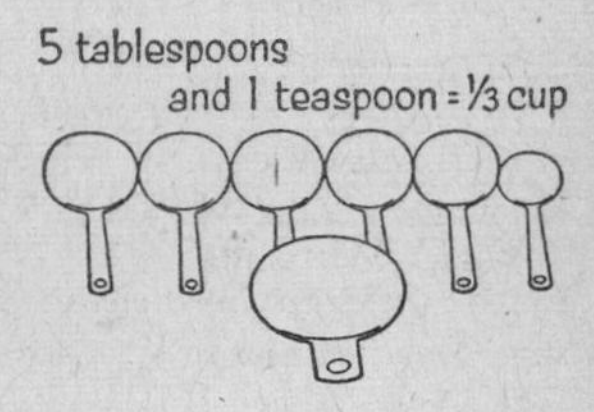

TO MEASURE BUTTER

When you use *quarter-pound* bars, cut off portion you need.

¼ lb. bar	=	½ cup
½ of a bar	=	¼ cup
¼ of a bar	=	2 tablespoons
⅛ of a bar	=	1 tablespoon
1 pound	=	2 cups

Planning Family Meals

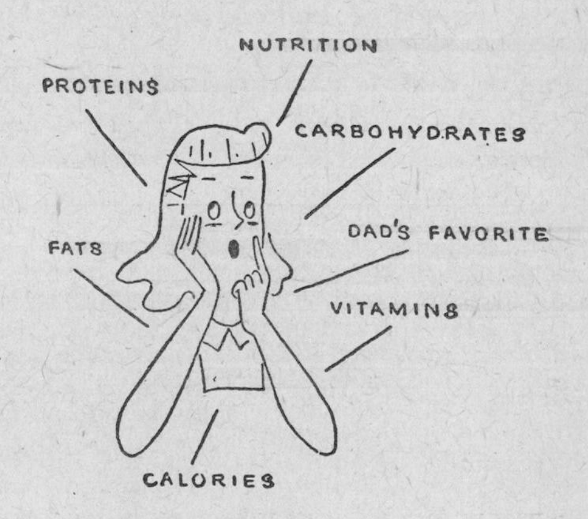

Meal planning—a problem or pleasure? Nevertheless, it's an important part of a homemaker's routine.

The following pages offer some useful information . . . . Refer to the Daily Food Guide as you plan well-balanced meals to include necessary nutrients. Use the Holiday Reminders and What To Have With What to find appropriate suggestions.

A DAILY FOOD GUIDE

Plan to include the following foods *every day* to help make sure your family's meals are nutritionally satisfactory. (Amount depends on age, sex, size, activity.)

Milk*	1 quart for children 2½ to 3 glasses for adults
Meat, poultry, fish	1 serving
Eggs	1 (at least 4 a week)
Vegetables	
green, leafy, yellow	1 or more servings
others (potato and raw vegetables often)	2 servings
Fruits	
citrus or tomato	1 serving
other	1 serving
Breads, cereals, other grain products, whole-grain or enriched	some every day
Butter or fortified margarine	some every day
Sugar, syrups, preserves	in moderate amount for flavor and sweetening

*As beverage and in milk recipes and in one or more of milk's various forms.

The National Research Council recommends the use of 400 U.S.P. or International units of vitamin D daily for children. A qt. of vitamin D milk contains this amount.

NUTRIENTS

WHAT nutrients do for us and WHERE we find them

	Function	Where found (good sources)
PROTEIN	builds bones, blood, skin, all body tissue necessary for body repair and for life itself	milk, all kinds meat eggs fish poultry cheese legumes nuts
FATS AND CARBO-HYDRATES	needed for energy and for growth add flavor to food increase one's satisfaction in food	cream, butter, egg yolk, margarine, bacon, lard, nuts breads, cereals, other grain products, whole wheat or enriched potatoes, legumes, other vegetables fruits sugar, syrups, preserves
MINERALS		
CALCIUM	builds bones, teeth needed for all body tissues; for blood clotting; for regulation of heart beat; for contraction and relaxation of muscles	milk cheese greens such as kale and broccoli nuts legumes

	Function	Where found (good sources)
	coordinates activities of all the mineral elements	
	aids digestion	
IRON	needed for building blood and other tissue cells	liver meat molasses egg yolk enriched and whole grain breads and cereals legumes green leafy vegetables dried apricots dried prunes
VITAMINS		
VITAMIN A	needed for growth, healthy skin, eyes, gums, tooth enamel, hair, nails essential for health of respiratory tract, digestive tract	green vegetables yellow vegetables apricots peaches tomato cantaloupe egg yolk whole milk butter fortified margarine fish liver oils liver
VITAMIN D	helps body to use calcium and phosphorus to make strong, well-formed bones and teeth	vitamin D milk fish liver oils

	Function	Where found (good sources)
THIAMINE	helps keep up good appetite, good digestion and healthy nerves needed by body to make good use of sugars and starches	pork liver legumes nuts enriched cereals whole grain cereals milk meat eggs green leafy vegetables
RIBOFLAVIN	helps to protect health and vigor at all ages helps body cells use oxygen helps resist infection influences health of mouth, skin, eyes	milk cheese liver legumes green leafy vegetables meat eggs
NIACIN	helps stimulate appetite helps with digestion helps protect nerve tissue	liver meat poultry legumes nuts peanut butter enriched and whole grain breads and cereals
ASCORBIC ACID (vitamin C)	helps build healthy gums, teeth, bones, blood vessels, other tissues	citrus fruit juices cantaloupe strawberries raw cabbage tomato green leafy vegetables

WHAT TO HAVE WITH WHAT

Puzzled about what to serve with your main course? Here are some natural go-togethers.

MEAT	VEGETABLES	SALAD	BREAD	DESSERT
Beef	baked potatoes browned potatoes corn, cauliflower mushrooms fried onion rings	mixed greens	Yorkshire pudding popovers	fruits apple pie cream pie cherry tarts a la mode
Fish	creamed potatoes mashed potatoes French fries tomatoes broccoli Hollandaise spinach with lemon Harvard beets	tomato aspic jellied vegetable	hard rolls corn bread	sherbet lemon pie tart fruits
Ham	sweet potatoes creamed potatoes corn pudding asparagus succotash peas, dried or fresh	pineapple cabbage slaw potato	spoon bread corn bread rye bread cheese biscuits peanut bread	pumpkin pie raisin tarts custard gingerbread ice cream
Lamb	parsley potatoes creamed potatoes asparagus curried rice minted peas carrots green beans	head lettuce pear with currant jelly mixed fruit	whole wheat rolls nut muffins	fruit gelatine grapefruit rhubarb sherbet
Pork	sweet potatoes creamed potatoes sauerkraut baked beans lima beans Brussels sprouts	cranberry gelatine Waldorf	steamed brown bread dressing	baked apple apple Betty jelly roll
Poultry	sweet potatoes mashed potatoes squash, noodles onions, corn celery hearts asparagus mushrooms	avocado and orange cucumber	hot biscuits waffles dumplings dressing	shortcakes ice cream chocolate cake caramel cake cheese cake
Veal	scalloped potatoes eggplant, rice cauliflower tomatoes mushrooms	jellied apricot tomato	nut bread raisin bread	prune whip fruit cobbler cider gelatine fruit compote rice pudding

NOTE: Suggested sauces—FOR BEEF—horseradish. FOR FISH—Tartare, Hollandaise, egg, lemon, tomato, parsley butter. FOR PORK—applesauce. FOR HAM—mustard, raisin, cider. FOR LAMB—mint, curry, currant. FOR POULTRY—cranberry, mushroom. FOR VEAL—currant.

HOLIDAY REMINDERS

Celebrate holidays with something special.

New Year's Day.......Egg nog; fruit cake

Lincoln's Birthday.....Log cabin and top hat shaped cookies

Valentine's Day........Heart-shaped tomato aspic salad; Valentine candies

Washington's Birthday..Cherry pie, tarts or sundae; Hatchet Cakes, page 133

Saint Patrick's Day.....Emerald Salad, page 73; pistachio ice cream; lime sherbet

Easter................Lamb with mint jelly; hot cross buns; Easter egg candies

Memorial Day.........Poppy seed rolls; Flower Pots. page 182

July Fourth ....Ding Dong Bell, page 159
Rocket Spray, page 160
Sweet Firecracker, page 161

Labor Day ....Banana Split, page 166

Columbus Day ....Pint-Size Pizzas, page 45

Halloween.............Spooky Ice Cream Cup, page 161 mulled cider and toasted doughnuts

Election Day..........Ballot Box, page 179

Armistice Day.........Drum Major Salad, page 69 star-shaped cookies

Thanksgiving..........Turkey; cranberry sauce; Pumpkin Pie, page 150

Christmas.............Roast beef with Yorkshire pudding; turkey; plum pudding

Menus

Need some new ideas for party fare . . . or just want some help with daily planning? We think you'll find this section handy. There are party menus for grownups and children; there are countless ideas for special occasions (weddings to picnics)—suggestions for almost every holiday on the calendar.

CHILDREN'S PARTIES

CIRCUS GET-TOGETHER

Party Clowns, page 160 or Circus Wagons, page 158
Delicious Butter Cookies, page 140
(Cut in Animal Shapes)
Taffy Mint Cooler, page 191

SMALL FRY SNACK

Graham Cracker Ice Cream Sandwich
Pink Confection, page 196

LITTLE FOLKS LUNCHEON

Pea Soup with Star-Shaped Croutons
Potato Puffs on Tomatoes, page 54
Jam Baskets, page 109
Humpty Dumpty, page 159 Milk

HAPPY BIRTHDAY PARTY

Birthday Cake Quickie, page 179
Gaily Frosted Cup Cakes
Chocolate Drink

TV PARTY LUNCHEON

Tomato Juice
Small Hamburgers
Baked Potatoes Buttered Carrots
Toasted Bread Triangles Butter
Brown Beanie, page 158
Milk

TODDLERS PARTY REFRESHMENTS

Easter Egg Nest, page 159
Cookies
Milk

CAROLERS' DINNER

Cranberry Juice   Cheese Bells, page 13
Little Chicken Pies, page 35
Buttered Green Beans
Cottage Fruit Salad, page 72, in Christmas Tree Molds
Caramel Cheese Rolls, page 93   Butter
Jolly Ice Cream Santa, page 159
Milk   Cocoa

GAMES PARTY DESSERT

Snowballs, page 160   Holiday Loaf Cake, page 133
Hot Spiced Chocolate Toddy, page 191

MORE MENUS FOR HAPPY OCCASIONS

Wedding Fare

BRIDAL BREAKFAST BEFORE 11 O'CLOCK

Orange Juice with Orange Sherbet
Chicken a la Regent, page 33   Buttered Peas
Buttermilk Blueberry Muffins, page 97   Butter
Coffee with Cream
Little Boxes of Wedding Cake

RECEPTION BANQUET

Fresh Fruit Cup with Mint Leaves
Turkey Croustades, page 36
Fresh Asparagus
Hearts of Lettuce   Snappy Dressing, page 90
Sweet Dinner Rolls   Butter
Vanilla Ice Cream   Lemon Sherbet
Wedding Cake
Coffee with Cream

Anniversary Parties

BUFFET DINNER

Centerpiece of Fruit
Hot Consomme in Punch Cups
Turkey-Ham Oriental, page 36
Buttered String Beans — Tossed Green Salad
Hot Biscuits — Butter
Vanilla Ice Cream with Grenadine Sauce
Milk — Coffee with Cream

DESSERT PARTY

Baked Alaska Cake, page 156
Assorted Candies — Salted Nuts
Coffee with Cream

JUNE PUNCH PARTY

Fruit Sherbet Punch
Party Sandwich Cake, page 111
Macaroons — Chocolates — Mints

WEDDING ANNIVERSARIES

Anniversary	Gift
First	paper
Second	cotton
Third	leather
Fourth	flowers
Fifth	wood
Sixth	candy
Seventh	copper
Eighth	bronze
Ninth	pottery
Tenth	tin or aluminum
Eleventh	steel
Twelfth	silk or linen
Thirteenth	lace
Fourteenth	ivory
Fifteenth	crystal
Twentieth	china
Twenty-fifth	silver
Thirtieth	pearl
Thirty-fifth	coral
Fortieth	ruby
Forty-fifth	sapphire
Fiftieth	gold
Fifty-Fifth	emerald
Seventy-fifth	diamond

Outdoor Picnics

NEW ENGLAND CLAMBAKE

Barrel Baked Clams — Baked Lobster
Melted Butter
Sweet Corn-on-the-Cob — Baked Potatoes
Watermelon — Oatmeal Cookies
Milk — Coffee with Cream

NEIGHBORHOOD PARTY

Hot Dogs — Kabobs
Scalloped Potatoes, page 55
Sliced Tomatoes — Celery Hearts — Pickled Beets
Carrot Sticks — Pickles — Olives
Sunshine Sponge Shortcake, page 130
Milk — Iced Tea

Card Party Fare

GRAND SLAM LUNCHEON

Apricot Nectar with Orange Sherbet
Broiled Lamb Chops
Buttered Peas — Tomato-Cheese Aspic, page 77
Tiny Berry Muffins — Butter
Sunshine Sponge, page 123
Tea

DESSERT BRIDGE DELIGHT

Strawberry Cream Carnival Cake, page 135
Coffee with Cream
Mints — Assorted Candies

IN-BETWEEN HANDS

Ginger Ale Lime Sherbet Punch
Garland Sandwiches, page 110
Assorted Tiny Cookies — Salted Almonds

Teen-age Get-togethers

RUMPUS ROOM SUPPER

Frankfurters on Toasted Buns
Three Decker Chicken Salad-Sliced Tomato Sandwich
Black and White Soda   Brownies

AFTER-THE-GAME BUFFET

Cider
Bacon Sprinkles, page 13
Pint-Size Pizzas, page 45
Seafoam Salad Rings, page 76   Vegetable Salad
Hot Crusty French Bread   Butter
Whatsit Sundae, page 173
Milk   Hot Chocolate

SUMMER REFRESHER

Fruit and Nut Bars, page 142
Raspberry Freeze, page 196

WHEN COMPANY COMES

Out-of-the-Ordinary Breakfasts

HOLIDAY BRUNCH

Broiled Grapefruit
Baked French Toast, page 95   Crisp Bacon   Tiny Sausage Links
Maple Syrup   Cottage Cheese and Jam
Milk   Coffee with Cream   Cocoa

BREEZEWAY BRUNCH

Fresh Strawberries with Ice cream
Creamed Eggs and Mushrooms   Buttered Peas
Corn Bacon Squares, page 92   Butter   Cherry Preserves
Milk   Coffee

TV Tray Lunches

COOL-OFF LUNCH

Frosty Jellied Consomme
Blushing Pear, page 63
Tomato and Cucumber Sandwich Triangles
Chocolate Cup Cake   Chilled Buttermilk

HAVE THE NEIGHBORS IN

Pumpernicks, page 112
Hearts of Lettuce   Yogurt Thousand Island Dressing, page 203
Peach Halves a la Mode
Milk   Coffee with Cream

SCORCHER SPECIAL

Summer Fruit Salad Plate, page 84
Jelly Muffins, page 96
Coffee Ice Cream Soda

WINTER WARM-UP

Champion's Chowder, page 20
Stewed Apricots   Brownies, page 138
Cocoa

Special Dinners

STAG DINNER

Shrimp Cocktail
French Onion Soup
Beef Stroganoff, page 24
Fluffy Mashed Potatoes   Buttered Peas
Fig, Orange and Cheese Salad, page 63   Piquant Dressing, page 90
Hot Rolls   Butter
Crispie Ice Cream Pie, page 180
Coffee with Cream

NEW ENGLAND DINNER

Spiced Tomato Juice
Boiled Corned Beef — Cabbage
Buttered Carrots — Parsley Potatoes
Parkerhouse Rolls — Butter
Peach Melba, page 171
Milk — Tea with Lemon

DINNER IN A COMPANY MANNER

Fresh Fruit Cup with Sherbet
Roast Fresh Ham
Whipped Potatoes — Broccoli
Cheese Biscuits, page 92 — Butter — Jam
Date, Nut and Cheese Pie, page 147
Milk — Coffee with Cream

COMMITTEE DINNER

Vegetable Juice — Cheese Shortbits, page 8
Seafood Newburg
Buttered Lima Beans
Mixed Green Salad
Hot Rolls — Jam — Butter
Lemon Sherbet
Milk — Coffee with Cream

Party Refreshments

BIRTHDAY PARTY

Peanut Balls, page 171 — Rainbow Party Cake, page 135
Chocolates — Mints
Milk — Coffee with Cream

SURPRISE SHOWER

Spring Baskets, page 160
Candied Walnuts, page 154 — Fruit Balls, page 154
Coffee with Cream

Lincoln's Birthday

PATRIOTS' DINNER

Grapefruit and Orange Sections
Pork Chops in Cream Gravy, page 30
Applesauce Brussels Sprouts
Buttered Herb Corn Muffins, page 97
Strawberry Ice Cream
Log Cabin and Top Hat-Shaped Cookies
Coffee with Cream

Valentine's Day

SCHOOL LUNCH VALENTINE

Heart-Shaped Ham Sandwiches
Heart-Shaped Strawberry Jam Sandwiches
Pink Grapefruit Sections in Valentine Paper Cup
Heart-Shaped Cookies
Milk

Washington's Birthday

MT. VERNON DINNER

Tomato Juice
Roast Prime Ribs of Beef
Harvard Beets Pan Browned Potatoes
Tossed Green Salad with Olive Dressing, page 90
Cloverleaf Rolls Butter
Cherry Sundae Hatchet Cakes, page 133
Milk Coffee with Cream

St. Patrick's Day

LEPRECHAUN LUNCHEON

Cream of Spinach Soup
Emerald Salad, page 73 Mint Jelly Sandwiches
Pistachio Ice Cream
Shamrock Cookies
Milk

NEIGHBORS' HOUSEWARMING

Sandwich Tray of American Cheese and Ham; Chicken Salad; Cottage Cheese and Chopped Dried Apricots
Radish Roses Green and Ripe Olives
Stuffed Celery Hearts
Cherry Drops, page 138 Pineapple Egg Nog, page 195

TV SNACK-TIME MENU

Fluffy Cottage Cheese Dip, page 12
Spicy Beet Cheese Dip, page 13
Carrot Curls Olives Pickle Fans
Cauliflower Tidbits
Crispy Potato Chips Toasted Crackers
Hot Chocolate

HOLIDAY GET-TOGETHERS

Turkey Sandwiches with Cranberry-Orange Relish
Celery Olives Carrots Nuts
Flaming Plum Pudding Sealtest Egg Nog

A YEAR OF HOLIDAY MENUS

New Year's Day

NEW YEAR'S EVE SUPPER

Sherbet Fruit Cup
Elegant Veal Birds, page 31
Romaine and Celery Salad French Dressing
Olives Cottage Cheese Spiced Peaches
Holiday Egg Nog Bavarian, page 125
Milk Coffee with Cream

EGG NOG OPEN HOUSE

Party Sandwich Loaf, page 110
Radish Roses Carrot Curls
Green Pepper Sticks
Egg Nog

Lent and Easter

EASTER SUNDAY DINNER

Vegetable Juice Cheese Shortbits
Roast Spring Lamb
Mint Jelly
Spinach Ring Filled with Fluffy Mashed Potatoes
Tossed Green Salad
Hot Cross Buns Butter
Strawberry Shortcake, page 130
Milk Coffee with Cream

Memorial [illegible]

[illegible]RST PATIO PICNIC

[illegible]lled Hamburgers on
[illegible] Poppy Seed Rolls
Macar[illegible] Ring, page 70
Celery [illegible] Sticks
Flower [illegible]
Purple Cow, page 19[illegible]

July 4th

STAR-SPANGLED SUPPE[illegible]

Pineapple Juice with Raspberry Sherbe[illegible]
Savory Meat Loaf, page 24
Buttered Lima Beans
Hearty Summer Slaw, page 71
Boston Brown Bread Cut in Star Shapes Butter
Ding Dong Bell, page 159 Cookie Stars
Milk Iced Tea with Lemon

Halloween

SPOOK PARTY

Spooky Ice Cream Cups, page 161
Chocolate Ice Cream
Halloween Lollypop Cookies
Halloween Candies
Milk Cider

Election Day

VOTERS' REFRESHMENT

Ballot Box, page 179
Flag-Shaped Cookies
Coffee with Cream   Cocoa with Whipped Cream

Thanksgiving

TRADITIONAL THANKSGIVING DINNER

Fresh Cider Cocktail
Roast Stuffed Turkey with Dressing
Sweet Potatoes Chantilly, page 56   Green Peas with Mushrooms
Lettuce Wedges
Yogurt Thousand Island Dressing, page 203
Hot Buttered Rolls   Cranberry Sauce   Watermelon Rind
Pumpkin Pie, page 150
Milk   Coffee with Cream
Mints and Nuts

Christmas

CHRISTMAS DINNER

Cream of Onion Soup
Roast Stuffed Turkey or Goose
Fluffy Mashed Potatoes   Mashed Turnips
Buttered Lima Beans
Caramel Cheese Rolls, page 93   Butter
Cranberry Pineapple Salad, page 63
Plum Pudding
Hard Sauce or Whipped Cream
Milk   Coffee with Cream

MERRY CHRISTMAS BUFFET

See page 79

Milk and other Dairy Foods

.... important nutrition facts

A Sealtest cookbook just wouldn't be complete without a word or two about dairy products. On the following pages you will find interesting facts on milk and milk products—their nutritional value; how they are processed; how they may be used.

MILK

Milk is the most nearly perfect food available to us, supplying some of every dietary essential . . . protein, fat, carbohydrate, minerals and vitamins. It is the one article of diet which is specifically prepared by nature to serve as a food. It owes its importance to many factors:

. . . it is an excellent source of *protein, fat* and *carbohydrate* each of which occurs in a very favorable form. It is important for body building, body repair and for energy.

. . . it has a rich and varied assortment of *mineral* elements and *vitamins* which occur in exceptionally well balanced proportions.

. . . it is outstanding as a source of *calcium* and *riboflavin*, the two specific nutrients with which our dietaries most often need strengthening. Its richness in calcium and phosphorus makes it indispensable for good growth of bones and teeth.

. . . it has a very liberal amount of vitamin A and a considerable amount of thiamine.

. . . if fortified, it contains all the vitamin D recommended for children.

. . . it is one of our most easily digested foods due primarily to its fluid form.

. . . above all, it is a *delicious* food . . . a favorite throughout the world and throughout life.

HOW MUCH MILK DO WE NEED?

A quart or more a day for every child; 2½ to 3 glasses a day for adults.

COMPOSITION OF MILK

PROTEIN 3.5% — Essential for growth, maintenance and life itself

CARBOHYDRATE 4.9%
MILK FAT 3.9% — Provide energy for work and play

MINERALS 0.7% — Body builders and regulators, essential for health

VITAMINS — Body regulators essential to life and exerting great influence on health

WATER — Body regulator, essential to life. (Over 60% of the body is water)

CALORIES IN 1 QUART — 660

High in nutritive value, milk is low in calories.

WHY IS MILK SO IMPORTANT FOR GROWING BOYS and GIRLS?

1 quart of homogenized vitamin D milk daily will furnish all of the following percentages of essential nutrients recommended by the National Research Council for a 12-year-old boy or girl:

95% of the *calcium* and 74% of the *phosphorus* . . . in ideal proportions for building strong bones and teeth. Milk is our best source of calcium.

48% of the *protein* . . . for growth, maintenance and life itself. Milk protein is of the highest quality, containing all of the essential amino acids.

35% of the *vitamin A* . . . for growth; health of skin, hair, nails, tooth enamel, gums, eyes, respiratory tract, digestive tract.

31% of the *thiamine* . . . for growth, appetite, good digestion and healthy nerves.

91% of the *riboflavin* . . . for growth; vigor; health of mouth, skin, eyes and body; resistance to infection. Milk is our outstanding source of riboflavin.

ALL of the *vitamin D* . . . for growth, strong bones and teeth, prevention of rickets.

26% of the *calories.*

No other food gives the same valuable nutritive return for so little money.

HOMOGENIZED MILK

Homogenized milk is pasteurized whole milk whose fat globules have been broken up into tiny, uniform-size globules which are dispersed evenly throughout the milk, thereby giving it an over-all creamy quality, smoothness and palatability. During digestion, a softer curd is produced from homogenized milk which aids the digestive process. Homogenized milk is usually fortified with vitamin D which gives it additional nutritive value.

BUTTERMILK

The tangy, clean taste of Sealtest buttermilk has the refreshing goodness and flavor of real, old-fashioned buttermilk from the churn. In the olden days, buttermilk was the end-product from the laborious hand churning of cream into butter. Today, modern scientific methods add a specially prepared lactic acid culture to pasteurized fresh skim milk and allow the combination to develop, under controlled conditions, until just the right flavor and consistency are reached, when the product is cooled and bottled.

Since buttermilk contains the valuable nutrients of milk, is low in calorie content and has the extra benefits of lactic acid fermentation, it is an important member of the dairy family. In cooked main dishes and desserts, in refreshing beverages and chilled summer soups, buttermilk gives a flavor and zestiness that are unique.

SKIM MILK

Skim milk is an especially important member of the dairy family today with the present interest in the number of calories in food. Skim milk is regular whole milk from which the butterfat has been removed reducing its calorie content in half. It retains the food value of regular whole milk except the butterfat and the vitamin A contained in butterfat. Skim milk can be used in practically all of the ways in which regular milk is used.

CHOCOLATE DRINK

Because of the universal liking for chocolate flavor, chocolate milk or chocolate drink has become a popular dairy food. It is made from fresh sweet milk or skim milk under the same sanitary care and precautions as other dairy products. Children especially like this product which is recommended as a supplementary drink to regular milk rather than a substitute for it. Chocolate drink or milk is a wonderful after-school snack or party favorite. It is delicious when heated and served with a blob of whipped cream.

COTTAGE CHEESE

Cottage cheese contains, in a compact form, much of the nutriment of milk. It is an especially valuable source of high quality protein, of riboflavin, and phosphorus, and has a significant amount of calcium. It is low in calories (only 87 in ⅓ cup) and exceptional as a "light" but satisfying and easily digested food.

Because it is concentrated, cottage cheese is doubly valuable in feeding children, whose capacities are smaller. Many child care experts recommend adding cottage cheese to meals for little children in their second year. Starting with a teaspoonful at first, the amount may be gradually increased. Throughout childhood and throughout life cottage cheese offers an excellent way to increase the amount of milk nutrients in meals. Its high nutritive value, its soft tender consistency and delicate delicious flavor make it a valuable food for young and old.

ICE CREAM

One of America's favorite foods is ice cream, a frozen product made from cream, milk solids, sweetening, and flavoring which may include fruits or nuts. The pleasing texture of ice cream depends on controlled processing, and careful freezing which whips in the right amount of air. Without air, ice cream would be a solid icy mass and would be unpalatable.

Ice cream is a good source of the fine proteins, the minerals calcium and phosphorus, vitamin A and riboflavin that are all found in milk. Contrary to popular belief, ice cream is not a high calorie food and compares favorably in calorie content with other popular foods. For instance, an average serving of ice cream (about ⅙ of a quart) contains only about 200 calories—approximately the same number found in ½ cup of chocolate pudding or one medium baked apple or a very small serving of angel cake.

The handy, rectangular ½-gallon package of ice cream is a great convenience to the busy homemaker. This package stores easily in the freezing unit of the refrigerator or in the freezer; it is easily opened and is always ready to serve. Because of its carefully planned design, several ½-gallon packages can generally be stored at one time without cramping storage facilities.

SHERBET

First cousin to ice cream, sherbet is steadily gaining in popularity due to its delightfully refreshing flavor. Consisting of a combination of milk solids, water, sugar and tangy fresh fruit flavoring, this frosty favorite gives sparkle to any course. Served in fruit cup, or a fruit or meat salad plate, the inviting tartness of sherbet is especially complimentary. In punch or any of the carbonated beverages, it is truly delicious—and as a dessert, sherbet is tops.

SOUR CREAM

Sour cream, sometimes sold under the name of cultured cream or Devon style cream, is made from pasteurized, homogenized sweet cream of about 18% butterfat. A lactic acid culture is added to it and the mixture allowed to incubate until the proper flavor and consistency have been reached. The product is then cooled and packaged. Like many dairy products, sour cream is rich in the protein, minerals, and vitamins found in milk, and it also contains nature's unique and nutritious fat, butterfat. Sour cream adds a gourmet touch to many dishes and is used by eminent cooks the world over.

YOGURT

Yogurt, sometimes spelled yoghurt, or yogourt, is a cultured milk of custard consistency. It is made by adding a specially prepared culture to whole milk, and allowing it to incubate, under controlled conditions, until the proper flavor and custard consistency have been attained. The calorie content of yogurt is usually about the same as or a trifle higher than in regular milk. Like other cultured dairy products, yogurt has a beneficial effect on the digestive system and usually aids the digestive process. It can be eaten as it is or may be used in many fascinating combinations of salads, side dishes, and desserts, where its unique blandness gives an intriguing flavor to food.

INDEX

Abbreviations 255
Alaska
  birthday 157
  cake, baked 156
  grapefruit 157
  orange 157
  tarts, baked 156
Almond cookies 137
Aloha sundae 166
Ambrosia salad 62
Anchovy egg sandwich
  filling 110
Appetizer cheese cake ... 8
Appetizers 7
  canapes 11
  hors d'oeuvres 8
  salads 14
Applesauce cheese pie ... 146
Apricot
  cheese sandwich filling . 104
  custard 118
  fizz 187
  half'n half 199

Bacon
  balls 10
  muffins 96
  sprinkles 13
Baked
  Alaska cake 156
  Alaska tarts 156
  bananas and sweet pota-
    toes 56
  custard 118
  French toast 95
  squash 56
Baking powder biscuits .. 92
Ballot box 179
Banana
  cheese sandwich 105
  chocolate cooler 190
  cream cake 131
  cream cheese yummy .. 105
  cream sundae topping . 174
  dessert salad 62
  egg nog trifle 125
  marshmallow cream ... 114
  milk float 198
  milk shake 195
  nog 194
  shake, creamy 198
  split 166
  split salad 62
Basic cream soup 16
Beef stroganoff 24
Beet
  cream cheese filling ... 13
  salad, jellied 74

Beets in sour sauce 53
Beverages 186
buttermilk drinks, tangy 199
apricot half'n half .. 199
buttermilk egg nog .. 199
buttermilk fruit smoothies 199
chocolate frosted deluxe 199
creamy buttermilk fizz 199
dreamy coffee frost .. 199
grape freeze 200
pineapple buttermilk pickup 200
prune float 200
saucy buttermilk ... 200
strawberry buttermilk fancy 200
vegetable cocktail ... 200
chocolate drinks, flavorful 190
banana chocolate cooler 190
chocolate malted .. 190
float 191
choc-orange
float 190
frosted 190
coffee chocolate 190
hot spiced chocolate toddy 191
mocha flip 191
super chocolate malted milk 191
taffy mint cooler 191
cream drinks, heavenly 198
banana milk float ... 198
creamy banana shake 198
custard cream smoothie 198
raspberry sparkle ... 198
egg nog drinks, holiday 194
banana nog 194
buttermilk egg nog .. 199
frosted flip 194
honey egg nog flip .. 195
pineapple egg nog .. 195
strawberry nog float . 194
ice cream drinks, dreamy 187
apricot fizz 187
cola cooler 187
currant delight 187
frosted custard 187
Honolulu punch 187
peach ginger frappe . 188
soda
caramel 189
chocolate 188
lemon 189
strawberry 189
vanilla 188
sparkling root beer .. 188
strawberry deluxe .. 188
milk drinks, refreshing . 195
banana milk shake .. 195
mocha cooler 196
molasses smoothie .. 196
pink confection 196
prune cooler 196
purple cow 197
raspberry
freeze 196
quencher 197
sparkling milk 197
strawberry
tantalizer 197
yogurt milk shake . 203
tropical malted 197
sherbet drinks, frosty .. 191
blueberry lemon fizz 192
cranberry punch 191
frosty lemonade 192
grape frappe 192
minted apricot freeze 192
orange
cola 193
julep 193
shrub 193
yogurt drinks
fruit refreshers 204
strawberry milk shake 203
Bing cherry sauce 174
Birthday
Alaska 157
cake quickie 179
ice cream ring 180

Black
night 167
witch 158
Black and white
parfait 161
sundae 166
Blintzes 42
Blueberry
lemon fizz 192
pancakes 99
peachie 161
puffs 131
roll 128
sauce 128
scones 94
shortcake 129
sundae topping 174
Blushing pear 63
Bologna roll-ups salad
plate 84
Bread pudding
milky chocolate 122
old fashioned 122
Breads 91
baking powder biscuits 92
California fruit loaf ... 93
caramel cheese rolls ... 93
corn bacon squares ... 92
croustades 36
fig nut bread 95
French toast 94
baked 95
buttermilk 94
Melba toast 97
muffins 96
bacon 96
buttermilk blueberry 97
cheese 96
deluxe buttermilk .. 96
herb corn 97
jelly 96
nut 96
raisin 96
rich 96
surprise 97
nut bread 95
pancakes
blueberry 99
featherweight 98
popovers 98
scones, blueberry 94
spoon bread 99
waffle toast 100
waffles
buttermilk 100
corn meal 100
yogurt
graham bread 205
oat crisps 205
Broiled
oranges with sherbet .. 165
peach coupe 167
Brown
and white parfait 114
beanie 158
top custard 119
Brownie sundae 167
Brownies 138
Buttermilk 233
beef
pinwheels 25
puffs 24
blueberry muffins 97
drinks 199
egg nog 199
French toast 94
fruit smoothies 199
lemon tarts 150
oat crisps 138
strawberry whip 126
waffles 100
Butterscotch
goober 167
nut sundae 167
sauce 174
surprise 167
trifle 121
Cabbage
carrot slaw 77
in cream 53
Cake
banana cream 131
birthday ice cream ring 180
blueberry puffs 131
chocolate icebox 131

creamy cocoa 132
dark mystery chocolate . 132
goblins 133
hatchet 133
holiday loaf 133
Hungarian cream 134
pear upside-down 134
quick mocha 135
rainbow party 135
scrumptious mincemeat 136
strawberry
cream carnival 135
festival 136
California
fruit loaf 93
sundae topping 175
three deckers 109
Calories in dairy foods ... 256
Canapes 11
bacon sprinkles 13
cheese bells 13
parsley flowers 13
party cream puffs 11
snappy triple deckers .. 13
tasty dips and spreads . 12
chicken olive 12
chili cheese 12
clam cheese 12
cottage cheese
date coconut 12
relish 12
deviled ham cheese .. 12
fluffy cottage cheese . 12
horseradish cheese .. 12
pimiento cheese 12
pineapple cheese 13
spicy beet cheese .. 13
tangy Roquefort ... 13
toasted bread cut-outs . 11
Candied walnuts 154
Candle magic 179
Candy 153
candle 158
Cantaloupe
pineapple sherbet cup .. 165
Caramel
cheese rolls 93
custard 118
nut sundae 167
rice raisin custard 119
sauce 175
soda 189
Carnival sundae 168
Carrot
apple cheese salad 69
cheese bowl 69
Celery seed dressing 88
Champion's chowder 20
Cheese
and noodle casserole .. 42
bells 13
biscuits 92
bowl 114
cake 143
appetizer 8
cream, pint-size 144
cottage, pint-size 144
pineapple refrigerator 145
tartlets 147
cucumber onion sandwich 105
custard pie, hearty 44
fondue 49
macaroni and 51
muffins 96
noodles and, casserole .. 42
pastry 29
pastry straws 9
pie
applesauce 146
date, nut 147
strawberry 146
pinwheels 92
sandwich barbecue 42
shortbits 8
souffle 49
soup 17
toast sandwiches 50
Cheesecake tartlets 147
Cherry
drops 138
parfait 162
sauce 176
tarts with cottage cheese 151
Chicken
a la regent 33
and broccoli Mornay ... 33
baked in cream 33
curry soup 22

fricassée, creamy 35
olive spread 12
pies 35
Children's ice cream
desserts 158
black witch 158
brown beanie 158
candy candle 158
circus wagon 158
ding dong bell 159
Easter egg nest 159
fruit baskets 182
funny face 158
Halloween pranks 183
Humpty Dumpty 159
jolly
ice cream Santa 159
Santa's sleigh 159
lolly-mike 159
party
clown 160
ice cream 184
pops 160
pink ice cream sandwich 160
rocket spray 160
snow ball 160
space planet 160
spooky ice cream cup .. 161
spring basket 160
sweet firecracker 161
Chili
cheese buns 106
cheese spread 12
dressing 88
Chilled yogurt soups 202
Choc-coconut pudding ... 120
Chocolate
chip pie 148
cream
charlotte 115
fudge 153
dipped almonds 162
drink 233
drinks, flavorful 190
frosted deluxe 199
ice box cake 131
ice cream dreams 185
malted 190
malted float 191
maple sundae 168
marshmallow
fudge 153
parfait 162
molded dream 126
sauce 176
soda 188
Spanish cream 127
souffle 124
waffles a la mode 181
Choc-orange
float 190
frosted 190
Christmas
cookies 140
cottage pudding 122
sundae 168
Circus wagon 158
Clam
cheese spread 12
chowder 16
Coconut cheese sandwich
filling 104
Coffee
chocolate 190
frost, dreamy 199
praline sundae 168
souffle 124
Spanish cream 127
supreme 168
Cola cooler 187
Colored sugar 140
Colored sugar cookies ... 139
Concord cool-off 162
Confectioners sugar
frosting 140
Confections 153
candied walnuts 154
chocolate
cream fudge 153
marshmallow fudge .. 153
Creole pralines 154
fruit balls 154
Cookie donkeys and elephants 179
Cookies 137
almond 137
brownies 138
buttermilk oat crisps .. 138

- cherry drops 138
- Christmas 140
- cottage cheese
  - brown edge 139
  - pastry 139
- date squares 141
- delicious butter 140
- donkeys and elephants . 179
- fruit and nut bars 142
- Halloween lollypop 141
- milk chocolate drop .. 142
- pumpkin 142
- shortbread 140

Cool-as-a-cucumber salad . 68

Corn
- bacon squares 92
- custards 53

Corn meal waffles 100

Cottage
- cheddar souffle 43
- dessert cream 115
- fruit salad 72
- maple creme 115
- Melba 116
- tuna tomatoes 68

Cottage cheese 234
- brown edge cookies 139
- crisps 10
- date coconut spread ... 12
- dessert
  - ring 124
  - topping 115
- dressing 88
- frozen New Orleans ... 116
- herbed onions 44
- in main dishes 41
  - blintzes 42
  - cheese
    - noodle casserole .. 42
    - sandwich barbecue 42
  - cottage
    - cheddar souffle ... 43
    - cheese herbed onions 44
    - cheese souffle 43
  - hearty cheese custard pie 44
  - lasagna 46
  - mainstay potatoes .. 45
  - peppy cheese peppers 46
  - pint-size pizzas 45
  - puffy omelet wedges . 47
  - scrambled eggs with cottage cheese .. 47
  - top-of-stove souffle .. 43
- pastry 9
- pastry cookies 139
- pastry hors d'oeuvres .. 9
- pops 10
- relish spread 12
- souffle 43

Cranberry
- cottage cheese salad ... 73
- cream 116
- parfait 162
- pineapple salad 63
- punch 191

Cream cheese cloverleaves 77

Cream
- custard 119
- drinks 198
- puffs 185
  - petite party 11
- sauce 58
- soup 16
- spirals 152

Creamed
- dried beef 25
- eggs in bologna cups ... 50
- shrimp and eggs 39

Creamy
- banana shake 198
- buttermilk fizz 199
- chicken fricassee 35
- chocolate sauce 176
- cocoa cake 132
- corn custards 53
- currant dressing 88
- lemon pie 148
- mint dressing 88

Creme brulee 120

Creole pralines 154

Crispie ice cream pie 180

Croustades 36

Crystallized mint leaves .. 193

Cucumber
- cheese sandwich 105
- dressing 89

Currant
delight 187
dressing 88
tempter 162
topping 175
Curried
dried beef 26
lamb and rice 30
Curry
accompaniments 34
crisps 22
dressing piquant 89
Indienne 34
Custard
baked 118
apricot 118
brown top 119
caramel 118
cream 119
large 118
marshmallow 118
caramel rice raisin 119
cream smoothie 198
creme brulee 120
floating island 120
frosted 187
rice raisin 119

Daily food guide 211
Dairy foods, calories 256
Dairy measures 255
Dark mystery chocolate
cake 132
Date
cheese sandwich filling . 104
nut cheese pie 147
nut cheese sandwich
filling 104
squares 141
Deep dish peach pie 149
Delectable sour cream
raisin tarts 151
Delicious butter cookies .. 140
Deliciously different sandwiches 105
Deluxe buttermilk muffins 96
Desserts 113
Deviled
egg baskets 10
egg cheese filling 112
eggs a la India 10
ham cheese sandwich .. 106
ham cheese spread 12
Dill dressing 89
Ding dong bell 159
Doughnut split 179
Dreamy coffee frost 199
Dreamy ice cream drinks . 187
Dried beef
cheese sandwich filling . 104
creamed 25
curried 26
goldenrod 26
Drum major salad 69
Dusty road 169

Easter egg nest 159
Egg
aspic appetizer 14
cream cheese sandwich 106
salad sandwich 106
Egg nog
Bavarian, holiday 125
Bavarian torte 125
buttermilk 199
drinks, holiday 194
parfait pie 181
sauce 122
trifle, banana 125
Eggplant, escalloped 54
Eggs
and shrimp, creamed .. 39
creamed, in bologna cups 50
deviled 10
scrambled with cottage
cheese 47
Elegant veal birds 31
Emerald salad 73
Escalloped eggplant and
tomato 54

Fan-tan fruit salad 63
Fanfare salad 70
Featherweight pancakes . 98
Fig
  nut bread 95
  nut fingers 111
  orange cheese salad ... 63
Filled pastry cookies 139
Fire ball 182
Fish 37
  mariner's casserole 40
  roll-ups 38
  salmon
    a la King 38
    loaves, little 37
    mousse, hot 37
  scalloped oysters 39
  shrimp and eggs, creamed 39
  tuna
    dinner treat 40
    scallop 39
Flaming duet 182
Flavorful chocolate drinks 190
Floating island dessert .. 120
Flower pots 182
Fluffy
  cottage cheese spread .. 12
  turnips 57
  whipped cream 137
Four point sandwich 108
Frankfurter
  macaroni casserole 27
  stew 27
French
  chocolate cream pudding 121
  coconut cream pudding 121
  coffee cream pudding .. 121
  maple cream pudding .. 121
  toast 94
  vanilla cream pudding . 121
Frosted
  custard 187
  flip 194
  green grape sundae 168
Frosting
  confectioners sugar 140
  golden yogurt 204
  strawberry 180
Frosty
  lemonade 192
  rainbow skyrocket 163
  sherbet basket 164
  sherbet drinks 191
  tomato buttermilk soup . 21
  tricks and treats 179
Frozen
  eclairs 180
  fruit salad 64
  New Orleans cottage cheese 116
  pineapple salad 78
  strawberry salad 78
Fruit
  and cottage cheese salads 62
  and nut bars 142
  and sherbet salad plate 84
  balls 154
  baskets 182
  meringues 169
Fruit cups, sherbet 164
  cantaloupe pineapple .. 165
  frosty sherbet basket .. 164
  melon balls 165
  orange avocado 165
  peaches a la sherbet ... 166
  pineapple potpourri .. 165
  sherbet ambrosia 166
Fudge
  chocolate cream 153
  chocolate marshmallow . 153
Funny face 158

Garden green souffle 57
Garland sandwiches 110
Ginger
  nut dressing 89
  pear salad 64
  treat 169
Gingerbread sundae 169
Gingersnap pie shell 148
Glazed fruit tarts 152
Goblins 133
Golden yogurt frosting .. 204
Goldenrod salad 67

Goober sauce 176
Grape
  frappe 192
  freeze 200
Grapefruit Alaska 157

Halloween
  lollypop cookies 141
  pranks 183
Ham
  and turkey Oriental ... 36
  'n cheese double deckers 67
  tetrazzini 29
  turkey salad 79
Harvest salad 79
Hatchet cakes 133
Hawaiian delight 116
Hearty
  cheese custard pie 44
  dinner pie 29
  frankfurter stew 27
  salad 78
  summer slaw 71
Heavenly cream drinks .. 198
Herb corn muffins 97
Herring cream cheese filling 13
Highland treat 163
Holiday
  egg nog Bavarian 125
  egg nog drinks 194
  loaf cake 133
  reminders 216
  salad ring 79
Homogenized milk 233
Honey
  cake sundae 170
  egg nog flip 195
  of a sundae 170
Honolulu punch 187
Hors d'oeuvres 8
  appetizer cheese cake . 8
  cheese
    pastry straws 9
    shortbits 8
  cottage cheese
    crisps 10
    pastry 9
  deviled
    egg baskets 10
    eggs a la India 10
  lily nibbles 9
  olive pinwheels 9
  ruffled cheese rounds .. 9
  simple 'n speedy 10
    bacon balls 10
    cottage cheese pops .. 10
    nut shells 11
    perky cucumber slices 11
    salmon pops 11
Horseradish
    cheese spread 12
    dressing 90
Hot
  fudge sundae 170
  main course sandwiches 108
  salmon mousse 37
  spiced chocolate toddy . 191
How to measure 208
Humpty Dumpty 159
Hungarian cream cake .. 134

Ice cream 155, 234
  Alaskas 156
  at breakfast 184
  cottage pudding 183
  drinks, dreamy 187
  Hawaiian 183
  parfaits 161
  sherbet fruit cups 164
  small fry favorites 158
  sundae glamour 166
  toppings 173
  tricks and treats 179

Jam baskets 109
Jam dandy 170
Jellied
  beet cottage cheese salad 74
  stuffed prunes 73

Jelly
muffins 96
rounds 139
Jiffy quick toppings 173
Jolly ice cream Santa 159
Jolly Santa's sleigh 159
Julienne veal stew 32

Key West salad 74

Lamb and rice, curried .. 30
Large custard 118
Lasagna 46
Lazy day salad loaf 75
Lemon
julep 193
pie, creamy 148
sauce 183
soda 189
syrup 189
tarts 150
Waldorf salad loaf 75
yogurt meringue pie .. 204
Lemonade, frosty 192
Lily nibbles 9
Lime
appetizer salad 14
cucumber salad 80
sponge 205
Little chicken pies 35
Little salmon loaves 37
Lolly-mike 159
Lone star salad 64

Macaroni
and cheese 51
cheese ring 70
frankfurter casserole .. 27
tuna salad 83
Main dish pastry turnovers 30
Mainstay baked stuffed
potatoes 45
Make your own salad plate 83
Malted
chocolate 190
float, chocolate 191
milk, super chocolate .. 191
tropical 197
Maple
chantilly 170
chocolate sundae 170
nut sauce 176
Maraschino cherry sundae 170
Mariner's casserole 40
Marshmallow
cream dream 126
custard 118
goober 171
sauce 177
Measuring 208
Meat
and cottage cheese salads 66
loaf 24
Meats 23
beef
pinwheels, buttermilk 25
puffs, buttermilk 24
stroganoff 24
dried beef
creamed 25
curried 26
goldenrod 26
frankfurter
macaroni casserole .. 27
stew, hearty 27
ham tetrazzini 29
hearty dinner pie 29
lamb and rice, curried . 30
main dish turnovers ... 30
meat loaf, savory 24
pork chops in cream
gravy 30
savory squares 28
Southern style casserole 28
veal
and noodle casserole . 32
birds, elegant 31
savory 31
stew, julienne 32

Melba
  sauce 177
  toast 97
Melon balls 165
Menus 217
Meringue shells 169
Merry-go-round cheese
      salad 70
Mexican chocolate sauce . 176
Milk 229
  chocolate drop cookies .. 142
  composition of 231
  drinks, refreshing 195
  homogenized 233
  importance of for
      children 232
  skim 233
Milky chocolate bread
      pudding 122
Mince-apples a la mode .. 184
Mint leaves, crystallized . 193
Minted
  apricot freeze 192
  magic 163
Mocha
  cooler 196
  flip 191
  fudge marvelous 163
  fudge sauce 177
Molasses smoothie 196
Molded desserts 124
  banana egg nog trifle .. 125
  buttermilk strawberry
      whip 126
  chocolate molded dream 126
  cottage cheese dessert
      ring 124
  egg nog Bavarian torte . 125
  holiday egg nog Bavarian 125
  lime sponge 205
  marshmallow cream
      dream 126
  Spanish cream 127
    chocolate 127
    coffee 127
  tart strawberry mousse . 127
Molded salads with cottage cheese 72
Mongole soup 22
Mousse
  salmon, hot 37
  tart strawberry 127
  turkey 82
Muffins 96
Mushroom
  sauce 30
  soup 21

New England-style clam
      chowder 16
Nineteen intriguing salads 61
Noodle cheese casserole .. 42
Nut
  bread 95
  muffins 96
  shells 11
Nutrients 212

Old-fashioned
  bread puddings 122
  strawberry shortcake .. 130
Olive
  dressing 90
  pinwheels 9
Omelet wedges, puffy ... 47
Onion
  milk soup 18
  orange cheese salad ... 65
  soup deluxe 17
Onions, herbed 44
Open face sandwiches ... 108
Orange
  Alaska 157
  avocado cup 165
  blossom 171
  cola 193
  julep 193
  onion cheese salad 65
  shrub 193
  tea biscuits 92
  Waldorf salad 203
Oven temperatures 255
Oyster stew 18
Oysters, scalloped 39

Pancake sandwich 108
Pancakes
blueberry 99
featherweight 98
Pantry shelf sandwich
fillings 104
Paradise cheese salad ... 80
Parfait
black and white 161
blueberry peachie 161
brown and white 114
cherry 162
chocolate marshmallow . 162
Concord cool-off 162
cranberry 162
currant tempter 162
frosty rainbow skyrocket 163
highland treat 163
ice cream 161
Melba 163
minted magic 163
mocha fudge marvelous 163
pie
egg nog 181
strawberry 185
pineapple 164
raspberry refresher 164
royale 163
sherbet 164
tapioca cream 117
Parsley flowers 13
Party
clown 160
ice cream 184
oyster stew 18
pops 160
sandwich
cake 111
loaf 110
sandwiches 109
Pastries 148
Pastry
cheese 29
cottage cheese 9
hors d'oeuvres 9
turnovers, main dish ... 30
Peach
berry cottage ring 76
flip 171
ginger frappe 188
Melba 171
pie, deep dish 149
treat 171
Peaches a la sherbet 166
Peanut
balls 171
butterscotch sauce 178
cheese sandwich filling . 104
Pear
salad, ginger 64
upside down cake 134
Peas in cream 53
Pecan pie 149
Peerless potatoes 54
Peppers, cottage cheese .. 46
Peppy
cottage cheese peppers . 46
potato salad 81
Perky
cucumber slices 11
dressing 90
Petite party cream puffs . 11
Pickle cheese sandwich
filling 104
Pies
cheese custard, hearty .. 44
hearty dinner 29
little chicken 35
Pies, dessert 148
applesauce cheese 146
chocolate chip 148
creamy lemon 148
crispie ice cream 180
date, nut cheese 147
lemon-yogurt meringue . 204
parfait
egg nog 181
strawberry 185
peach, deep dish 149
pecan 149
pumpkin 150
strawberry cheese 146
Pimiento
bisque 19
cheese spread 12
Pineapple
buttermilk pickup 200
carrot slaw 80

Pineapple (cont.)
cheese spread 13
egg nog 195
glow 171
mint sauce 178
parfait 164
sauce 177
sherbet potpourri 165
topping, cheesecake ... 144
upside down shortcake . 128
Pink
confection 196
ice cream sandwich 160
Pint-size
cottage cheese cake ... 144
cream cheese cake 144
pizzas 45
Pinwheels 112
Piquant dressing 90
Pizzas, pint-size 45
Planning family meals ... 210
Popcorn dixie 171
Popovers 98
Pork chops in cream gravy 30
Potato
cheese salad ring 71
chowder, savory 19
puff souffle 55
puffs on tomatoes 54
salad
peppy 81
sour cream 81
soup
sour cream 19
vichyssoise 21
turnip duet 57
Potatoes
peerless 54
scalloped 55
stuffed 45
sweet, chantilly 56
Poultry in main dishes .. 33
chicken
a la regent 33
and broccoli Mornay 33
baked in cream 33
fricassee, creamy ... 35
little pies 35
curry indienne 34
turkey
croustades 36
ham Oriental 36
Praline sauce 178
Pralines, Creole 154
Pretzel crunch 172
Prune
cooler 196
float 200
nut cheese sandwich
filling 104
wheel salad 65
Prune-cot buttermilk
shortcakes 129
Prunes, jellied stuffed ... 73
Puddings 120
bread
milky chocolate 122
old-fashioned 122
butterscotch trifle 121
choc-coconut 120
Christmas cottage 122
French cream
chocolate 121
coconut 121
coffee 121
maple 121
vanilla 121
seafoams 123
souffle, dessert
chocolate 124
coffee 124
vanilla 124
sunshine sponge 123
Puffy omelet wedges 47
Pumpernicks 112
Pumpkin
cookies 142
pie 150
tarts a la mode 151
Purple cow 197

Quick
caramel sauce 175
mocha cake 135
waffles a la mode 181

Rainbow
allure 172
party cake 135
Raisin
muffins 96
tarts 151
Raspberry
freeze 196
quencher 197
refresher 164
sparkle 198
Red
bow sandwich 108
raspberry tartlets 152
Refreshing milk drinks .. 195
Refrigerator pineapple
cheese cake 145
Rice
and raisin custard 119
griddle cakes 26
Rich muffins 96
Ripe olive cheese sandwich
filling 104
Rocket spray 160
Ruffled cheese rounds ... 9

Salad
bowl 71
dressings 87
celery seed 88
chili 88
cottage cheese 88
creamy currant 88
creamy mint 88
cucumber 89
curry piquant 89
dill 89
ginger nut 89
horseradish 90
olive 90
perky 90
piquant 90
snappy 90
sweet sour fruit 203
tangy tartare 90
yogurt Thousand
Island 203
fixin's 60
plates 83
bologna roll-ups 84
fruit and sherbet ... 84
make your own 83
other suggestions ... 85
summer fruit 84
Salads 59
appetizer 14
fruit salads
ambrosia 62
banana
dessert 62
split 62
blushing pear 63
cranberry pineapple . 63
fan-tan fruit 63
fig, orange, cheese ... 63
frozen
fruit 64
pineapple 78
strawberry 78
ginger pear 64
lone star 64
orange
onion, cheese 65
Waldorf 203
pineapple carrot slaw 80
prune wheel 65
South Sea 65
sunburst 66
Waldorf cheese 66
meat salads
cottage tuna tomatoes 68
goldenrod 67
ham'n cheese deckers 67
hearty 78
shrimp and rice 80
stuffed tomato rosettes 66
tuna
macaroni 83
spring 67
turkey
ham 79
mousse 82

molded salads
cottage fruit 72
cranberry cottage
cheese 73
emerald 73
holiday salad ring ... 79
jellied
beet cottage cheese 74
stuffed prunes 73
Key West 74
lazy day salad loaf .. 75
lemon Waldorf loaf .. 75
lime
appetizer 14
cucumber 80
paradise cheese 80
peach berry ring 76
seafoam salad rings . 76
tomato cheese aspic . 77
turkey mousse 82
zesty cheese aspic ... 76
vegetable salads
cabbage carrot slaw . 77
carrot
apple, cheese 69
cheese bowl 69
cheese cloverleaves .. 77
cool-as-a-cucumber .. 68
drum major 69
fanfare 70
harvest 79
hearty summer slaw . 71
macaroni cheese ring 70
merry-go-round cheese 70
peppy potato 81
potato cheese ring .. 71
salad bowl 71
sour cream
potato 81
spinach 82
stuffed tomatoes 82
tomato cheese rosette 72
vegetable medley ... 72
Salmon
a la king 38
loaves, little 37
mousse, hot 37
pops 11
Sandwich
breads 102
fillings 104
anchovy egg 110
apricot cheese 104
beet cream cheese ... 13
coconut cheese 104
date cheese 104
date nut cheese 104
dried beef cheese .. 104
herring cream cheese 13
peanut cheese 104
pickle cheese 104
prune, nut cheese ... 104
ripe olive cheese ... 104
tuna sour cream 104
turkey olive 110
Sandwiches 101
deliciously different ... 105
banana
cheese 105
cream cheese 105
cheese, cucumber and
onion 105
chili cheese 106
cucumber cheese 105
deviled ham cheese .. 106
egg cream cheese ... 106
egg salad 106
turkey salad roll 106
hot main course 108
cheese sandwich 42
pancake 108
toasted cheese 108
open face 108
four point 108
red bow 108
silvery sardine 109
party 109
California three
deckers 109
fig nut fingers 111
jam baskets 109
garland 110
pinwheels 112
pumpernicks 112
sandwich cake 111
sandwich loaf 110

triple deckers 107
Sauce
blueberry 128
egg nog 122
mushroom 30
tangy tomato 25
Sauces and toppings 173
Saucy
buttermilk 200
sundae 172
Savory
cheese soup 17
crackers 22
crisps 22
meat loaf 24
potato chowder 19
salmon sandwich filling 112
squares 28
veal 31
Scalloped
oysters 39
potatoes 55
Scot-mallow sundae 172
Scrambled eggs with cottage cheese 47
Scrumptious mincemeat cake 136
Seafoam salad rings 76
Seafoams 123
Sherbet 235
ambrosia 166
drinks, frosty 191
fruit cups 164
parfait 164
Shortbread cookies 140
Shortcakes 128
blueberry 129
blueberry roll 128
pineapple upside-down . 128
prune-cot buttermilk .. 129
strawberry 130
sunshine sponge 130
Shrimp
and eggs creamed 39
and rice salad 80
Silvery sardine sandwich . 109
Simple 'n speedy hors d'oeuvres 10
Skim milk 233
Slaw
cabbage carrot 77
hearty summer 71
pineapple carrot 80
Small fry favorites 158
Snappy
cottage cheese sandwich filling 112
dressing 90
triple deckers 13
Snow
ball 160
cap split 184
Souffle
cheese 49
chocolate 124
coffee 124
cottage
cheddar 43
cheese 43
garden green 57
potato puff 55
top-of-stove 43
vanilla 124
Soups 15
basic cream 16
champion's chowder ... 20
chicken curry 22
clam chowder 16
mongole 22
mushroom 21
onion
milk 18
soup deluxe 17
party oyster stew 18
pimiento bisque 19
potato
chowder, savory 19
sour cream 19
vichyssoise 21
savory cheese 17
tomato 22
frosty, buttermilk ... 21
surprise 20
tureen tricks 21
vichyssoise 21
yogurt, chilled 202

Sour cream 201, 235
  potato
    soup 19
    salad 81
  raisin tarts 151
  spinach salad 82
South Sea salad 65
Southern belle 172
Southern-style casserole . 28
Space planet 160
Spanish cream 127
Sparkling
  milk 197
  root beer 188
Spicy beet cheese spread . 13
Spinach souffle 57
Spooky ice cream cup .. 161
Spoon bread 99
Spring basket 160
Squash, baked 56
Strawberry
  buttermilk fancy 200
  cheese pie 146
  cream carnival cake ... 135
  deluxe 188
  festival cake 136
  fluff 117
  frosting 180
  ice cream puffs 185
  mallow 117
  mousse, tart 127
  nog frosted float 194
  parfait pie 185
  shortcake 130
  soda 189
  sundae 172
  tantalizer 197
  topping, cheese cake .. 146
  trifle 172
  yogurt milk shake 203
Stuffed tomato
  rosettes 66
  salad 82
Summer fruit salad plate 84
Sunburst salad 66
Sundae
  buffet 173
  tarts 173
Sundae toppings 173
  banana cream 174
  Bing cherry 174
  blueberry 174
  butterscotch 174
  California 175
  caramel 175
  cherry 176
  chocolate 176
    creamy 176
    Mexican 176
  currant 175
  goober 176
  jiffy-quicks 173
  maple nut 176
  marshmallow 177
  Melba 177
  mocha fudge 177
  peanut butterscotch ... 178
  pineapple 177
    mint 178
  praline 178
  quick caramel 175
  toffee 178
Sundaes 166
  aloha 166
  banana split 166
  black
    and white 166
    night 167
  broiled peach coupe .. 167
  brownie 167
  buffet 173
  butterscotch
    goober 167
    nut 167
    surprise 167
  caramel nut 167
  carnival 168
  chocolate maple 168
  Christmas 168
  coffee
    praline 168
    supreme 168
  dusty road 169
  frosted green grape 168
  fruit meringues 169
  ginger treat 169

gingerbread 169
honey
cake 170
of a 170
hot fudge 170
jam dandy 170
maple
chantilly 170
chocolate 168
maraschino cherry 170
marshmallow goober ... 171
orange blossom 171
peach
flip 171
Melba 171
treat 171
peanut balls 171
pineapple glow 171
popcorn dixie 171
pretzel crunch 172
rainbow allure 172
saucy 172
scot-mallow 172
southern belle 172
strawberry 172
trifle 172
tarts 173
whatsit 173
Sunshine sponge 123
shortcake 130
Super chocolate malted... 191
Surprise
muffins 97
tomato soup 20
Sweet
firecracker 161
potatoes
and baked bananas . 56
chantilly 56
sour fruit dressing 203

Taffy mint cooler 191
Tahiti special 185
Tangy
buttermilk drinks 199
Roquefort spread 13
tartare dressing 90
tomato sauce 25
Tapioca cream parfait ... 117
Tart strawberry mousse .. 127
Tarts
cherry 151
glazed fruit 152
lemon, buttermilk 150
pumpkin 151
raspberry tartlets 152
sour cream raisin 151
Tasty dips and spreads .. 12
Thousand Island dressing . 203
Toast cases 26
Toasted
bread cut-outs 11
cheese sandwich 108
Toffee topping 178
Tomato
cheese aspic 77
cheese rosette 72
sauce 46
soup 22
frosty buttermilk ... 21
surprise 20
stuffed rosettes 66
Tomatoes
cottage tuna 68
in savory sauce 58
Top-of-stove souffle 43
Toppings, ice cream 173
Triple decker sandwiches . 107
Tropical malted 197
Tuna
dinner treat 40
macaroni salad 83
scallop 39
spring salad 67
sour cream filling 104
tomatoes, cottage 68
Tureen tricks 21
Turkey
croustades 36
ham Oriental 36
ham salad 79
mousse 82
olive sandwich filling .. 110
salad roll 106

Turnip potato duet 57
Turnips, fluffy 57
Turnovers, main dish 30
turnips, fluffy 57
white sauce 58
Vichyssoise 21

Vanilla
dessert souffle 124
soda 188
syrup 188
Veal
and noodle casserole .. 32
birds, elegant 31
savory 31
stew, julienne 32
Vegetable
and cottage cheese salads 68
cocktail 200
medley salad 72
Vegetables in main dishes . 52
beets in sour sauce 53
cabbage in cream 53
corn custards, creamy .. 53
eggplant and tomato .. 54
peas in cream 53
potato
puff souffle 55
puffs on tomatoes ... 54
turnip duet 57
potatoes
peerless 54
scalloped 55
spinach souffle, garden green 57
squash, baked 56
sweet potatoes
baked bananas and .. 56
chantilly 56
tomatoes in savory sauce 58
turnip potato duet 57

Waffle toast 100
Waffles
buttermilk 100
chocolate, a la mode ... 181
corn meal 100
quick, a la mode 181
Waldorf cheese salad 66
What makes a good cook . 207
What to have with what .. 215
Whatsit sundae 173
Whipped cream, fluffy ... 137
White sauce 58

Yogurt 201, 235
fruit refreshers 204
frosting, golden 204
graham bread 205
lemon meringue pie ... 204
lime sponge 205
oat crisps 205
orange Waldorf salad .. 203
soups, chilled 202
strawberry milk shake .. 203
sweet-sour dressing ... 203
Thousand Island dressing 203

Zesty cheese aspic 76

DAIRY MEASURES

Approximate

1 lb. cottage cheese	=	2 cups
8 oz. pkg. cottage cheese	=	1 cup
12 oz. pkg. cottage cheese	=	1½ cups
½ pint whipping cream (1 cup)	=	2 cups after whipping
½ pint coffee cream	=	6 to 8 servings in coffee
1 lb. butter	=	2 cups
¼ lb. butter	=	½ cup
1 lb. Cheddar cheese	=	3 cups grated
1 qt. ice cream	=	4 to 6 servings
1 qt. milk	=	4 cups
1 pt. milk	=	2 cups

ABBREVIATIONS

tsp.	=	teaspoon	min.	=	minute
tbsp.	=	tablespoon	hr.	=	hour
qt.	=	quart	doz.	=	dozen
oz.	=	ounce	pkg.	=	package
fl. oz.	=	fluid ounce	°F.	=	degrees Fahrenheit
lb.	=	pound	"	=	inch

med. = medium

OVEN TEMPERATURES

Very slow	250°F.	Moderately hot	375°F.
Slow	300°F.	Hot	400°F.
			425°F.
Moderate	325°F.		
	350°F.	Very hot	450°F.

DAIRY FOODS ARE LOW IN CALORIES

Dairy Food	Amount	% Butterfat	Calories
Whole milk	1 glass, 8 fl. oz.	3.9	165
Sweet or coffee cream	2 tbsp.	20.0	62
Sweet whipping cream	1 tbsp.	40.0	57
Sour cream	2 tbsp.	18.0	57
Chocolate drink	1 glass, 8 fl. oz.	2.0	178
Skim milk	1 glass, 8 fl. oz.	0.1	84
Cultured buttermilk	1 glass, 8 fl. oz.	0.5	86
Sweetened condensed milk	1 tbsp.	8.0	61
Evaporated milk	½ cup	7.9	171
Dried skim milk	1 oz. or 4 tbsp.	1.1	102
Ice cream, vanilla	⅙ qt.	12.0	189
Sherbet	⅙ qt.	1.5	186
Butter	1 pat or 2 tsp.	80.5	73
American process cheese	1 oz.	30.2	104
American Cheddar cheese	1 oz.	32.3	112
Cream cheese	1 oz.	34.0	97
Cottage cheese, creamed	⅓ cup	4.0	87